W9-AXH-888

PLAIN AND ORDINARY THINGS

SUNY Series, Feminist Theory in Education
Madeleine Grumet, editor

About the Cover Illustration

Artist: Judy Natal, born: 1953 in Chicago, Illinois
Title: Fan Series #4 (Self Portrait with Snow Geese and Shell)
Medium: Photogravure (artist proof)
Date: 1978
Artist's Statement: This print grew out of a series of self portraits that I
made when I moved to Rochester, NY, to attend graduate school in
photography at Rochester Institute of Technology in 1976. I knew no one and I
found tremendous solace in the few things that I had brought with me. The
shell was given to me by my mother upon my departure from Chicago. She
remembered how, as a child, I loved the magic of holding the shell to my ear, eyes
closed, listening to the distant echoes of the waves against the shore. In
the print, I grasp the shell as if clutching my past as I stood on the threshold of the
uncertain. The lovely, fragile, white flowers were snow geese that I clipped
from George Eastman's gardens as a photographic monument to
the life I was about to embrace.

PLAIN AND ORDINARY THINGS

Reading Women
in the Writing Classroom

Deborah Anne Dooley

PE
1404
.D66
1995

STATE UNIVERSITY OF NEW YORK PRESS

Rn

Published by
State University of New York Press, Albany

© 1995 State University of New York

All rights reserved

Printed in the United States of America

No part of this book may be used or reproduced in any
manner whatsoever without written permission. No part of
this book may be stored in a retrieval system or transmitted
in any form or by any means including electronic,
electrostatic, magnetic tape, mechanical, photocopying,
recording, or otherwise without the prior permission in
writing of the publisher.

For information, address State University of New York
Press, State University Plaza, Albany, NY, 12246

Production by Dana Foote
Marketing by Dana E. Yanulavich

Library of Congress Cataloging-in-Publication Data

Dooley, Deborah Anne.
    Plain and ordinary things: reading women in the writing classroom
  / Deborah Anne Dooley.
      p.   cm. — (SUNY series, feminist theory in education)
    Includes bibliographical references and index.
    ISBN 0–7914–2319–0 (alk. paper).—ISBN 0–7914–2320–4 (pbk.:
  alk. paper)
      1. English language—Rhetoric—Study and teaching.   2. Authorship—
  Sex differences.   3. Feminism and education.   4. Women—Language.
  5. Women teachers.   I. Title.   II. Series.
  PE1404.D66   1995
  808'.042'07—dc20   94–21538
                                                                CIP

10 9 8 7 6 5 4 3 2 1

FTW
AHC7414

For Madeleine,
who gave me back my voice

CONTENTS

FOREWORD

It's not polite to quibble with a dedication; nevertheless, I, who have argued that knowledge marks the path of human relationships, admit to being somewhat taken aback to find myself in Deborah Dooley's dedication of this book. Dedications are places where writers often skip over the conversations that have fed their texts to first conversations, ones they have held with their parents or children. The reclamation of biological family at the beginning of a book suggests apology, as if to say, despite the pretense of objectivity and worldly sophistication that this book projects, I admit that I am a child of my parents.

Free of these pretensions of lonely subjectivity, Deborah Dooley's text requires no such confession. This dedication is in absolute keeping with the project of this text, for Dooley is arguing that naming our connections to persons, places, to the pulse of life, is the motive and reward of writing.

My quibble is not one of modesty but of mutuality. Deborah Dooley found the voice that speaks here in the conversation we shared when she enrolled in a course that I was teaching on feminist theory. I taught the course and she took it for one reason: not so much to learn about feminist theory, but to talk to someone else who cared about it. Deborah's dedication reminds me of the importance of that conversation to student and teacher alike.

When I received my degree from the University of Rochester at the age of thirty-nine, the dean of the school brought me into his office for some parting advice. I, he said, should not bother to apply for assistant professorships. Instead, I should just concentrate on my writing. Then someday, already distinguished by the publications necessary for tenure and promotion, I could simply sail into an advanced position at a prestigious university. That was what he, the dean, would have done, had he been able to write as well as I. He did not understand what I already knew, that it was through the very labor that he was advising me to avoid, teaching, that I would discover what I had to say. Classrooms are for conversations about the world, and, despite his sincerity, I felt as if the dean had just banished me from the vivid world to the shelter and gloom of Jane Austen's sitting room.

The Dean's advice was probably not as sexist as it seemed, although it is hard to imagine him advising a male graduate to stay home and write. It also represented the split in his own experience. This man, a Japanese-American and a sociologist of higher education, longed for the spirituality and aesthetics of his traditions. In sending me home he was sending me to the residence of his own soul.

The fault lines that split our emotional and cultural experience—home/school, writing/teaching, knowing/loving—are bridged in this text. Deborah Dooley has written a text for teaching that fully explores the ways that teaching takes up and engages all of our intelligence, perception, and competence. This integration is utterly critical to our classrooms, that despite our efforts, relentlessly slide toward simplistic and reductive technologies of knowledge. Recent celebrations of student expression have spawned writing classrooms that emphasize student pro-duction of texts but ignore the issues and world that those texts address. They are classes without curriculum. In this book Deborah Dooley re-turns books to the writing classroom. She has chosen books by writers who reveal the connections to the world that ground them. Dooley offers a reading of those texts that is simultaneously literary—read against the discursive traditions that have surrounded them—and pedagogical—read against the conversations with her students that will surround her.

From these readings she draws a vision of teaching and writing that you will recognize. You will remember the conversations you have with the colleagues who have become your friends, snatches of talk from lunch, the walk to the parking lot, late at night over the phone. Sometimes they start with a book you are teaching, with something a student wrote, or didn't say, and they lead to what you want to write yourself, to the connection that, once but vaguely intuited, is now grasped and confirmed.

Plain and Ordinary Things is finally, despite our recognition and fond familiarity, neither plain nor ordinary. It is an extraordinary text of teaching and represents a genre that deserves to be fruitful and multiply. I am thinking about essays such as Lionel Trilling's "On Teaching Mod-ern Literature" and of Muriel Rukuyser's collection *The Poet in the World* or Alice Walker's *In Search of Our Mothers' Gardens*. Unlike texts on critical pedagogy that express their authors' desires to change the world without taking the world into account, these texts are full of the sights and sounds, the hesitations and resistance, that take place when real people come together to decide what they can say to each other about their experiences of the world they share. Deborah Dooley's remarkable book reveals how feminist theory in education can encourage and sup-port this literature and its compelling teachings.

Madeleine R. Grumet

PREFACE

As a naive reader, and later as a more sophisticated respondent to literature, my first impulse was always to wonder what was behind the mask of
character. The texts told the *stories* of the hero *without,* but I wanted
always to know the *name* of the hero *within.* I never questioned the
writer's sincerity. For me, authenticity was always the real issue: not the
calling but the naming, not the lines but between the lines; the image
but also the object, the thing itself; the word but also the shape of the
lips and the wet, fuzzy touch of tongue to teeth; the spray of spittle in
the effort to pronounce: the transpiration and the expiration but also the
inspiration. And so, forever less interested in *what* the writer did than
why, I read the private documents—letters, journals, notebooks. Through
them I came to realize the power of writing to compose not only the text
but the self. I came to see public texts—the poems, the narrative fictions—
as invitations not only to hear stories as sequences of events unfolding in
time, but to overhear, besides, the authentic voices of those women
writers whose surrogate narrators retold them.

In addition to being a reader, I was a young writing teacher coming from a typical American graduate school English program where it
was assumed that if one could do it, one could teach it. And I was, as
well, a young feminist teacher of women's literature for whom theory in
the midst of sixteen new preparations in five years was at best a gleam in
other women's eyes. My professional situation was such that exposure to
reasonably sophisticated writing theory came early and with a reasonably
systematic formality. The feminist work came like the paradigm of most
women's lives, in fragments, in intuitions, piece after piece composed
into syllabi that became my portion of a larger women's studies curriculum, but mostly composing me as I composed them.

The Greek *paidagogos* signifies both the school building and the
school teacher. As it moves into English—pedagogue, pedagoguery—it
carries with it the disparaging taint of inadequacy and ineffectualness.
Yet, ironically, pedagogy is defined as "the science that treats of the
principles and art of teaching as a profession: the theory of education and
its application in order to assure the best results in instruction and training; the science and art of teaching."[1] To the old saw "Those that *can,*
do, those that *can't,* teach," I felt I should add the disclaimer "And those

that *can* often teach something contrary to what they think and do."

For years in the writing classroom, I taught students to become chameleon selves, responding skillfully and efficiently to the exigencies of rhetorical situations with multiple masks donned to suit variable purposes, audiences, and subjects. And in the discussion that distinguished logic from rhetoric, and truth from validity, I taught them to be sincere but finally inauthentic. In my literature classes I taught students that women had claimed the personal narrative form as their own because it was the ground where identity making could begin and the fragments of authentic self composed. In women's literature, the term *mask* appears as an expression of anguish, of the public construct that represents women's work as sisters, wives, mothers, daughters, lovers, friends, (what they do), belying the private work of naming themselves—the work not of doing but of being. In my literature classroom I taught my students that the task of identity making was one of unmasking, of discovering one's own voice. In the writing classroom, I was teaching them, finally, to wear every mask—and to give voice to every experience—except their own. In the gradual dawning of that dichotomy upon my teacherly consciousness—and conscience—this book took form.

My own interest began with journal literature, and developed toward studying their journals' relationship to women's personal narrative,[2] fiction, and to their poetry. Journal literature is inherently paradoxical. Its form is perhaps more precise than any other in its "accounting" of time and space, specific in the overt demand for "entries" to a ledger that holds a relatively short, linear record of successive days' events. Yet its very specificity frees the writer: to use fragmented compartments to explore wholeness; to negate the false consciousness that the linear sequence of events is the only measure of time, that progress means hurtling ever forward into a future whose success is measured by the ability to leave the past behind; to affirm that the journal's real project is going backward in order to go forward, actualizing and accessing the past and resignifying its language so we can become authentically accountable to ourselves for the reality that we construct.

Without benefit of theory, my work with women's journals, letters, notebooks, and the fictive narratives that emerged from them suggested a series of affirmations that caused me to experience increasing discomfort in the theoretical justification for my own writing pedagogy. In her poem "The Sabbath of Mutual Respect," Marge Piercy enjoins us: "Praise the lives you did not choose./They will heal you, tell your story, fight/for you. You eat the bread of their labor./You drink the wine of their joy."[3] In this spirit, I came to see that if I wanted to learn something about the contradiction between these two compartments of my professional life, I needed to ask what these writers could teach me about reading, writing, and teaching. This book is about what I am learning from them.

In part 1, "Song and Sexuality: A Theory of Women's Writing," I place modern women writers in the Romantic tradition and offer a renewed understanding of their relationship to orality and thus to rhetoric and to song.

In chapter 1, "Songs of Silence: Women's Writing and the Recovery of the Romantic Project," I argue that this generation of women affirms our Romantic legacy. They not only understand it as the problem of integrating feeling and thought; they also recognize that language not only describes experience but makes it what it is. "Imagination," Coleridge reminds us, "is a repetition in the finite mind of the eternal act of creation in the infinite I AM" (*Biographia Literaria,* chap. 13). The actual role of Eve aside for a moment, at the heart of the Genesis myth is the power and responsibility that adhere to naming. While "out of the ground the Lord God formed every beast of the field and every bird of the air," nevertheless "he brought them to the man to see what he would call them; and whatever the man called every living creature, that was its name" (Genesis 2:19).[4] Journal work is the ground for the radical resignifying that is women's project with language, and with the reality that language constructs. It is their first claim to the power of language offered in the Genesis myth.

So, first, I propose that journal work is inherently conversational in impulse, and that its literary-historical roots lie in the oral narratives of preliterate cultures. This legacy of storytelling is recovered successively, albeit differently, by nineteenth-century Romantic lyric poets and by women writing in the personal narrative tradition.

Secondly, journal writers use its compartmentalized form to argue the failure, in fact the danger, of extending technological specialization— with its concomitant compartmentalization of language and thought—to the work of human relationships, be they with self, selves, or others. Essentially, they warn how dangerous it is to mistake productive values for reproductive values.[5] They demonstrate at the same time how much human cost is borne by those men and women trapped in social roles and in self-constructs that demand the utter dichotomization of private and public selves. They use the form, in other words, to deconstruct the very dichotomy the form appears to sanction.

Idiomatic usage reflects how deeply we have embraced this dichotomy. "What is your name?" we ask—that is, "How do you name yourself?" or "What have your parents named you?" Yet the social reality of identity often fails to distinguish person from object. We do not ask "Who are you named?" but "What are you called?" "I am called . . . ," we reply, so busy about the calling and being called that we forget the naming and the request that we be named in return. Personal narrative is about a lifetime effort to *name.* This occurs in a world that offers a birthrite of name-giving/taking during ritual rites of passage—birth, baptism, *bris,* confirmation, *bat* or *bar mitzvah*—but excises these rituals' significance from most other parts of human experience. Being "named" is the private reality; being "called" the public experience. Journal writing is about the effort to bring together the naming and the calling, to name both our experience and ourselves.

Thirdly, these journal writers argue that reproductive values are always about object relations, an intuition that most (with the exception of psychoanalyst Joanna Field) appear to reach without the benefit of the nevertheless valuable and careful work of object-relations[6] theorists now available to us. "[P]eople themselves need to be reproduced both daily and generationally," Nancy Chodorow writes. "Most theoretical accounts agree that women as wives and mothers reproduce people—physically in their housework and child care, psychologically in their emotional support of husbands and their maternal relation to sons and daughters." However, "Men are socially and psychologically reproduced by women, but women are reproduced (or not) largely by themselves" (*The Reproduction of Mothering,* 36).

This idea of women "reproducing themselves" has, I believe, significant implications for women's narrative, which will be explored throughout the second half of the book; indeed, it is a primary thread connecting parts 1 and 2. However, the use of the term itself raises two issues that relate to my use of the phrase *women's writing* throughout this text and also to my use of French feminist theorists as they address what is itself the complex relation of the body and the text—of sexuality and textuality.[7]

To claim that we can refer to "women's writing" as a category suggests more than simply acknowledging that women have produced texts. Among other things, it presupposes an earlier question (what Judith Gardiner characterizes as a chief question of feminist literary criticism): "Who is there when a woman says 'I am'? "[8] And it leads to a subsequent question: "Is women's writing different from men's?"

I do not deny that biological and sociocultural and psychological constructs figure into any understanding of the term *woman.* Nevertheless, my argument presupposes that the woman saying "I am," and especially, for my purposes here, the woman writing, is engaged in formulating an identity that she can name. By speaking about writing as an act of identity making, and by arguing the complexity of the identity-making act for women, I have again presupposed something—that "woman" is more than solely a biological category or a sociocultural or psychological construct. If their identity-making process is of a different order from men's process, and if writing is part of the process of identity making, then it stands to reason that differences will mark women's writing (and perhaps women's writing process, too). Exactly what these are, and specifically *why* these are, if they can be adequately named, is the subject of much debate, which is as irresolvable here as it has been in other very multidisciplinary quarters.

This book makes one primary claim about women's writing: that it has a narrative affinity with an oral tradition influenced both by women's relation to their mothers and their mothers' songs and by their multifaceted position(s) as Other in many cultures and societies. This affinity with an oral tradition is common to the literatures of oppressed groups; certainly the massive recovery of African American and other postcolonial literatures makes this point eminently clear. But this book is not a comparative study of the relative influences of gender and oppression on writing—men's or women's. "Myths of gender"[9] continue to be perpetuated by even the most well-intentioned theorists, and they must be examined and exposed. But among the available directions for research, feminist revisions of psychoanalysis seem to me to be most helpful in positing some basis for the common "differences"—for instance, of preference for particular kinds of narrative, of relation to images and the things they represent, of thematic interest—I have seen in the women's writing I have studied. It is not my intention to claim that these differences emerge in every woman's writing in every culture, nor do I wish to claim that they never occur in men's writing; I only wish to propose that they have made a sufficiently repetitive appearance in the writing I have studied to make the term *women's writing*, so stipulated, available as a category for consideration.

My argument is situated in object-relations theory. My definition of "reproductivity" as it is applied to the social relations of gender and writing and teaching writing in classrooms, my understanding of women's identity making, as well as my discussion of Virginia Woolf's notion that women "think back through their mothers" is informed by the work of object-relations theorists, most particularly by Nancy Chodorow. As Gardiner notes, many feminist critics report the attractiveness of object-relations theory to feminists whose critical model has emphasized the social construction of knowledge: it is a social and psychological rather than a biologically based theory. My complementary use of French feminist theory should suggest that I am not so ready to dismiss biology as an influence either in the social relations of gender, in the process of women's identity making, or as a factor in women's writing. The problem seems to be that once a notion of women's bodies in relation to time/space (and consequently to writing their songs) is introduced, we are headed down the road of "biological *determinism*" rather than a more richly dialectical understanding of the relationships among individual gendered subject, literature, culture, and society. By the same token, I reject the reduction of the term *reproductivity* to a descriptor of a biological act. I cannot accept the statement, nor do I intend the book to argue that "a theory of 'biological *determinism*' shaping a common response to patriarchy in its various forms"[10] makes sense. Biology is not, and never has been, destiny. On the other hand, to dismiss out of hand the specificity of the body's (be it closer on the spectrum of possibility to male or to female) relation with the world and with the text that mediates the relationship between the world and the body in the name of social and cultural constructions of experience seems equally foolish.

Reporting on the multiplicity of sex characteristics *and* gendered behaviors manifesting themselves in this culture as well as in those far different from our own, whatever these may be, should surely by now have silenced the hydra-headed voices of biological determinists, sociobiology notwithstanding. That the explosion of gender studies in all disciplines has failed to do this is, indeed, from my perspective, attributable to an entrenched patriarchal abasement to the god of binary opposition. The kind of reductionism represented by the word *determinism* is what I intend to dismiss when I suggest later that *l'écriture feminine* has been misread (and therefore itself dismissed) as being of necessity *deterministic*. To me this is neither a question of dissembling authors (I'm not saying that the French women are saying that biology is destiny when they don't really mean it) nor of theorists reading poorly (I'm not saying that their work is so complex that everyone with the exception of me has misread them), but a matter of emphasis and a manifestation of the inevitable tendency to privilege one or the other part of a proposition when the parts are expressed in a relation characterized by difference. Even Chodorow, after all, refers to a "sex-gender system" and argues that the male child turns from the mother in recognition of his *difference* from her, and the female child struggles for a lifetime with her *likeness* to her. Surely biology must have something to do with the conclusions children reach about difference. Rejecting the biological basis for women's mothering, Chodorow nevertheless writes: "We are, of course, biological beings, and our embodiment needs accounting for" (*The Reproduction of Mothering*, 16).

Finally, I want to point out that, in addition to Chodorow's book, the reproductive metaphor has a rich scholarship in feminist psychoanalytic theory, in feminist critique of traditional political thought (cf., for example, Mary O'Brien's *The Politics of Reproduction*), and in curriculum theory (cf., for example, Madeleine Grumet's *Bitter Milk*). Some other theorists of reproductivity include Sara Ruddick *(Maternal Thinking)*, Nell Noddings *(Caring)*, Julia Kristeva *(Desire in Language)*, and Jessica Benjamin *(Bonds of Love)*.[11] Furthermore, questions about reproductivity are not only *women's* questions. To try to talk about the mother tongue and about "plain and ordinary things" in the context of a discussion of reproductivity is to try to reclaim the maternal/material from its appropriated position as a cultural product. Kim Chernin writes in *Reinventing Eve*, "When a woman seriously asks herself what it means to be a woman she is pulling at a thread that can unravel an entire culture" (25). There are many ways to begin to do this, and I hope that *Plain and Ordinary Things* is one of them.

In chapter 2, "Reading Women's Songs: A Theory of Orality," I relate women's narrative tradition to that of preliterate peoples, especially Australian Aboriginals, and to the concept of song. I pose three problems: maintaining a relationship to the literal in an essentially figurative universe, expressing the vision that "everything is not one thing," and effecting a merger of the apparently disparate experiences of knowing and being. I read Virginia Woolf's *Between the Acts* as the literate complement to Aboriginal materials and as the fictional expression of the theory of orality proposed by Walter Ong in *Orality and Literacy*.

My decision to study Australian Aboriginal peoples was somewhat serendipitous. I had just stumbled upon Bruce Chatwin's book *The Songlines* and, shortly thereafter, Diane Bell's book *Daughters of the Dreaming*. I also read some other formal anthropological studies about tribes from the same region. First, I was fascinated by a people whose bodies were so intimately connected to the things of their world and whose rituals so embedded in their everyday lives that the paths they walked—their "Dreaming-tracks"—were understood to be trails of song bringing the world into existence. For their descendants, walking and singing were the same thing, reproducing the ancestral act of creating the world they lived in. I felt that an important lesson could be learned by a postliterate people about the power of narrative and the risks of our disconnection from the oral tradition upon which literacy is founded.

But reading about the same people from three very different positions, those of a male travel writer, two female anthropologists who lived among tribal women and focused on them, and male anthropologists who studied male ritual from a position that seemed clearly outside, also offered a more complex way to rethink a traditional understanding of men's and women's relation to rhetoric, expressed by one colleague as the binary of "male dominance and female resistance."[12] The multiple readings of this culture offer an example of how complex and careful a reading of a presupposed, gendered, dominance/resistance model must be. For example, there is the problem of the recorder/investigator's relationship to the person giving evidence, a problem of interpretation shared by investigators of preliterate *and* literate cultures. Aboriginal narratives about their ritual practices have been interpreted almost exclusively by male anthropologists; deliberate obfuscation on the part of both men and women was common practice to protect these sacred rituals and songs from the potential for desecration by (male, Western) outsiders. When Diane Bell, a female anthropologist, lived among tribal women, learning their language and earning their trust, she uncovered this tradition of lying to the interloper studying their culture, and in the process learned a great deal about how inappropriate earlier interpretations of the *separation* of men's and women's ritual practices as *necessarily* signaling dominance had been. For me it was a helpful lesson in avoiding a dualistic interpretation of narrative practices that would be reductive of the way I want to address the problematic of women's access to the public rhetoric in literate cultures, as well as the problematic of the ways the term *public* in connection to rhetoric has been defined, in Aboriginal culture and in our own.

Part 2 of the text, "Reading Women Writing," the last four chapters of the book, focuses on selected work of Virginia Woolf, Joanna Field, and Adrienne Rich. Their journals, essays, poetry, and fiction are writings through which these women reproduce themselves, exploring the gap between being called and being named, and renaming *themselves* as a critical part of the reproductive process. These texts are, in fact, cradle songs that enable a harkening back through time and consciousness to those first object relations in a world awash with sensations—colors, lights, shapes, smells, touches, sounds—mediated through a mother's voice. "In my sensory education," Eudora Welty says, "I include my physical awareness of the *word*" (*One Writer's Beginnings*, 11). The connection to the classroom comes in recognizing that, as teachers, women reproduce people, too, and that, especially as writing teachers, their ongoing mediative function in this regard is a critical one.

"Reproducing themselves" for these women also involves finding the place and the space from which they have come, and a place and a space to claim as their own—a "ground of being"[13] as Heidegger terms it; "a room of one's own," as Woolf terms it; "a life of one's own," as Joanna Field terms it. It involves the affirmation that we must go backward in order to go forward, that a writer must have the capacity to actualize these moments—"moments of being,"[14] Woolf calls them—if she is to reproduce her experience, if she is to reproduce herself.

As Woolf recognized, this actualizing capacity is both a literal and a narrative act. Journals are about the insights that signal and affirm this reproductive act. Writing is about the discovery of these insights. So the composers of these journals have much to teach the writing teacher. And the lessons of their journal work become first principles for their fiction, poetry, and the theory that follows from it. In short, writing is not solely a productive but also a reproductive act, and this is a crucial insight that must inform pedagogical theory and practice.

"Childhood's learning is made up of moments," Eudora Welty writes. "It isn't steady. It's a pulse." Returning with her father to his father's house, she becomes aware that "The trips were wholes unto themselves. They were stories. Not only in form, but in their taking on direction, movement, development, change. They changed something in my life: each trip made its particular revelation . . . with the passage of time, I would look back on them and see them bringing me news, discoveries, premonitions, promises—I still can; they still do" (*One Writer's Beginnings*, 10). Because this is a work about space, it is of course also a work about time. "The events of our lives happen in a sequence of time," she writes, "but in their significance to ourselves they find their own order, a timetable not necessarily—perhaps not possibly—chronological. The time as we know it subjectively is often the chronology that stories and novels follow: it is the continuous thread of revelation" (75).

Because writing is about our arrangements in space and time, this is also a book about ritual. I talk most fully about ritual in chapter 5, "Rituals of Happiness: Joanna Field's Method of Following the Image." Like teaching, writing is a ritual activity. The classroom is a space that can be made into a ritual place. Ritual in its richest sense evokes mythic (circular, not linear) time, bringing people together to make a sacred *place* of a space. In his article on the relation between ethnopoetry and ritual, Richard Schechner remarks that, unlike ape ceremonial centers, human ritual sites are spaces "permanently transform[ed]" by being written on or having "a lore" attached to them ("Towards a Poetics of Performance," 43). This "writing," either visual or oral (oral because

aboriginal people's songs function like "writing," in Schechner's understanding of them) is basic to the cyclic "gathering, performing and dispersing" (44) that is the paradigm for ritual everywhere—including the
classroom space itself. His remarks intensify our sense of the relationship
between the Pilbara rock drawings of Aboriginal women dancing,[15] and
the marks in the sand by which Aboriginal women teach their children
about the things of their world. And his remarks connect us to our
experiences in contemporary classrooms, too. Sadly, too often, the rituals
that happen in classrooms finally disconnect—rather than connect—our
students from each other and from significant experiences and aspects of
themselves. In several chapters, I try to suggest why this is so. In chapters 2 and 3, and in successive chapters, examining the ritual places of
preliterate people, the poetry they sing, the lore they tell, and the drawings they make is part of my effort to reread connection back into the
modern experience of classrooms. In chapter 3, I theorize this connection as a proposal for a phenomenology of intimacy, and I situate the
discussion in many literary gardens, studying the garden as image. In
chapter 5, Field's method of following the image emerges as one way of
addressing the reader/writer's need for connection between the individual body and the body politic of our culture and our world.

And so in several ways and places in the book I ask these questions:
How do we make the classroom space authentically "place" in its richest
sense, through new rituals of connection that replace the old, disconnect-
ing ones? How can we help students see both the classroom and the page
as more than a space to be read or written upon, but as a *place* where a
ritual gathering and performing is a collaborative opportunity for rich
kinds of celebratory activity? What does it mean to think about the classroom as a reproductive space?

This is a book about writing, and the conclusion of each chapter
seeks direct application to the writing classroom. Yet in many chapters
the *reading* of others' texts is of paramount concern. There are a number
of reasons for this choice. First, while it is commonly held that writers
give notoriously unreliable testimony about the specific content of their
work, I believe they are extraordinarily accurate and helpful when they
talk about writing processes.[16] I have found writers' journals inordinately
helpful in reading their fiction and, for my purposes here, particularly
lucid in the readings they offer of the ways they explore and use writing.

Virginia Woolf and Joanna Field, whose published journals are rich
and detailed (the former voluminously so), wrote in the early decades of
this century, a time when the collocation of many persons and events

both reflected and were stimulated by a remarkable renaissance that we now call "modernism." The surge of imagination that marked the modernist enterprise was spun from the energy of Wyndham Lewis's vortex[17] and the broken fragments of cubist art; both were posed in dialectical relation to numerous efforts aimed at envisioning a new whole.

Woolf's and Field's works reflect both parts of this modernist effort. In her journals, essays, and fiction, Woolf uses a new prose form—a kind of intersection of fiction and poetry—to announce that the old order is broken and with it the old ways of connecting persons with their world and consequently the old ways of being in the world and knowing what is "real." Her work is the fictional counterpart of the larger phenomenological effort, most obvious in Heidegger, to revise and reconstruct the connections among language, thought, and reality, between being and time, and therefore between people and the spaces/places they inhabit.[18] Woolf's most significant contribution to the subject of the literature/writing relation is her ability to capture the place "between" in the dialectics of chaos and the new order she envisions, a place of equal fascination to Heidegger in his effort to locate Truth in the work of art. As the titles of her books reveal, this is the place where most of us live most of the time if we live authentically—always somehow "between the acts," on the way "to the lighthouse," always on "the voyage out." Her writing is a touchstone for this whole book, but the single chapter most closely focused on her work is chapter 4, "Virginia Woolf and the Problematic of Intimacy."

It is no metaphor to say that this is where most writers—and teachers and students—live, too, in the place *between* the chaotic, sensory bombardment of everyday life and the relentless linearity of conventional English syntax. Woolf's work is both a philosophy of language and a model for the creative uses of this dialectical tension; I read it not so that we can write like her, but so that we can get a taste of what riding the waves of this kind of adventurous process is like. Her fiction pioneers the way for a broken generation to reclaim its connection to the object, to the texture of an experience severely damaged by urban industrial capitalism and the imperialist conception of an Other and of otherness. Her books are, and are about, ritual. Both the journals and the fiction lay open to us a quality of consciousness that shows us the way to grieve what we have lost and to reconnect.[19]

Although not herself a fiction writer, Joanna Field (née Marion Milner) joins Woolf in offering us systematic ways to find and follow the images of our imaginative lives back to things themselves. Biologist turned psychoanalyst, Field uses her keen skills as an observer to watch the world and so to watch herself in relationship to it. As a writer she finds voice first by finding the ways that she was silenced and had silenced herself. Field's interest in education is lifelong, and her three journals respond to the three great educational questions of her life: "What makes me happy?" *(A Life of One's Own)*; "What blocks my creative process?" *(On Not Being Able to Paint)*; "What are the ways of knowing that will make my life less fragmented, more whole, and how can I cultivate them?" *(An Experiment in Leisure)*. Field's method for following the image as a painter, writer, and psychoanalyst makes a great contribution to thought and practice in the writing classroom. Reading her read herself, a dialectical process[20] she actively engages in all three journals, we become ourselves engaged in a model process for doing the same.

The link to contemporary poet Adrienne Rich comes through the social relations of gender, its consequences for language, and the way that Rich embeds her images in the crucible of human relationships. Though Rich herself is not a published journal writer, her theory is nevertheless informed by the relentless honesty that the connections between the personal and the political demand. Numerous essays record her own growth as woman and poet; they scrutinize with self-conscious lucidity her early need, as both of these, to be her father's daughter, and they record the gradual confrontation, in poetry and theory, with the oppressive silence this need imposed. Rich's work extends and explicates Woolf's imperative that every woman, if she writes, must look back to her mother. In so doing, she both deconstructs and reconstructs *mother* and the mothering relation.

Her lesbian voice offers yet another bridge between the work of these three twentieth-century women and the preliterate songs of Yugoslavian poets and Austrialian Aboriginal peoples, the subject of chapters 2 and 3. To the majority of the West, both are profoundly Other. I argue implicitly in this book that in the dialectical relation to the Other—in fact only there—can we truly find ourselves. This means that we must find the Other in ourselves, a process that is, of course, central to ritual activity. According to Schechner ("Towards a Poetic of Performance"), in the healing rite, in order to effect their cure, shamans transform themselves into other beings, the healing transformation occurs, and they return to their former selves (52); in theater, actors and audience are transformed in the ritual reenactment of story that may have permanent consequences for all three (49). Writing is one way to explore our connection to the Other that resides in our world and in ourselves.

Of equal importance to the concept of Otherness[21] is the recognition of how much its denial has cost. As Adrienne Rich knows well, the

study of the Other offers the opportunity to examine our own brokenness and the self-directed violence that is its consequence. In an early
poem, she laments grimly: "The tragedy of sex/lies around us, a woodlot/
the axes are sharpened for" ("Waking in the Dark," (1971), *The Fact of
A Doorframe*). Sylvia Wynter explicates her comment this way:

> As western man 'pacified' New World nature, eliminated the
> "savage," penned them up in reservations, he did the same with
> whole areas of his Being. Indeed it would be difficult to explain
> the extraordinary nature of his ferocity if we did not see that it
> was, first of all, a ferocity also wrought, in psychic terms, upon
> himself. Western man—as defined by the bourgeoise—retained
> those areas of Being whose *mode of knowing* could sustain the
> narrative conceptualizations (the heraldic vision) of his new
> world picture, but eliminated, penned up on reservations, those
> areas of *cognition* which were, by their mode of knowing,
> *heretical* to the conceptualized orthodoxy that was required.
> THE MODE OF COGNITION THAT WAS PENNED UP
> WAS A MODE WHICH WESTERN MAN (ALL OF US
> SINCE IT IS NO LONGER A RACIAL BUT A CULTURAL
> TERM) REMAINS AWARE OF ONLY THROUGH
> POETRY—AND POETRY AS THE GENERIC TERM FOR
> ART.... THE SALVAGING OF OURSELVES, THE
> RECLAMATION OF VAST AREAS OF OUR BEING, IS
> DIALECTICALLY RELATED TO THE DESTRUCTION
> OF THOSE CONDITIONS WHICH BLOCK THE FREE
> DEVELOPMENT OF THE HUMAN POTENTIALITIES
> OF THE MAJORITY PEOPLES OF THE THIRD WORLD.
> ("Ethno or Socio Poetics," 82)

Susan Griffin and numerous other feminist theorists[22] have recognized with Rich that women have been victims to the act of pacification
and exorcism Wynter describes, and of the concomitant deprecation of
the ways of knowing that follow it. The burning of tens of thousands of
"witches" says it all.[23]

This is a book about recovery in both senses—about finding what
has been silenced and lost, and about healing. For too long, teachers
have confronted the fragmented experience of living in a house whose
eclectic and carefully partitioned reconstruction has rendered them ultimately homeless. Actualizing the relationships among reading and writing, the songs of preliterate peoples, nineteenth- and twentieth-century

literary history, feminist theories about gender and language, women's writing, and writing pedagogy, can help us to renovate this house, and show us how to make it home. Finally, in this book I call us to explore the relations between our private and public selves, between our roles as teachers and writers, and to examine the authenticity of the voices with which we speak to our students, to our colleagues, and to ourselves.

ACKNOWLEDGMENTS

Many spiritual and psychological traditions recognize that there are no accidents. This book was conceived as a paper in a postdoctoral seminar I stumbled into as part of a master's program in education leading me to a counseling degree. That course, "Feminist Theory in Education," was taught by Madeleine Grumet, now Dean of the College of Education at Brooklyn College. It was she who told me that the paper begged to be a book, and she who made it possible for this stepchild of many disciplines to write it. The language of my dedication statement means exactly what it says: Madeleine showed me a way to find a voice in the scholarship of my discipline, and to connect that scholarship to other disciplines—philosophy, psychology, education, anthropology—in a way that felt rich to me. She mentored me in a way that I most needed to be mentored, at a time when I most needed the mentoring she could offer. And in the process, she became my friend. My first acknowledgment goes to her with admiration and love.

Many others have supported this work. My colleague Richard Kalinoski read the whole of this manuscript more than once. His hard questions and critical concerns kept me honest and helped me to sort ways of bridging the gap between what I needed to write and what audiences needed to hear. And at my lowest point in the process, he encouraged me to go on and to finish. For all of this I owe him great thanks.

Susette Graham and Jane Koenen read chapters, lending their many years of experience and their expertise as, respectively, literary critic and philosopher. As I wrote, I thought often of how much I learned in their classrooms when I was their student. Laura Kroetsch and Nancy DeJoy each gave me a summer of their editorial expertise. Nancy's judicious reading, her unfailing ability to point me in the direction of some new and helpful piece of research, her research skill, her ongoing interest and support, all have meant a great deal. That Nancy is now my colleague is a source of delight to me. Other colleagues in the Women's Studies Program at Nazareth and in the English Department graciously read and commented on portions of the book; their support and suggestions helped me both intellectually and emotionally. These women and men have my gratitude, as do the innumerable students, some of whose writing you will read here, without whom there would have been no book.

Sandra Jamieson of Drew University read the manuscript with an astuteness and a thoroughness that enabled me to clarify my thinking on a number of issues, most particularly those related to the problems of biological determinism and the use of the generalized term *women* in my text. She was also instrumental in guiding me toward secondary critical sources about Heidegger that were crucial in helping me sharpen my understanding of how his work can aid a reading of Woolf's. I have tried to cite in my text all the places where I recognize her helpful suggestions and textual references.

Dana Foote, Production Editor, responded graciously to my many questions and offered excellent advice. Wendy Nelson was an intelligent and careful editor of the manuscript, struggling valiantly with my many inconsistencies of noting and reference, and polishing sentences thoughtfully and judiciously. Lois Patton and her assistants at SUNY Press were forever supportive and gracious throughout the long period that this manuscript has been in preparation.

Along with George Ford, my thesis advisor and a superb humanist scholar of Victorian literature, my teachers and colleagues at Nazareth College have given me, over a period of twenty years, the intellectual foundation that made this book possible. Dr. Dennis Silva, Vice-President for Academic Affairs at Nazareth College, supported the summer grants and the sabbatical leave that enabled me to complete this book.

And last, but first, come my parents, who have always been there for me, whose values of loving care inform this text, without whom I *truly* could not have written it. Thank you all.

PART ONE

SONG AND SEXUALITY:
A THEORY OF WOMEN'S WRITING

plain and ordinary things
speak softly
      —Adrienne Rich, "From an Old House in America"

The temperature has dropped to -10 this morning, and everywhere crystals of white snow crunch underfoot. Yet each day the sun shines—cruel, cold, beautiful. Odd that those qualities are often found in combination. The body shell has its own response as well; my skin has bleached an ivory-white, and blusher applied in a thin layer rests on the surface like a soft, rose mist. All the other colored features—green eyes, black lashes and brows, stand out in finely detailed portraiture. I have had my hair cropped very close to my head, the shortest it has ever been, and the effect is that large green eyes stare out at visitors with the intensity that is produced by an absence of all other distractions. This month I am living inside of those eyes, lips enforcing silence upon speech, hands free of all rings but one that I have bought for myself, enjoying the freedom of nakedness and of simplicity. The body curls up inside wool and fur, rubbing itself silently against warmth and holding the cold at bay. Long hours of sleep are the luxury of each day, comparable only to reading that is savored, a deliberate, delicious, silent entry into the past. A bad cold has closed my ears to extraneous sounds—I live for a while happily in a white-noise world; even the sound of my own words comes to me from far away.

Creating the ultimate luxury, I have asked my students to prepare an essay for today—we shall not speak to each other aloud, then, in that difficult interchange that is the classroom. The struggle to find the right word, the right phrase, is put off for another day; yet they have the gift of struggling today, on their own. I have asked them to write to me about survival; they do not yet realize that the kinds of survival they write about are particular to the writer, incorporated in stories of men and women as far apart as Eudora Welty and Ernest Hemingway: a return to the past so that it can be explored once again at a distance, relived with pain in the tranquility of the present moment, suffered again so that a space might be made for understanding to fill; fantasy—the day-dream that provides us with that most temporary but most creative respite from reality drenched in a cold day's sun; the journey, when the fantasy has passed, through the landmarks of each day, refusing to stop, determined to endure—

otherwise known as the strength to complete a hard day's work of living; dialogue, communication, love, gift—the entry into relation with other persons that catapults us out of ourselves in the demand that we give ourselves away . . . It goes on, that rhythmic list of survival tactics that rocks us into and out of ourselves with the motion of the birthing cradle. (Whitman knew what he was doing when he traced his poetic voice to the sea, to the cradle, to the cry of a bird in search of its mate.) But for now the beginning is enough.

This should perhaps have been a journal entry, but I keep no journal— better been a poem, but I write no poems. So I send it along to you, reflections of an English teacher on a cold morning.

I

Songs of Silence:
Women's Writing and the
Recovery of the Romantic Project

Introduction

The first day in a freshman writing class is inevitably one in which the sound of an anxious and expectant silence deafens real speech. Its first spoken words are often a recitation of the syllabus: papers to be written, books to be read, first words then sentences then paragraphs to be understood, then forms of writing to be mastered (or sometimes the reverse), a jargon to be learned like those in all the other college classrooms. Next to the mathematics class, it is probably the place of more anxiety than any other college classroom. It is the place where mistakes will be corrected with varying degrees of embarrassment to corrector (teacher) and correctee (student), where inevitably some hidden fault will come to light, no matter how hard its author tries to cover her confusion. It is a place of many assumptions about what should be known before we come—or, worse, what has never been known and seemingly never will. Here, being and knowing play hide-and-seek on expectant faces, suspicious, and rightly so, that despite all the talk about process (the being) the grade will evaluate a product (the knowing) pure and simple.

Is it any wonder, then, that following the first, tentative written piece, dashed off in varying degrees of hurry and confusion (often the "writing sample") a first questioner turns out of the peer group sharing each others' work toward the place in the room where the teacher stands: "Is this right?" "Am I right?" "Is this what you want?" "How many pages should it be?" "Is this too short?" "Is this long enough?" "My teacher said that you should always/never do it this way." Clearly, there is a silent, conspiratorially enforced agreement: this will never be the place of "plain and ordinary things." Thus, the anxiety: these students sense that they are somehow broken writers who have come to the college writing class, with understandably varying degrees of desire, in one last effort to be "fixed."

5

The effort to separate process and form (or content), the ecstatic
and the rational, the natural and the human, the private and the public,
the *re*productive world of conceiving, gestating, nurturing children and
the *pro*ductive one, is a hallmark of the separation of ontology from
epistemology, of being from knowing. Relating these two worlds of experience, or, better, recognizing that being and knowing are dialectical
processes informing our experience of one world, is crucial to making art
(the "piece" is, after all, an intersection of many kinds of knowing-in-
the-world and being-in-the-world). And this recognition is crucial to
making *meaning* in a written text. In short, the piece gives speech to
what both William Wordsworth and Adrienne Rich think of as "plain and
ordinary things." In so doing, as utterance, it connects us to them and
enables us to "compose" our brokenness. In composing the text, we
compose, as well, the self.

To rethinking the art of writing and the art of teaching writing, the
feminist movement's revisioning activity can make a radical contribution.
Exploring that contribution, it is finally not necessary—and not the project
of this book—to ask if women's writing is "different" in some particular
way. Nevertheless, the intersection of women's arts and theories encourages us to rethink the ways we read and write, and the ways we teach
students to do both, as well. A revisioned literary history is important to
this enterprise. New ways of reading texts in light of that historical
revision offer insights about the relationship between reading and writing, about writing processes and writing pedagogy.

This chapter looks at the efforts of some women to recover, read-
dress and reintegrate the work of the Romantics, which writers like
Matthew Arnold and T. S. Eliot strove so hard to repudiate. Their project
has three dimensions: it involves, first, women's definition of the object;
second, their sense of the perceiving subject's relations *with* (not *to*) the
object; and last, the nature of knowing/being expressed in the written
record of that seeing-in-relationship.

The Problem of Romanticism

As the Romantic experiment failed[1] and as efforts to repress the questions it raised and to repudiate the relationships it deemed important
intensified, the nineteenth century[2] experienced a gradual, horrifying
numbness. This "denaturing" of experience was marked by a growing
rift between human and natural, human and human, between aspects
of the self, between knowing and being, between the song and the
text. If our connection with the world and with each other is broken,

and if significant aspects of the self are repressed, the text that explores and constructs meaning will be broken, too. I propose that, as teachers of writing in the twentieth century, we are facing in our students' texts the consequences of that brokenness. Women's literature frequently records the effort to come to terms with this actual—and literal—brokenness. In part, this is because women write from the position of Other. In Peter Duerr's terms, we have consistently stood, or been placed, in the "wild" space outside of the culture's enclosure,[3] a position that often facilitates the critique of the relation between sameness and difference and a recognition of the dialectical nature of that relation. Consequently, I believe that we can learn a great deal from women's work.

If we must discover new forms to reconstruct meaning from brokenness, as teachers of writing we must find new forms to help students reestablish the relationships that Romantic writers understood and brought into their texts as crucial to a fulfilled, authentic life. These new forms are essential for making meaning of learning processes, too. So pedagogical and aesthetic questions are never mutually exclusive; that is, both practices—the pedagogical and the aesthetic—remain rooted in *ethos,* in questions about how to live authentically.

Where have students learned this sense of brokenness, and how have we come to suggest to them—and perhaps believe ourselves—that the writing class is higher education's last-stop repair shop? In part, it is because they come convinced that they have no story to tell.[4] In part, it is because Wordsworth's triumphant experiment "to ascertain how far the language of conversation in the middle and lower classes of society is adapted to the purposes of poetic pleasure"[5]—an experiment about language, but really an experiment about connecting people to their world and to one another—finally failed. And, in part, it is because the potential fruits of his experiment were finally buried under an avalanche of competing cultural demands unleashed upon everyone by the growth of the modern city.

During the nineteenth and early twentieth centuries, English and American people found themselves confronting city life as a reality and as an image—or, better, an icon—of the impact its technology would have on their lives. A pervasive brokenness—real and imaginative—begins here. So, too, begins the human lament for what is lost. In Byron's *Don Juan,* London is

A mighty mass of brick, and smoke, and shipping,
Dirty and dusky, but wide as eye

> Could reach, . . . a wilderness of steeples peeping
> On tiptoe through their sea-coal canopy. (X, lxxxii, 1–3, 5–6)

For Wordsworth, it is a "monstrous ant-hill on the plain/Of a too busy world!" (*Prelude* VII, 149–50).

> A work completed to our hands, that lays,
> If any spectacle on earth can do,
> The whole creative powers of man asleep! . . .
> . . . What a shock
> For eyes and ears!
> What anarchy and din,
> Barbarian and infernal,—a phantasma,
> Monstrous in colour, motion, shape, sight, sound!
> (*Prelude*, VII, 679–81, 685–88)

In Charles Dickens's *Martin Chuzzlewit*, it is "this crowd of objects" (162), and in *Bleak House:* "Smoke lowering down from chimney pots, making a soft black drizzle, with flakes of soot in it as big as full grown snow flakes—gone into mourning, one might imagine, for the death of the sun. . . . Fog everywhere. Fog up the river, where it flows among green aits and meadows; fog down the river, where it rolls defiled among the tiers of shipping and the waterside pollutions of a great (and dirty) city" (1). For Eliot, it is simply "Unreal" (*The Wasteland*, 60), for Joseph Conrad, surreal: "Then the vision of an enormous town presented itself, of a monstrous town more populous than some continents and in its man-made might as if indifferent to heaven's frowns and smiles; a cruel devourer of the world's light. There was . . . darkness enough to bury five million lives" (*The Secret Agent*, 12).

In the midst of this mesmerizing city stood the Crystal Palace, a paradox of steel and glass erected in 1851 on the green in Hyde Park, an industrial exhibit hall and a pervasive symbol of Victorian worship of progress. But the psychological reality was a pervasive sense of their own brokenness. Wordsworth would write in his Preface to the *Lyrical Ballads:* "For a multitude of causes unknown to former times are now acting with a combined force to blunt the discriminating powers of mind, and unfitting it for all voluntary exertion to reduce it to a state of almost savage torpor. The most effective of these causes are the great national events which are daily taking place, and the increasing accumulation of men in cities" (*Prose Works*, 128). "I am past thirty, and three parts iced over—and my pen, it seems to me is even stiffer and more cramped than my feeling," Arnold had written to his friend in 1853 (Foster, *The Letters of Matthew Arnold to Arthur Hugh Clough,* 128).

Arnold's remarks come at the midpoint of a century whose pervasive themes are broken geography and broken object-relations—country and city, organism and mechanism, parent and child, person and nature, person and person, self and selves—and a desperate effort to find appropriate connection. The early part of the century had witnessed a Romantic revival of the lyric; its singers sought with varying degrees of success to make the object into an image, an imaginative leap through which their transcendence of brokenness might be achieved. Tintern Abbey and the natural landscape that surrounded it became for Wordsworth a reminder of a certain kind of childhood vision of a time when "Their colors and their forms, were then to me/An appetite; a feeling and a love" ("Lines: Composed A Few Miles Above Tintern Abbey," 79–80). It was a vision to be repudiated by the adult mind. Abbey and landscape became as well vehicles for an extraordinarily abstract (and one might say finally highly suspect) feeling of "connection" to "humanity."

> . . . I have learned
> To look on nature, not as in the hour
> Of thoughtless youth; but hearing oftentimes
> The still, sad music of humanity,
> Nor harsh nor grating, though of ample power
> To chasten and subdue. And I have felt
> A presence that disturbs me with the joy
> Of elevated thoughts; a sense sublime
> Of something far more deeply interfused,
> Whose dwelling is the light of setting suns
> . . . and in the mind of man . . .
> ("Lines: Composed A Few Miles Above Tintern Abbey," 88–99)

The struggle with abstraction is reflected in what becomes of things, and persons, in some of Wordsworth's work. One might say, for example, that only a man of Wordsworth's class privilege (and distance from certain kinds of people and objects) could romanticize the "dignity" of a leech-gatherer's life, immersed in frigid ponds, attracting the bloodsuckers for later sale with his warm-blooded, quickly chilling, old legs. These poems begin in specificity—a ruined abbey, daffodils, a nightingale, an urn—but they end with the object-made-image—thus somehow no longer itself. The lament of Keats ("Cold Pastoral!") seems inevitable. Entombed in his hedgerow, he recognized the failure—or at least the unbearable transiency—of this project of transcendence: "Was it a vision, or a waking dream?/Fled is that music:—Do I wake or sleep?" ("Ode on a Grecian Urn," 45; "Ode to a Nightingale," 79–80). A failure to connect lurked in the hedgerow, and in the heart.

By midcentury, the voice of Arnold would be heard claiming, emphatically and repeatedly, a new, back-to-basics project: "to see the object as in itself it really is" ("On Translating Homer," *Complete Prose Works*, 1: 140). Arnold rode the railroad all over Europe for thirty-five years, inspecting schools and producing several volumes of essays on the problem of education in England and on the Continent. He and his fellow Victorians were, at least early in their careers, obsessed with form as a means of managing a psychically unmanageable content. Their poems, like his, were a poignant lament over their disconnection from history, from other persons, from nature, from the imaginative faith of their Romantic predecessors, and from themselves. (It was, after all, not an accident that the Romantic lyric gave way to the dramatic monologue, a poem of implied, not actual, conversation, and a poem of intellectual relativism that was the form perfected by this latter part of the nineteenth century.) Defeated by his inability to fulfill his own classical prescription that poetry should "inspirit and rejoice the reader" (*Complete Prose Works*, 1:2), Arnold concludes the Preface to his *Poems, 1853* with a resounding exhortation to formal excellence:

> if it is impossible for us, under the circumstances amidst which we live, to think clearly, to feel nobly, and to delineate firmly; if we cannot attain to the mastery of the great artists;—let us, at least, have so much respect for our art as to prefer it to ourselves. Let us not bewilder our successors; let us transmit to them the practice of poetry, with its boundaries and wholesome regulative laws, under which excellent works may again, perhaps, at some future time, be produced, not yet fallen into oblivion through our neglect, not yet condemned and canceled by the influence of their eternal enemy, caprice. (*Complete Prose Works*, 1:15)

But neither tinkering with form nor tinkering with content worked. Arnold simply stopped being a poet and turned to writing about poetry, politics, and society instead. The ultimate terror of this self-exploration was, of course, solipsism, what he called in the 1853 Preface "the great disease of modernism, the dialogue of the mind with itself." While his classicism called him to epic, his inherently Romantic legacy made him, at his best, a lyric poet, but one frightened by what his poetic self-confession might reveal. In fact, only quite late in his career, after he had stopped writing poetry, did Arnold put aside his terror of the emotional anarchy the Romantics' exploration of the feeling self seemed to threaten and celebrated the vital promise offered by their *"lyrical cry"* ("On Translating Homer," *Complete Prose Works*, 1:209). While his Scholar Gipsy was "born in days when wits were fresh and clear" ("The Scholar Gipsy," 201), his nostalgically Romantic, Victorian consciousness experienced itself, "With its sick hurry and its divided aims" (204), "Wandering between two worlds, one dead, / The other powerless to be born" ("Stanzas from the Grand Chartreuse," 85–86). And in "The Buried Life" he stutters rhetorically,

> Only—but this is rare—
> When a beloved hand is laid in ours, . . .
> When our world-deafen'd ear
> Is by the tones of a lov'd voice caress'd
> . . . then he *thinks* he knows
> The Hills where his life rose,
> And the sea where it goes.
>   (77–78, 82–83, 96–98; emphasis added)

The object as image was insufficient to the Victorian imagination, and genuine connection—to object or person—seemed an impossibility.

Arnold's legacy in the twentieth century is Eliot's "Prufrock," who "dares" not even "think he knows." Eliot's "objective correlative" is a catchphrase that seeks to achieve the same promise as Arnold's "imaginative reason"[6]—appropriate connection of the feeling subject to an object "in itself, as it really is." His work demonstrates a visceral struggle with the problem of integrating feeling and the necessity to provide an "objective" description of experience. While it reflects the failure of William Blake's triumphant proclamation that imagination itself might "buil[d] Jerusalem/In England's green pleasant land" ("Preface," from *Milton*, II, 15–16), Eliot's struggle demonstrates that the dream was not yet dead.

Feminist criticism has pointed out that disconnection, the denaturing of the lived experience, had inevitably to be accompanied by a devaluing of the feminine—life—principles, and thus a devaluing of "woman," and of individual women in the culture. This devaluing was acted out in the creation of forms, the Victorian "Angel in the House" and her whalebone corset not the least of them. These forms could capture and possess her energy and her potency, thus mastering and sanitizing (dreadful corruption of the world) a terrifying array of natural processes—among them conception, birth, and the nurturing of children—through mastering her.

If this poetry of male Romantics and their legatees expressed their yearning for connection, it was complemented by the separation imposed on women. Many "forms" were erected on the conventional ground of language itself. Pregnancy was called "confinement." Middle and upper class working women who married were abruptly and immediately "retired" to the home to await the birth of children without any cultural ritual to ease that drastic change of lifestyle. "Rest" cures for "hysterical" symptoms focused on eliminating factors that had caused them—underlying disturbances of women's reproductive organs and functions—and were conducted with the demand for complete control by a male physician whose female nurses dispensed milk diets and douches while he himself prescribed aliments and nutriments, the potables heavily laced with alcohol.[7] Massive furniture, some of it heavily and elaborately carved, crowded every room, its weight and mass bringing a kind of solid security in a rapidly changing world, and a massive cleaning problem, too. Multiple patterns covered walls, drapes, and rugs as though frantically to fill up every possibility of empty space. The nursery was removed to the top of the house; in *Jane Eyre* only the attic where Rochester's "nymphomaniac" wife was kept and from which her mad laugh echoed was at further remove from the everyday work of the household. As Charlotte Perkins Gilman's short story recording her own "rest cure" reveals, more than one attempt was made to "confine" women there with their children and to use infantilization itself as a primary means of control; thus, the Victorian sexual fascination for the child-woman.[8]

And gradually, relentlessly, male and female writers in the latter half of the century, their texts strewn with lovers, brokenhearted in one way or another, tell stories of efforts—largely unsuccessful—to bind up and thus to control those demonic and ecstatic elements that were the great fascination of an earlier Romantic generation. It is a tribute to the power of this Romantic inheritance and the women who came to embody it that, despite relentless efforts at repression, this feminine energy would not be contained. The child Jane throws herself furiously against the locked doors of her dead stepfather's blood-red bedroom, and they do not yield. But she is delivered unconscious from this room, reborn in the identity of a confirmed defiance that causes Jane the woman to refuse Rochester's efforts to dress her as his doll, and infuses her refusal to return to him until his dreadfully maimed state guarantees her mastery of their married life together. Rochester's wife emerges from her attic, and the fire of her bounded rage burns down his house and wreaks upon him a terrible, castrating revenge. Keats's sinuous Lamia and Coleridge's Christabel find expression in Tennyson's Vivien and Rossetti's often halo-bound recreations out of myth and literature. Despite her reduced social status at court, the prostituted quality of her sexuality, and the pitiful tenor of her jealousy, Viven works her magic, entombing Merlin for eternity like no mean Circe. And the sinuous hands of Rossetti's women, along with the sheer mass of their hair and torsos, threaten always to burst from the confinement of his frames. In short, as Nina Auerbach argues of texts whose women are apparently more submissive (the saintly child Helen is clearly Jane's foil in this regard), these women's stories are the fulfillment of "a vital Victorian mythology whose lovable woman is a silent and self-disinherited mutilate, the fullness of whose extraordinary and dangerous being might at any moment return through violence. The taboos that encased Victorian woman contained buried tributes to her disruptive power" (*Woman and the Demon*, 8). Again, "Burne-Jones and his Victorian associates force us to look into the serpent-woman's face and to feel the mystery of a power, endlessly mutilated and restored, of a woman with a demon's gifts" (*Woman and the Demon*, 9). Seeking to master nature—and the nature in ourselves—we confront increasingly the fact that we have instead unleashed a monster—many monsters, in fact. But the warnings of these consequences were present already in nineteenth-century images of women over whom for centuries patriarchal cultures had sought control as part and parcel of this ongoing obsession for mastery over life and, thus, over death.

The complement to this sense of broken relationship, to the disconnection from the objects of our experience that images cannot heal, to the separation and silencing of women in culture, is the loss of song, the loss of story itself. In his book, *The Singer of Tales*, Albert Lord reflects that "if the way of life of a people furnishes subjects for story and affords occasion for the telling, this art will be fostered. . . . The songs have died out in the cities not because life in a large community is an unfitting environment for them but because schools were first founded there and writing has been firmly rooted in the way of life of the city dwellers" (20). Why did writing silence song? Because in Europe, culture and literacy had gradually come to be synonymous. "Culture and humanity resided in writing. Without writing there was a void. The oral culture of the indigenous civilization was a non-culture, was barbarous. By a process of repetition, 'humanity' came to be synonymous with being European: with the 'possessor' of European culture. . . . The myth of the cultural void of the non-West—The Other—was to be central to the ideology which the West would use in its rise to world domination."[9]

Silencing women's efforts to represent their experience is of a piece with male efforts to culturally dominate the "barbarian" Other, because women's project shares important connections to that of oral cultures. Women's writing takes as one of its projects a return through memory to a time and a culture that is not "illiterate" as it is typically described, but "preliterate," to an oral tradition in which the word is conceived as "utterance," the "outering" of self in order that the self can find a creative and fluid intersection with an ongoing cultural tradition. Madeleine Grumet speaks of it as "recovering our own possibilities, ways of knowing and being in the world that we remember and imagine and must draw into language that can span the chasm that presently separates what we know as our public and private worlds" (*Bitter Milk*, 15). This is, of course, what the Romantic lyric, which is first and foremost a song, was about.

In women's writing, this reclamation has often involved the recovery of personal history, partly, yet significantly, what Virginia Woolf called "think[ing] back through our mothers" (*A Room of One's Own*, 79), a task that every woman writer must inevitably do at some point—or at many points—in her ongoing process. Secondly, it involves the rediscovery and the reaffirmation of the senses and the sense of time, of history, that are the hallmarks of this preliterate time of life and this preliterate relationship to language. This is no conventional history, but the history of our own Otherness and, by dialectical extension, the record of the ways that we, too, have been possessed and colonized in the West. In short, just as there is an oral tradition emerging from the preliterate period in the history of a culture's literature, a period when "composition and performance are two aspects of the same moment" (Lord, *The Singer of Tales*, 13), so too is there a preliterate period in the history of an individual's struggle toward written language and the sense of fixity and "conventionalization" that the mastery of written language inevitably brings.[10]

In their effort to move back behind erected linguistic conventions that have fixed their identity in a language foreign to their experience and a linearity foreign to their understandings of time and space, these women, too, seek a return to a kind of Romantic consciousness in which being and knowing—composition and performance—are at least dialectically understood if they can no longer in a literate society be conceived as one. Preliterate men, bards, and troubadours,[11] and their Romantic legatees, sang the poetry that shaped and was shaped by culture, but lost the song when their literacy became obsessed with fact, with linearity, with progress defined only as a relentless hurtle toward technocracy. Reminding us of what we had lost and seeking a way to recover it in song was preeminently Romantic work. Blake's *Songs of Innocence and Experience* was among the first of these efforts.

Contemporary women writers, like their Romantic counterparts, seek the recovery of this oral tradition. Their interest is not its formed, or formal, but its form*ing* possibilities and its connection to mythic time. They seek the song as utterance. But, unlike their predecessors, they seek the song, not to *make* the object image, but to *forge a relationship* between the two. They seek the moment of relation and the many moments that become history, that place "between" that Virginia Woolf calls "the moment of being." They seek what Rich calls "the thing itself and not the myth" ("Diving into the Wreck," I.63).[12] They are both willing, and in fact recognize the need, to suspend fact for facticity,[13] expecting to find and articulate not "truth" but "truth-in-relation," and to "know" it by its "being" there in relation to them.

Despite current cultural pressure to make students write in conformity to standard English, the first battle of the writing classroom is, ironically, against the conventionalization of language. This is, it seems to me, a renewed Romantic battle in the oral tradition particular to the project of women's literature, and women's work in this regard can be significantly instructive to writing pedagogy. Its aim is to help students discover, to hear, or perhaps best, to overhear, their own voices—voices that many writing teachers I know will lament as having been absent from students' texts for a very long time—and once they have overheard them, in Eliot's phrase, to "dare" to *trust* them.[14] Eudora Welty writes of her own process:

> Ever since I was first read to, then started reading to myself, there has never been a line read that I didn't *hear.* As my eyes followed a sentence, a voice was saying it silently to me. It isn't my mother's voice, or the voice of any person I can identify, certainly not my own. It is human, but inward, and it is inwardly that I listen to it. It is to me the voice of the story or the poem itself. . . . I have supposed but never found out, that this is the case with all readers—to read as listeners—and with all writers, to write as listeners. It may be part of the desire to write. The sound of what falls on the page begins the process of testing it for truth, for me. Whether I am right to trust so far I don't know. By now I don't know whether I could do either one, reading or writing, without the other. (*One Writer's Beginnings,* 12–13)

The work of these women writers is crucially about memory, a chief fascination for Romantic and Victorian alike (although each group regarded its activity and its fruits very differently). It is also about discovering techniques that can link sensation to experience and to feeling. This work leads ultimately, as Robert Langbaum *(The Mysteries of Identity)* describes the Romantic understanding of these, to *self* (what Keats called "Soul"), to *identity* (the continuity of self over time), and, I would argue, to *voice* emerging from a written text. For *self* and therefore *voice*, in my view, is dependent on the capacity to do exactly what Madeleine Grumet describes: to remember ways of knowing and being in the world, the childlike and the playful not the least of these; to imagine the possibilities for other ways of knowing and being, and to have the capability of calling them into language.

Tracing nineteenth-century understandings of "self" through Locke, Hume, and (chiefly) Wordsworth, Langbaum argues that, for Hume, "the self is a retrospective construction of the imagination, and for this reason 'memory not only discovers the identity, but also contributes to its production.' Only through memory can we create the self by seeing continuity between past and present perceptions. . . . Memory above all will remain the creator, the artist-fabricator, of self" *(The Mysteries of Identity,* 27). But "[Hume] lacks the Wordsworthian notion that the forgotten past comes suddenly alive in the present and establishes when it does the only continuity of self that matters" (28).

This movement backward in order to go forward is, as Langbaum notes, a chief characteristic of Wordsworth's "processive self." It is also a hallmark of the personal narrative work of countless women writers, and it spills richly into their fiction, as well. The object relation happens by remembering the object and imaginatively reproducing it. In this relationship, the self is formed and transcended at the same time, a circular— or spiraling—evolution both celebratory of and dependent upon a faith in the relational possibilities of human experience.[15]

Yet while the object-made-image may evoke archetypal dimensions of the human self and of human experience, the risk is always that the semiosis of the object may disconnect it from its reality as a thing in the world. This is one dimension of the kind of solipsism most feared by the Romantic generation, and it underlies Keats's lament about the veracity of his own ecstatic experience as the nightingale flees from his hedgerow.

Often their inability to grasp multiple levels of meaning attached to image and symbol as they are claimed and elaborated by individual writers and cultures causes contemporary students to be labeled "literalist." But as legatees of the Romantic struggle with the same issue, they are finally, it seems to me, certainly *not* literal—and this is the problem—they are simply not connected to these objects at all. How, then, does writing teacher help these students to begin to recover connections?

I suspect the answer is not to forget, as Wordsworth felt he had to, the time of "thoughtless youth," but to begin to remember it. These memories and imaginings are first called into language—first given voice—in song. This is where the troubadours began, this is where the Romantic poets began, and this is where many contemporary women writers begin as well. "My mother," Welty says, "always sang to her children" (*One Writer's Beginning*, 12). Traditionally, the lyric, the formal hallmark of nineteenth-century Romanticism, has been understood to be the place of song, of utterance, but to harvest its rich potential, and to grasp the extent to which this potential has been lost to literate cultures, necessitates a return to an understanding of its oral roots.

Orality and Memory

The thematic and formal qualities of oral narrative have been well documented by Scholes and Kellogg in *The Nature of Narrative,* and by Albert Lord in *The Singer of Tales.* I suspect, in fact, that Matthew Arnold intuitively recognized and effectively exploited the oral *formula,* "a group of words which is regularly employed under the same metrical conditions to express a given essential idea,"[16] as a rhetorical strategy. But what is most interesting is the way Lord describes the epic songs of illiterate Yugoslavian mountain poets recorded almost eighty years ago, and what his description offers to writing classroom theory. First, Lord notes that the oral poet is not merely a transmitter but also a creator of cultural tradition: his key point—and the key point of the relationships among these oral poets, romantic writers, and contemporary women's work—is that the act of composition and the act of performance are one and the same. Unlike the Western, postliterate ballad passed on exactly from generation to generation, "an oral poem is not composed *for* but *in* performance.... We must eliminate from the word 'performer' any notion that he is one who merely reproduces what someone else or even he himself has composed.... Our singer of tales is a composer of tales. Singer, performer, composer, and poet are one under different aspects *but at the same time.* Singing, performing, composing are facets of the same act" (*The Singer of Tales,* 13).

"[S]uch a price/The Gods exact for song;/To become what we sing" ("The Strayed Reveller," 232–34), Arnold had written in this poem richly reminiscent of Keats. "I do not believe in separation," says Bernard in Virginia Woolf's *The Waves.*[17] "The human voice has a disarming quality—(we are not single, we are one)" (221). In an important sense, students' questions—"Is it right?" "Is it long enough?" "How do I do that?"—suggest the extent to which we have communicated to them a false linearity in the writing process: first we compose it, then it is read, usually in silence, by the teacher at her desk, to determine if it is "right." This implies that writing and making texts are the same activity, that writing involves fixed forms to be learned and imitated rather than fluid processes to be entered into. From this it follows that students experience themselves as mere transmitters of cultural convention rather than as creative voices to be added to the chorus of those who have come before. Writing so often with a frightened sense of how their texts will look (rarely sound) to their teacher-audience, students lose both a sense of ownership of their work (words pass through them but do not come from and so do not belong to them) and a validation of their own voices. Thus the brokenness of their relationship to fact—the negation of facticity: these voiceless students simply never tell their own stories because they never feel invited, in the world of school, to tell them, nor have they inherited the tools or the attitude of mind that would make the telling possible. How many of our students feel able to risk the act, or to pay what Arnold calls (and Woolf demonstrates is) the price—in self-exposure, in effort, and in time—to be genuinely connected to the object? And how often have they learned from the academy a false sense of appropriateness that has negated their experience and in some cases invalidated the fullness of experience itself?

It was the urge to invite back into their songs all kinds of experiences proscribed by past formal constraints that gave impetus to the Romantic movement. This same impetus informs contemporary women's writing—and should inform contemporary teaching as well. Woolf's poet, Neville, one voice of the six who compose *The Waves,* speaks about experience in a way that prescribes how Woolf's prose poem is to be read—or, better, how it is to be listened to—and what the nature of the relationship between person and person, person and world, person and self or selves, reader/listener and narrator must be:

> Certainly, one cannot read this poem without effort. The page is often corrupt and mud-stained, and torn and stuck together with faded leaves, with scraps of verbena or geranium. To read this poem one must have myriad eyes . . . One must put aside antipathies and jealousies and not interrupt. One must have patience and infinite care and let the light sound, whether of spiders' delicate feet on a leaf or the chuckle of water in some irrelevant drainpipe, unfold too. Nothing is to

be rejected in fear or horror. . . One must be skeptical, but throw caution to the winds and when the door opens accept absolutely. Also sometimes weep; also cut away ruthlessly with a slice of the blade soot, bark, hard accretions of all sorts. And so (while they talk) let down one's net deeper and deeper and gently draw in and bring to the surface what he said and she said and make poetry. (313–14)

In addition, Lord's description of Yugoslav villages where oral poets perform can also speak richly to the writing classroom's pedagogy. In fact, it is a paradigm for the contemporary classroom with all its literal, cognitive, and emotional traffic.

> In the country villages, where the houses are often widely separated, a gathering may be held at one of the houses during a period of leisure from the work in the fields. Men from all the families assemble and one of their number may sing epic songs. Because of the distances between the houses some of the guests arrive earlier than others, and of course this means that some leave earlier. Some very likely spend the whole night. . . . The singer has to contend with an audience that is coming and going, greeting newcomers, saying farewell to early leavers; a newcomer with special news or gossip may interrupt the singing for some time, perhaps even stop it entirely. (*The Singer of Tales*, 14)

We think of the writing classroom as a place like so many others in which a certain amount of teaching/learning occurs in a specified amount of time. In reality, like Lord's description of Yugoslavian storytelling, it is not a place, but a time—a fluid and chaotic time without a defined beginning or ending—a moment of being together in which composing and performing are one activity. This conception can shed new light on curriculum, on our conception of writing as a solitary *versus* a communal activity, on the syllabus with its defined goals and fixed due-dates for paper completion, and, along with these poets' sense of "repertory" and "competence," on the revision process itself.

First, after the poet has listened much of his life to other singers and longs to join their ranks, an increase in the poet's competence involves not primarily increasing his "products"—the number of songs per se that he can sing—but facility with a process: "this does not involve memorizing a text, but practicing until he can compose it, or recompose it himself" (*The Singer of Tales*, 25). Consequently, there is no imaginary *Wasteland*—no imaginary fixed and unchanging text against which "correctness" can be measured. Secondly, he is a poet without a sense of linearity. His sense of the word involves its embeddedness in a relational group of sounds: "The word for 'word' means an 'utterance.' When the singer is pressed then to say what a line is, he, whose chief claim to fame is that he traffics in lines of poetry, will be entirely baffled by the question" (25). This extends to his consciousness of time, as well. When asked if he can learn a song he hears right away, he responds, "Yes, I could sing it for you right away the next day" (26). What is more, "The singers he has heard have given him the necessary traditional material to make it possible for him to sing, but the length of his songs and the degree to which he will ornament and expand them will depend on the demand of the audience" (25).

He sees the work not as a partial structure, beginning, middle, and end; the conception of "line" as a partial unit of meaning has no significance to him. His focus is a core of meaning out of which the structures that allow and enhance its expression emerge. The activity of composition is therefore organic, not self-consciously mechanical, and it is ultimately bound up with a consideration that it is sung to be overheard. Finally, the revision process is celebrated as an ongoing, lifelong one. Competence, artistry, involve having "a sufficient command of the formula technique to sing any song that he hears, and enough thematic material at hand to lengthen or shorten a song according to his own desires and to create a new song if he sees fit" (26). He can thus never, like contemporary students and teachers, ask the questions "Is this right?" "How many pages should it be?" "Is it good enough for an A, a B, a C?" but only the single question "Does this work?" This question can be asked only in the felt context of a supportive community, without the anxieties that we know block the composing process. It is a question that causes the modern writing teacher to rethink the concept of fact and originality, as well as the nature of the composing process itself.

Demo Zogic, one of the poets Lord interviewed in his study, comments on his ability to sing a song again that he has heard only once: "It's possible . . . I know from my own experience. When I was together with my brothers and had nothing to worry about, I would hear a singer sing a song to the *gusle*, and after an hour I would sing his whole song. I can't write. I would give every word and not make a mistake on a single one" (27). Yet Sulejman Makic, another poet responding to the question whether it is better to sing a new song right away, or a day later when it might be forgotten, argues: "It has to come to one. One has to think . . . how it goes, and then little by little it comes to him, so that he won't leave anything out . . . One couldn't sing it like that all the way through right away" (26–27). What he describes is a process not merely of recovering an original text, but of recreating, recomposing the initial experience of his hearing it—the Romantic experience of seeing/hearing, remembering, imagining, calling it back into language. His relationship to fact, then, is a relationship to story, to narrative, and never to words themselves. So the concept— oft repeated in the writing classroom—"in your own words" is a foreign one to him.

> We think of change in content and in wording; for, to us, at some moment both wording and content have been established. To the singer the song, which cannot be changed (since to change it would, in his mind, be to tell an untrue story or to falsify history), is the essence of the story itself. His idea of stability, to which he is deeply devoted, does not include the wording, which to him has never been fixed, nor the unessential parts of the story. He builds his performance, or song in our sense, on the stable skeleton of narrative, which is the song in his sense. (99)

"My mother always sang to her children," Eudora Welty had written, overhearing her mother's storytelling voice in the dark. "Long before I wrote stories I listened for stories. Listening *for* them is something more acute than listening *to* them" (*One Writer's Beginnings*, 12, 16). "Writing is to start," writes Chantel Chawaf, "it is always to push the beginning further back, because in language nothing of the body, nothing of the woman has, as yet, been integrated. . . . Everything starts from the body and from the living, from our senses, our desires, our imagination."[18] "I learn," May Sarton writes, "by being *in relation to*" (*Journal of a Solitude*, 107).

Journal writing, telling one's story to oneself, is one means of creating facticity, the relation of persons to the facts of their experience, remaking as it does so our sense of time and of our "place" in it. While it is clearly not song, journal writing, the personal narrative that is undisputedly a significant one for women, is a postliterate form participating in some of the rich possibilities of its roots in oral narrative. Like the lyric, its impulse is inherently conversational: as a conversation with the self, it offers to its composers/performers the opportunity to circle back upon our experiences and ourselves, revising, reseeing both. Rereading each successive diary entry, we may circle back not upon recorded experience per se, but on (a sometimes continually varied series of) fixed texts that record our memory of the experience reproduced there. Composing the narrative, in fact, we compose our selves; like the way an oral poet learns his song, one comes to it "little by little."

In Moffat and Painter's *Revelations,* women talk about their journal writing: In 1918, the young diarist Nelly Ptaschkina wrote of herself, "Two Nelly's live in me. Sometimes I would like to know which is the real one. When I am in that other world, 'that' Nelly seems the real one; when I am back again in my ordinary everday one it is 'this.' In fact, they complete each other and make up the real me" (59). Joanna Field speaks about her diary work in *A Life of One's Own:* "I seemed to have two quite different selves, one which answered when I thought deliberately, another which answered when I let my thought be automatic. I decided to investigate further the opinions of the automatic one, to ask it questions and write answers without stopping to think" (352). Anne Frank's journal is a series of letters written to an alter ego she calls Kitty: "I hid myself within myself . . . and quietly wrote down all my joys, sorrows, and contempt in my diary" (35–36).

Whether it is introduced as a book for free writing, prewriting, reaction, focused reflection, description, or dramatization, if its use is not distorted by an overzealous writing teacher anxious only to help her students find material to write about, the journal can be a safe place where conversation can begin. Because its truth is "my story," truth-to-me, as a form it can validate the kind of "playing around" with experience that schooling's passion for order and form so frequently condemns, and it can be a place where the resignifying process that marks feminist work with language can begin. It validates chaos as a means of making order. And in the guise of a linear record of time, it allows participation in a circular, recursive temporality so fascinating to the Romantics that is at the heart of "composing" anything, including ourselves. Virginia Woolf writes of her own journal:

> there looms ahead of me the shadow of some kind of form which a diary might attain to. I might in the course of time learn what it is one can make of this loose, drifting material of life; finding another use for it than the use I put it to, so much more consciously and scrupulously in fiction . . . The main requisite, I think on rereading my old volumes is not to play the part of censor, but to write as the mood comes or of anything whatever; since I was curious to find how I went for things put in haphazard, and found the significance to lie where I never saw it at the time. (Moffat and Painter, *Revelations,* 227)

Like her Romantic predecessors, what Woolf explores is her own creative process—her journals are the ground of her fiction making—and in the dialectic between journal writing and fiction writing, Woolf explores consciousness itself. Her particular interest is an inherently Romantic one: her work is an extended inventory of the objects and relations of her life in memory, but she seeks them less as images through which the transcendent can occur than as things themselves that are part and parcel of the "moments of being" punctuating the organic and orgasmic movement of her text.

Woolf's texts are the songs of many voices, all of which are her own. More than any other twentieth-century writer she seems to have grasped the capacity to become one with the object. Her effort is to reclaim the landscape out of which the colors and the voices of her experience are born, reclaiming not fact, but facticity, and negating the kind of portraiture in which writers "collect a number of events, and leave the person to whom it happened unknown" (*Moments of Being*, 69).

Like Blake's *Songs* and Wordsworth's *Prelude*, much of women's writing is a retrospective effort to reclaim their childhood with their mothers in order that they might reclaim both their own children and themselves: "Many bright colours; many distant sounds; some human beings, caricature, comic, several violent moments of being, always including a circle of the scene which they cut out: and all surrounded by a vast space—that is a rough visual description of childhood" (Woolf, *Moments of Being*, 79). This world begins in the nursery. Like her Romantic predecessors, Woolf seeks first to reclaim not solely childhood, but a childlike connection to the object. Remembering two "first memories" she writes:

> without stopping to choose my way, in the sure and certain knowledge that it will find itself—or if not it will not matter— I begin: the first memory.
>
> This was of red and purple flowers on a black ground—my mother's dress; and she was sitting either in a train or in an omnibus, and I was on her lap. I therefore saw the flowers she was wearing very close; and can still see purple and red and blue, I think, against the black; they must have been anemones, I suppose. Perhaps we were going to St. Ives; more probably, for from the light it must have been evening, we were coming back to London. But it is more convenient artistically to suppose that we were going to St. Ives, for that will lead to my other memory, which also seems to be my first memory, and in fact it is the most important of all my memories. If life

has a base that it stands upon, if it is a bowl that one fills and
fills and fills—then my bowl without a doubt stands upon this
memory. It is of lying half asleep, half awake, in bed in the
nursery at St. Ives. It is of hearing the waves breaking, one,
two, one, two, and sending a splash of water over the beach;
and then breaking, one, two, one, two, behind a yellow blind.
It is of hearing the blind draw its little acorn across the floor
as the wind blew the blind out. It is of lying and hearing this
splash and seeing this light, and feeling, it is almost impossible
that I should be here; of feeling the purest ecstasy I can
conceive.
          . . . . .

   Those moments—in the nursery, on the road to the beach—
can still be more real than the present moment. (*Moments of
Being*, 64–65, 67)

In *The Waves*, Virginia Woolf's Rhoda expresses her struggle for
identity as the desperate effort to reconnect with the objects of her
experience. She begins with a lament: "I have no face." She ends with
the intuition that identity is about relationship, about facticity: "Alone, I
often fall down into nothingness. I must push my foot stealthily lest I
should fall off the edge of the world into nothingness. I have to bang my
hand hard against some door to call myself back to the body" (203–4).
Woolf's own intuition is that while the object itself may be lost to us,
writing is a means to recover our relation to it. About her own mother
she writes an incessant elegy, in diaries, autobiographical fragments, and
in many fictional works:

   What one would not give to recapture a single phrase even!
   or the tone of the clear round voice. . . . past as those years
   are, her mark on them is ineffaceable, as though branded by
   the naked steel, the sharp, the pure. Living voices in many
   parts of the world still speak of her as someone who is actually
   a fact in life . . . as of a thing that happened, recalling, as
   though all around her grew significant, how she stood and
   turned and how the bird sang loudly, or a great cloud passed
   across the sky. Where has she gone? What she said has never
   ceased. (*Moments of Being*, 36, 39)

Later she would reflect of her mother: "She was keeping what I call in
my shorthand the panoply of life—that which we all lived in common—
in being" (*Moments of Being*, 83).

The order of the personal narrative form is not the scientist's: it is neither logical, nor quantifiable, nor subject to conventional forms of analysis. "It seemed," Joanna Field writes, "that I was normally only aware of the ripples on the surface of my mind, but the act of writing a thought was a plunge which at once took me into a different element where the past was intensely alive" (Moffat and Painter, *Revelations*, 352). "And the order," Sylvia Ashton-Warner insists, "will be its own. An order of *emotional* importance" (Moffat and Painter, *Revelations*, 216).

In their explorations of consciousness, these women share the postliterate scientist's interest in sifting evidence, in repeatedly circling back upon the facts of experience in search of insight. But journal keeping is not deductive analysis leading from hypothesis toward proof. Nor is it finally the search for an image to express the movement of reflective consciousness and the nature of its relation to time, to memory. It is a search "for the thing itself." "Sometimes," wrote Field, "the meaning of an experience would only begin to dawn on me years afterward, and even then I had often to go over the same ground again and again, with intervals of years in between. In fact, I came to the conclusion that the growth of understanding follows an ascending spiral rather than a straight line" (Moffat and Painter, *Revelations*, 393). Field's spiral is yet another refinement of the circle imposed upon the line. The journal is an instrument for exploring consciousness, for circling back in recorded memory upon past experience. Insight dawns with "the growth of consciousness," and we are lifted beyond the circle's endless round. With each return, we may know a bit more. For, as Charlotte Painter's journal reflects, "the levels of the unconscious mind are yet to be counted" (Moffat and Painter, *Revelations*, 398).

The willingness—in fact the inevitability—of becoming and confronting a divided self, of confronting our brokenness, is a central theme of women's journals. Its pervasive expression, crossing cultures, generations, and historical periods, suggests these writers' connections to personal, cultural, and historical pasts—in particular to childhood and to the metaphoric childhood of the beginning writer's discovery of process—that can facilitate the reconnection of the knowing subject and the object-in-relation-to-which she knows.

Dividedness need not be, although it often becomes, brokenness. This was perhaps one of the most significant, though least heralded, discoveries of the Romantic period: a dialectical consciousness (innocence/experience; imagination/reason; past/present; clod/pebble; tiger/lamb) that became the excited fascination of a Romantic generation and the despair of their Victorian descendants. Understood and affirmed as both the blessing and the curse of memory, that sense of being "two selves," private and public, childlike and adult, deviant and appropriate, can create a rich, dialectical tension out of which much creative activity is born. Most importantly, it can be a basis for validating other kinds of knowing central to the world of imaginative play, and to the activity of composition that is the writer's work, and life's work.

Writing "On Memory and Childhood Amnesia," Ernest Schachtel posited that we do not remember very early childhood (the pre-Oedipal period) because "the categories (or schemata) of adult memory" are inadequate descriptors of childhood experience and consequently unfit to support recollection of it. While these memories are "continuous," they are nevertheless "barren," like a "road with occasional signposts and milestones" bereft of its accompanying "landscape."[19]

Schachtel's description of adult memory's sterility is an appropriate one for so many "voiceless" and "landscape-less" student papers of which I have spoken earlier. What he argues here can be traced to another, far more negative consequence that Welty recognizes she must escape: the obsession with linear time.

> Through learning at my later date things I hadn't known, or had escaped or possibly feared realizing, about my parents—and myself—I glimpse our whole family life as if it were freed of that clock time which spaces us apart so inhibitingly, divides young and old, keeps on living through the same experiences at separate distances.
>
> It is our inward journey that leads us through time—forward or back, seldom in a straight line, most often spiraling. Each of us is moving, changing, with respect to others. As we discover, we remember; remembering, we discover; and most intensely do we experience this when our separate journey's converge. Our living experience at those meeting points is one of the charged dramatic fields of fiction.
>
> I'm prepared now to use the wonderful word *confluence*, which of itself exists as a reality and a symbol in one. It is the only kind of symbol that for me as a writer has any weight, testifying to the pattern, one of the chief patterns, of human experience. (*One Writer's Beginnings*, 111–12)

Julia Kristeva's work[20] adds to Schachtel's postulate the argument that these inadequate categories are learned, part of the vast cultural conspiracy to negate and silence our pre-Oedipal child's connection to mother and to her language. The record of this effort to silence and negate is embedded in literary history. Knowing this history reminds us that if categories are learned, they can be unlearned, too. For example, nineteenth-century literature is a poignant record of the culture's repudiation of women, but also of children, from Blake's lament for the London chimney sweeps crying "'weep, 'weep" in child voices to Dickens' fictional excoriation of his society's literal and metaphoric orphaning of its sons and daughters. The term *childlike* comes into the language in the short-lived Romantic attempt to preserve and validate certain kinds of imaginative ways of seeing and knowing that they perceived as central to making art. But the tide of technology, its insistent emphasis on linear time, descriptions, processes; the conventionalization of language and the intolerance of deviance imperative to making and measuring "progress"; an anxious sense of the speed of time; the increasing formalization of education and its appropriation by the public domain; the devaluing of leisure and of play—all worked against the continued affirmation of children and of childlike ways of seeing and knowing and being. And so the proverbial village idiot found himself insitutionalized as a ward of the state, and the child, dressed like a miniature adult, was remanded to the custody of the nursery, the boarding school, or the factory, all of which served to separate mothers and children, and served, as well, the industrial machine. Schachtel recognizes the profound irony in this process. While "early childhood is the period of human life which is richest in experience," education and learning both enhance and limit experiential knowing, dampening and finally eradicating both curiosity and wonder. "The average adult," says Schachtel, " 'knows all the answers,' which is exactly why he will never know even a single answer."[21]

It is exactly this curiosity, this capacity for questioning and wonder, that Kristeva argues we can—and must—recover.

Classroom Praxis

The typical freshman writing classroom, to pun on Schachtel's term, is a place of many brakes, and many breaks. At worst, it is jammed with squirming bodies, shifting, whispering, doodling, staring off disconnectedly into dead space. They wander in late, leave early, without books or with the wrong books, having read stories for "the facts" or not at all, docile recorders of everything heard from the teacher, carefully avoiding a record of student community lest they become confused. The overwhelming temptation is to urge students to "grow up" and demonstrate that they are "serious learners" with an interest in the world and their own development. Yet what we need to urge is that they grow "back" or "down" so that they can grow "out" into the world, becoming playful learners capable of climbing behind the conventional structures and significances of language. They need to discover their own voices and the multiple means, beyond the five-paragraph essay, by which facticity allows experience to be ordered, engaged, and celebrated.

Schachtel's description of contemporary disengagement from experience, the matter-of-fact absence of facticity, is a paradigmatic record of nineteenth-century literature's thematic threnody. It is also a record of the twentieth-century classroom and twentieth-century curricula's legacy of brokenness. In light of this discussion of the disconnection from pre-Oedipal childhood, Schachtel's food metaphor is a paradoxically rich one: "While Midas suffered tortures of starvation, the people under whose eyes every experience turns into a barren cliché do not know that they starve."[22]

For Welty and for numerous other women writers, journal writing spills fluidly over into fiction making, yet another ground for embedded self-discovering. Referring to Miss Eckhart in her story "June Recital," Welty writes: "in the making of her character out of my most inward and most deeply feeling self, I would say I have found my voice in my fiction" (*One Writer's Beginnings*, 111).

Like Virginia Woolf, Welty recognizes with explicit clarity that her own voice emerges out of "convergence," of "meeting points," of moments when being and knowing come together. "Of course," Welty concludes, "the greatest confluence of all is that which makes up the human memory—the individual human memory. . . . Here time, also, is subject to confluence. The memory is a living thing—it too is in transit. But during its moment, all that is remembered joins, and lives—the old and the young, the past and the present, the living and the dead" (113–14).

E. M. Forster began his wonderful novel *Howard's End* with the epigraph "Only connect." The writing classroom must become the place and the time where the means of fulfilling Forster's great urging can genuinely be explored. The writing teacher's task is not, then, to demand specificity in students' writing, but to help them discover the tools to recover their own experience; it is to teach not language conventions but the suspension of them in order that language might be remade, experience revisited, and significance revised to express the individual writer's connection to fact. It is the work of empowerment.

When my students come to their first writing class, and we have chatted awhile, named ourselves, and told an uncomfortable story or two about ourselves, I ask them to come back with two books, a writing book and a drawing book. The work of the first week is to subvert the word, of the second to subvert the sentence, of the first month to allay anxieties by talking about and playing with revision—recovering sight and coming to understand how it gestates insight. Frederik Franck's *The Zen of Seeing* inspires the first few days, sending students out beyond the classroom walls. Franck instructs his readers to make space around themselves, to focus on whatever is immediately before them, to sit for a time before it, eyes closed, then to open them, and to draw, focused on the object, not the drawing, never lifting the pencil, "let[ing] the hand follow what the eye sees" (xv). Sharing their drawings anonymously, little by little students are drawn toward the kind of empathy that enables them to climb behind the labels for things and experience themselves as connected to what they have drawn. My students read some of what Franck writes; we talk a bit about insight, about significance—meaning-making.

> Seeing and drawing can become one, can become SEEING/ DRAWING. When that happens there is no more room for the labelings. . . . Every insignificant thing appears as if seen in its three dimensions, in its own space and in its own time. Each leaf of grass is seen to grow from its own roots, each creature is realized to be unique, existing now/here on its voyage from birth to death. No longer do I 'look' at a leaf, but enter into direct contact with its life-process, with Life itself, with what I, too, really am. . . . Becoming one with the lilies in SEEING/DRAWING, I become not less, but more myself. For the time being the split between Me and not-Me is healed, suspended. (Franck, *The Zen of Seeing*, 7)

Little by little we move toward words, but our prewriting exercises do not end in sentences. Semantic networks[23] become the means of exploring the apparently random associative fiber-optics of memory, of leaping synaptic gaps and figuring out why. Word pictures lead to mind pictures; free-writing is yet another resource to inventory experience, to recall smell, taste, touch, sight, sound. Sentences begin in a journal, and these pieces are shared aloud if the writer so chooses; the sounds and rhythms of their own words and others' words can be heard and savored. Communities of writers are formed in smaller groups, part of the larger collective that begins to define itself in the risking experience of hearing and being overheard, of listening and being listened to. In this community, each person's work becomes everyone's work; originality resides in the uniqueness of the stories, the pictures, the experiences, the insights, not merely in the words. Multiple drafts in response to multiple readings and listenings battle back the tyrannical permanence of the word, integrate revision from before the beginning to after the end, and enforce a potent sense of the connotative nature of language and the interpretive activity of knowing. Finally, if it all works, there emerges gradually through the ritual of reading, writing, storytelling, listening, in the dialectic of public and private, a sense of the sacred, of something holy, whole, healthy, of being participating in Being; Annie Dillard's conception of insight. May Sarton's *Journal of a Solitude* is a rich reflection of what every Romantic poet seems eventually to have discovered: the song as utterance becomes, inevitably, prayer:

> I suppose that the only prayer—reached only *after* all pleas for grace or for some specific gifts have been uttered and laid aside—is: "Give me to be in your presence. . . . " Simone Weil says, "Absolute attention is prayer." And the more I have thought about this over the years, the truer it is for me. I have used the sentence often in talking about poetry to students, to suggest that if one looks long enough at almost anything, looks with absolute attention at a flower, a stone, the bark of a tree, grass, snow, a cloud, something like a revelation takes place. Something is 'given,' and perhaps that something is always a reality *outside* the self. We are aware of God only when we cease to be aware of ourselves, not in the negative sense of denying the self, but in the sense of losing self in admiration and joy. (99)[24]

Despite her professed atheism, like Franck and Sarton, Woolf too shares this sense as a consequence of becoming one with the object, not an outcome but an expression of this intense experience of fusion:

> I was looking at the flower bed by the front door; "That is the whole," I said. I was looking at a plant with a spread of leaves; and it seemed suddenly plain that the flower itself was a part of the earth; that a ring enclosed what was the flower; and that was the real flower; part earth; part flower.
>
>   . . . . .
>
> I feel that I have had a blow; but it is not, as I thought as a child, simply a blow from an enemy hidden behind the cotton wool of daily life; it is or will become a revelation of some order; it is a token of some real thing behind appearances;

and I make it real by putting it into words. It is only by putting it into words that I make it whole; this wholeness means that it has lost its power to hurt me; it gives me . . . a great delight to put the severed parts together. . . . From this I reach what I might call a philosophy, a constant idea of mine; that behind the cotton wool is hidden a pattern; that we—I mean all human beings—are connected with this; that the whole world is a work of art; that we are parts of the work of art. *Hamlet* or a Beethoven quartet is the truth about this vast mass that we call the world. But there is no Shakespeare, there is no Beethoven; certainly and emphatically there is no God; we are the words; we are the music; we are the thing itself. And I see this when I have a shock. (*Moments of Being,* 71–72)[25]

Being and knowing—what Woolf calls "telling the truth about my own experiences as a body" ("Professions for Women," 62) come together in community, when "performance and composition" are one: every writer, every singer, has an audience. But the last paradox, the lesson so difficult for the socially passionate nineteenth-century novelists to learn (busy as they were about the work of repudiating Romantic individualism in the name of social responsibility, busy as they were at imposing upon life a sequential march from cradle to grave), was that the ground of community is solitude, and that solitude is constructed upon the sense of being "composed," of being "at home" with oneself. To be "at home" we have to know where home is; to know where it *is,* we have to know where it *was.* Home is not a space but a place. I suspect this same difficulty confronts the contemporary student; I am certain this same difficulty confronts the contemporary teacher.

Denise Levertov sings this last message that was, finally, the intent of my own first reflection:

> . . . I sing those messages you've
> learned by heart . . .
> . . . You hear
> yourselves in them,
> self after self. Your solitudes
> utter their runes, your own
> voices begin to rise in your throats. ("Poet and Person," 7–12)[26]

Towards the end of *The Waves,* Bernard confronts the despair in what he calls "the contribution of maturity to childhood's intuitions—

satiety and doom; the sense of what is inescapable in our lot; death; the knowledge of limitations; how life is more obdurate than one had thought it" (363). We cannot help but hear the voice of Keats. But Woolf causes Bernard to answer the despair, although the response can by no means be any Wordsworthian conception of joy. The ecstasy is of a different order altogether: it is about wrestling meaning from experience through utterance.

> Some people go to priests; others to poetry; I to my friends, I to my own heart, I to seek among phrases and fragments something unbroken—I to whom there is not beauty enough in moon or tree; to whom the touch of one person with another is all, yet who cannot grasp even that, who am so imperfect, so weak, so unspeakably lonely. There I sat.
>
> . . . . .
>
> But if you hold a blunt blade to a grindstone long enough, something spurts—a jagged edge of fire; so held to lack of reason, aimlessness, the usual, all massed together, out spurted in one flame hatred, contempt. I took my mind, my being, the old dejected, almost inanimate object and lashed it about among these odds and ends, sticks and straws, detestable little bits of wreckage, flotsam and jetsam floating on the oily surface. I jumped up, I said, 'Fight.' 'Fight,' I repeated. It is the effort and the struggle, it is the perpetual warfare, it is the shattering and piecing together—this is the daily battle, defeat or victory, the absorbing pursuit. The trees, scattered, put on order; the thick green of the leaves thinned itself to a dancing light. I netted them under with a sudden phrase. I retrieved them from formlessness with words. (361, 363–64)

Without a knowledge of brokenness, connectedness cannot be understood. Without the experience of connectedness, our students' texts will be forever broken. These are the lessons Adrienne Rich explores in her search "for the thing itself." This is the legacy that Virginia Woolf, Joanna Field, that journalmakers, their work deeply embedded in the Romantic tradition, and in the songs of preliterate people, seek to learn in the effort "to become the thing"—to become themselves. This is the dialectic of the writing classroom's project.

They were women then
My mama's generation
Husky of voice—Stout of
Step
With fists as well as
Hands
How they battered down
Doors
And ironed
Starched white
Shirts
How they led
Armies
Headragged Generals
Across mined
Fields
Booby-trapped
Kitchens
To discover books
Desks
A place for us
How they knew what we
Must *know*
Without knowing a page
Of it
Themselves.

—*Alice Walker,* In Search of Our Mothers' Gardens

II

Reading Women's Songs:
A Theory of Orality

Australian Aboriginal Song and the Problem of Access

In their Dreamtime, believe the Australian Aboriginals, their "Ancestors sang the world into existence" (Chatwin, *The Songlines*, 11) scattering along the "footprints" of their wanderings "a trail of words and musical notes" (13).[1] These "Dreaming-tracks" became "both map[s] and direction-finders" (13), an episodic topography of sacred sites separated and marked by stretches of song, "melodies" that were one with the wandering footsteps of the ancestor. For Aboriginal people, the Greek understanding of *melos* ("limb," but also the root for our word *melody*) is a literal one: a man on Walkabout sings the song of those who share his dreaming by traveling down their songline. To depart from it is to risk death at the hands of another whose territory one has violated. To find oneself in a land whose things he had not "named" is to risk dehydration and starvation in a world that is a "jigsaw of microclimates."

Despite the fact that his songline crosses the territories of as many as twenty languages, a man knows his song by its "taste" or "smell," that is, by its tune: words might change, but the melody remains consistent from beginning to end. Each man has responsibility for a stretch of his Ancestor's songline, received at one stop or hand-over point and "handed-over" at another. His verses are title and deed to his inherited land, his songline a segment of their ancestral trade route. Songs, not things, are the primary media of exchange. And while the patterned songlines of their Ancestors were represented on the carved plaque, the *tjuringa*, the paternal totem itself—his Dreaming—was so powerful that it was never represented pictorially. To do so would be, again, to risk death.

Sometimes the clan would gather to sing the entire song cycle, each man in the prescribed order reciting his verses, risking death should he "uncreate the creation" by failure to maintain this proper sequence of his verses or his proper place in the cycle. For

35

> By singing the world into existence . . . the Ancestors had been
> poets in the original sense of *poesis,* meaning 'creation.' No
> Aboriginal could conceive that the created world was in any
> way imperfect. His religious life had a single aim: to keep the
> land the way it was and should be. The man who went
> 'Walkabout' was making a ritual journey. He trod in the
> footprints of his Ancestor. He sang the Ancestor's stanzas
> without changing a word or note—and so recreated the
> Creation. (Chatwin, *The Songlines,* 14)[2]

Albert Lord's comments (in *The Singer of Tales*) on the relation
between writing and the end of storytelling suggest that writing became
one among the many technologies emerging from (though not beginning
with) nineteenth-century urban industrialization. Song brings people together to hear the story the singer tells. Writing, like other technologies,
enables people to remain apart: the word comes to them, they need not go
to the word or to the place where others gather to hear it spoken. Despite
the extraordinary possibilities writing offers for the exchange of ideas as
well as their increased complexity, availability, and sophistication, the loss
in the shift from oral to written culture is significant. In simplest terms, it
can involve the disconnection of the knower and the known, and the
disconnection of knowers from each other. Supporting the rise of rational-
ism and of modern science, the privileging of writing supported at the
same time the dispossession of many groups of "savage Others," people of
many colors among them. Supporting the specialization of knowledge and
its disciplines, the advent of literacy drew increasingly rigid lines between
acceptable forms of private and public rhetoric, further enforcing the growing
schism between private and public lives, private and public selves. Understood in this context, the losses consequent upon literacy can be devastating to the core of human Being itself.[3]

In search of a model for connected knowing, and also of evidence
for women's relationship to song in oral culture, in this chapter I study
several groups of preliterate tribes among the Australian Aboriginals. The
Walbiri (Warlpiri) and to a lesser extent the Pintupi are the primary
interests of Bruce Chatwin, a travel writer whose book *The Songlines* is a
wonderful layperson's introduction to the surviving oral tradition in Australia. Selected anthropological literature offers the customs and myths of
several other Aboriginal tribes. Diane Bell's *Daughters of the Dreaming*
considers the Warlpiri, Warumungu/Warlmanpa, Kaytej, and the
Alyawarra. Her research appears to contradict John Morton's "The Effectiveness of Totemism"; Morton, citing the work of noted anthropolo-

gists Carl Strehlow, B. Spencer and F. J. Gillen, studies the Aranda. It is also apparently contradictory to that of Chris Knight, who studies the Rainbow Serpent myth as told by the peoples of northeast Arnhem Land in her article "Lévi-Strauss and the Dragon." All of these texts attempt to read Aboriginal myths and rituals as they express preliterate understandings of knowing and being in the world. Their conflicting readings of the data they gather suggest a point Walter Ong makes repeatedly in *Orality and Literacy:* the technology of writing forever transforms the ways we know and "be" in the world, and consequently the ways that we read our experiences and the experiences of others. For this reason alone, an extended look at the conflict among these anthropologists is useful.

As a parallel text to these and to Chatwin's, I read Virginia Woolf's *To the Lighthouse.* In this comparison I try to redefine and revalue the concept of song in relationship to public rhetoric in oral cultures, accompanied by a parallel revision in our own, literate culture as this is modeled by Virginia Woolf. Exploring women's relation to song, this chapter will ask three questions: First, to what extent have women had a voice in the public rhetoric of their "tribe," however that term is defined, literally and metaphorically, in pre- and postliterate cultures? Second, to what extent are our readings of women's access to that rhetoric gendered? Third, how can models for connected knowing emerging from oral traditions help us to recover this kind of knowing in the postliterate world?

The utter integration among singer, song, and world expressed in Aboriginal oral tradition is a powerful model for connected knowing. But despite the extraordinary connections between their world and the songs they sing about it, the preliterate Aboriginal song tradition cannot be idealized. On the other hand, it cannot be read solely through the eyes of literate investigators, either. These two caveats are at the core of the problem invoked in sorting out the contradictory readings of women's role in this oral tradition.

The majority of anthropologists have claimed that, as in literate cultures, public Aboriginal rhetoric and ceremony excludes and devalues women's voices in order to appropriate women's power. Using the feminist paradigm of developing data that is woman-centered, Diane Bell offers a persuasive contradiction: traditional views of women's marginalization and oppression in Aboriginal society result from male anthropologists' misreadings of what they see, and from tribal women's deliberate efforts to limit men's access to information about women's rituals. On the contrary, she argues, sex-segregated Aboriginal society allowed women to have a real and substantial power base. In fact, "women were not the pawns in male games but rather, daughters of the dreaming who proudly and forcefully made distinctions concerning their lives and heritage" (*Daughters of the Dreaming*, 209). Bell does not deny that damage has come to women's autonomy in this century, but she lays primary responsibility for it to the life of settlements on which Aboriginal tribes have been forced to live by a largely white male government. Women's loss of access to the land, and therefore to their sacred sites and the rituals they readily performed there, is particularly damaging. Unlike men, women have not been compensated for this loss of power by sharing in the privileges that males can earn through their affiliation with white male culture on the reserves.

Despite their losses, Bell says, Aboriginal women are "autonomous, independent ritual actors who actively participate in the creation, transmission and maintenance of the values of their society," insisting that "[t]hese values do not constrain woman to the domestic round of child-rearing and limit her contribution to her society to economic considerations" (226). Nevertheless, the loss of ready access to their lands has been paralleled by (in fact one can say it has caused) a loss of access to "the continuing dialogue which allowed women to participate actively in the construction of the cultural evaluations of their role in their society" (249). This "erosion" of "women's solidarity and autonomy" has been caused by, among other things, white male definitions of them as sex objects and domestic workers and a consequently changed regard for them by their own men. Recording "the shattering of the ritually maintained nexus of land as resource and spiritual essence" in Central Australia, Bell "locate[s] a shift from female autonomy to male control, from independence to dependence" (247). Although Bell does not yet see significant damage emerging in loss of *ritual* control, anthropologists have recorded this as occurring elsewhere. For example, in the Western Desert, observing men's intrusion upon the mother-daughter tie by changing kinship and marriage links to consolidate male intergenerational connections, anthropologist Annette Hamilton sees men "infiltrating women's hitherto autonomous worlds" (247). While the two anthropologists disagree on causal factors, they concur that losses are occurring in women's access to power, and that these losses are a consequence of an imposed white male model. The connections among land, song, and power are particularly important, and they remain important for women in postliterate culture. When these become disconnected, women lose voice. When they lose voice, they lose song. When they lose song, they lose power.

Both their substantial autonomy and male efforts to appropriate women's ritual practice point out the power of song in general and of women's songs in particular. The mother-daughter tie is particularly significant in ritual ceremonies. *To the Lighthouse* extends the concept of song in literate culture, reinforcing its connection to the maternal voice and exploring Woolf's struggle to hear her mother's voice behind her father's language. Ultimately, I argue that we must recover a kind of connected knowing that need not be repudiated by literate cultures, one that can underlie and support the writing process and the student who engages it, too.

Bruce Chatwin's *The Songlines,* from which the introduction to this chapter is drawn, is a rich source for examining understandings of song, and song's extraordinary role as the underlying construct of tribal rituals, economies, geographies, and topographies, and of its religious understandings and practices. Song is so utterly integrated in the lives of these oral/aural people, that to walk (to move one's limbs) and to sing is the same act; so "harmonious" are the two that "by spending his whole life walking and singing his Ancestor's Songline, a man eventually became the track, the Ancestor, and the song" (179). At the same time, Chatwin's silence about women's involvement in the Walkabout, as well as his relegation of women to the domestic sphere in his description of Aboriginal life, seem to support Bell's argument that how, and by whom, the data are read are as important as the data themselves.

So, these songs *can be read one way,* as part of an epic, inherently patriarchal tradition that serves specific, nationalistic ends: defining territory, supporting a national economy, and maintaining consistently a kind of conformity to its values by threat of death. While the totemic ancestor is never represented pictorially, the foot tracks of his wanderings are "written" on *tjuringa,* the sacred tribal territorial map that only "initiates" can view. (The impetus to make written language serve the public domain, territory, and economy is confirmed by philologists who trace our Roman letters *A* and *B* to the Phonecian graphic symbols *aleph* and *beth* ("house" and "ox")—that which, like his woman, a man owns (Gilbert and Gubar, "Ceremonies of the Alphabet," 22). That "the logocentric project [has] always been . . . to *found* (fund) phallocentrism, to insure for masculine order a rationale equal to history itself"[4] is amply demonstrated by the predominant masculinity of singer and song in the oral culture that precedes it. It is not only the technology of writing that leads to an exclusionary and finally disconnected understanding of song. Even in preliterate cultures like the Aboriginal Walbiri or Pintupi, from the male totemic ancestor to his wandering descendant, the singer appears almost always to be a man singing to and about other men, and the only valid rhetoric a public one—one in service of his territories, his economies and sacred rituals that control his loyalty to the tribe, the circumference of his life, and his return "to the place from which he has come," that is, his death.

Still, the uses of song in apparently patriarchal cultures remain problematic. Anthropologists like Morton point out that other rites demonstrate an additional use for song—the effort to claim and use female reproductive power. " 'Songs are the potent force of 'increase rites,' possessions believed 'to contain . . . magic virtues which [give] power over Nature and environment in the locality where they had originated' (Strehlow, 125–26). . . . To possess songs is to have *power to control* [italics added] not only animal or plant species which constitute one element of the totemic complex, but also the general vitality of local areas. 'Increase ritual' is a general enlivening of the country in all its aspects. It is, as Aranda people say, to 'look after' the country (and therefore trust it to look after them)" (Morton, "The Effectiveness of Totemism," 456).[5]

But the song is also intimately tied to the sowing of the ancestral male seed, and it is crucial to understand that the increase ritual is, as well, the means by which male appropriation of reproductive potency occurs: appropriating the woman and appropriating language are one and the same activity. "All ancestors originally possessed, as extensions of their heads, giant poles *(tnatantja)* appearing as huge phalli. . . . An ancestor's phallus was the source of all his *tjurunga,* [sacred objects] . . . often the precondition of ancestral creativity" (Morton, "The Effectiveness of Totemism," 456). While death is the "growing tired" that leads the ancestor and his sons to sink back into the ground, becoming *tjurunga* once again, reincarnation is possible through the opportunity for one's life cells, scattered by one's lifetime wandering, to leap into the body of a woman crossing his wandering track.

Like the secret caves in which *tjurunga* are normally kept hidden, in this model for understanding woman's cultural role, her womb appears to be essentially a passive receptacle in which preparation for the important work of men is to be made. Womb time and the youthful period of dependence on the mother involve alienation from one's *tjurunga.* Increase rites in the religious lives of men begin with initiation rites during which, segregated from mother and the domestic life of the tribe, adolescent boys "consume" secret knowledge and recover the "secret name" sung over their conception *tjurunga* (457). "Initiation is the creation of the inner autonomy of a man's spirit, and autonomy is marked by the ability of a man to "name himself" as an ancestor" (457), that is, to name himself as his father's, not his mother's, son.

In French linguist Julia Kristeva's terms it is to repudiate the semiotic and embrace, at the behest both of loss and desire, the symbolic language of the Father and with it his Law.[6] It is this relationship between an appropriated language and an appropriated sexuality that French feminist Hélène Cixous reflects when she writes:

Men still have everything to say about their sexuality, and everything to write. For what they have said so far, for the most part, stems from the opposition activity/passivity from the power relation between a fantasized obligatory virility meant to invade, to colonize, and the consequential phantasm of woman as a "dark continent" to penetrate and to 'pacify.' (We know what "pacify" means in terms of scotomizing the other and misrecognizing the self.) Conquering her, they've made haste to depart from her borders, to get out of sight, out of body. The way man has of getting out of himself and into her whom he takes not for the other but for his own, deprives him, he knows, of his own bodily territory. One can understand how man, confusing himself with his penis and rushing in for the attack, might feel resentment and fear of being "taken" by the woman, of being lost in her, absorbed or alone. ("The Laugh of the Medusa," in Marks and DeCourtivron, *New French Feminisms*, 247)

The colonizing act described here is legal, linguistic, and sexual. Its power is revealed by its elaboration in central tribal rituals whose blood-letting activities reflect male claims to the totality of the reproductive enterprise, both male and female. For example, in the kangaroo ceremony of Krantji Soak where the ancestor Krantjirinja was born, a circular ground painting decorated by feathers and blood surrounds a deep hole. The most secret of the ritual song's verses describe the plunging of young males' down-decorated *tnatantjas* deep into the hole filled with initiatory blood drawn from the subincised penises and opened arteries of their arms. This act, both creative and destructive, signals the simultaneous conception of the kangaroo (each down feather may be a potential kangaroo) and the return of the ancestor to the ground (his death). While in the Dreaming ancestors have no mothers because they emerge spontaneously from the earth, the incestuous nature of *this* act is clear: in the myth, "Krantjirinja's death was also incestuous intercourse with his father's sister" (Morton, "The Effectiveness of Totemism," 459; cf. 472 n. 5). Bloodletting and song-making interpenetrate; the ritual acts are orgasmic. Men drain themselves until they are "pure form, distilled into the tjurunga" (459), "pour[ing] out the Law [anything to do with the Dreaming] from the heart" (460).

The tripartite male inheritance of language, law, and reproductivity is also reiterated by *ingkura* ceremonies, which offer initiates access to knowledge revealed at night, traditionally the place and time of the female. When the game he has hunted and offered to his elders ("man meat," the "flesh of the father") is pressed to his own lips by those in possession of sacred tribal knowledge (*aralkalelama*, "to make open mouthed"), the previously imposed ban of silence is lifted:

> The 'gift of speech' was originally conferred in the Dreaming when men were also instructed about *tjurunga*, marriage and procreation (Gillen, 1986: 185). One may therefore interpret *aralkalelama* as symbolic of men's triple accession to language, exogamy and the Law. Without *aralkalelama* a man is not a man: without having his mouth 'opened' he would be unable to sing and 'speak for' his country or take a wife. (463)

The relentless separation of the reproductive and productive worlds represented by this act of menstrual appropriation, the fear and secrecy that accompany it, and its definition of song as access to the tripartite power structure of the tribe all suggest that while access to literacy indeed became (and remains) a powerful means of *class* oppression, even in preliterate (oral) cultures, women, chief sustainers of the reproductive economy, have rarely had access to the public rhetoric that is defined as the "real" song of the tribe to which they belong. In this single appropriative act, gender and class oppression intersect.

This is one reading. Sadly, as Bell points out, it might be more accurate *now* than when the original data it interprets were gathered some ten years ago.

The alternative reading emerges from Bell's ample evidence that Aboriginal women have sung, do sing.[7] Chatwin's book indicates that women do not go on Walkabout, and he suggests that because they are female and uninitiated, they do not have access to the tribal *tjuringa*. Their tablet, he writes, is not stone or wood, but sand. Their audience is not the carefully chosen, carefully prepared initiates whose rites are pre-scribed under pain of death, but the tribe's children. Their goal is not territory or production but reproduction: they sing a life-cycle song of beginnings and endings.

"Even in captivity," Chatwin writes,

> Pintupi mothers, *like good mothers everywhere* [italics mine] tell stories to their children about the origin of animals: *How the Echidna got its spines . . . Why the Emu cannot fly . . . Why the Crow is glossy black . . .* And as Kipling illustrated the *Just So Stories* with his own line drawings, so the Aboriginal mother makes drawings in the sand to illustrate the wanderings of the Dreamtime heroes.

She tells her tale in a pattern of staccato bursts and, at the same time, traces the Ancestor's 'footprints' by running her first and second fingers, one after the other, in a double dotted line along the ground. She erases each scene with the palm of her hand and, finally, makes a circle with a line passing through it. . . .

This marks the spot where the Ancestor, exhausted by the labours of Creation, has gone 'back in.'

The sand drawings done for children are but sketches or 'open versions' of *real* drawings representing the *real* Ancestors, which are only done at secret ceremonies and must only be seen by initiates. (*The Songlines,* 21)

That these mothers' words are song, and that singing to her children is part of what makes a "good" mother, is obvious in Chatwin's interpretation of the tribe's value system. Less obvious is the extent to which the value of these songs appears to be qualified and diminished by the tribe—or by Chatwin, looking at the evidence through male, Western, postliterate eyes. Unlike the *tjuringa,* the sacred board on which is written the formal tribal record of the ancestor's dreaming, these mothers' songs, he writes, are fingered in the sand and quickly "erased with the palm of her hand." They can never share the public acclaim of Kipling's illustrative line drawings, not because they emerge from an oral culture, but because they are at best "sketches," poor imitations of "*real* drawings representing *real* Ancestors," which women, uninitiates that they are, could know only in the loosest, most "open" way. In the public record, ironically enough, it is the *Ancestor,* not the child-bearing woman, who, "exhausted by the labours of Creation, has gone back in," the Aboriginal term for death. Because their labor appears to Western eyes to be without value, women's creation songs appear not to be part of the public rhetoric of the tribe. Because failure to learn them properly does not carry with it the penalty of death, their songs are perceived as harmless, powerless, useless. Because they are not overtly didactic in content or intent (of what use to the productive economy, after all, is knowing why the crow is black or why the emu cannot fly), their value is expressed only as an afterthought whose apparently unconscious irony is intensified by the quality of Chatwin's understatement: "*All the same,* it is through the 'sketches' that the young learn to orient themselves to their land, its mythology and resources" (*The Songlines,* 22, emphasis added).

Diane Bell's research contradicts much of Chatwin's implied interpretation of what he sees, and much of the anthropological interpretation that precedes her field work in Australia. The women she interviews

about their lives and ritual practice (both of which she observes extensively) respond with delight, because " 'White fellas always ask the men,
but we know too" (*Daughters of the Dreaming,* 25). The separation by
sex of Aboriginal people in economic and ritual terms means that men
and women operate from "separate, gender-specific power bases" (2);
consequently, neither can be an adequate witness to the life and practices
of the other. Through conversation and observation with the women,
Bell comes to understand that Aboriginal women's ritual, though largely
separate from men's, expresses their full access to the Law of the
Dreamtime *(jukurrpa);* she also learns that women go on Walkabout like
the men, that they have sacred sites, and that they have *tjurunga.* In
other words, they sing, they dance, and they incise boards *as well as* write
on sand to record their ancestor's wanderings. To a limited extent, women
participate in men's rituals, including initiation rituals, in which Bell
observes women playing what she calls "key decision-making" roles (247).
This last fact is somewhat startling in light of the apparent absence of
women in Morton's extensive writing about male initiation cited above
and in the next chapter. Men participate in women's rituals, too, but
when they arrive, what they do, and when they leave is clearly rigorously
prescribed. Bell observes great respect for women's prescription of this,
especially in the older men's behavior. Finally, she finds that

> in ritual women emphasize their role as nurturers of people,
> land and relationships. Through their *yawulyu* (land-based
> ceremonies) they nurture land; through their health and curing
> rituals they resolve conflict and restore social harmony, and
> through *yilpinji* (love rituals) they manage emotions. Thus in
> women's rituals their major responsibilities in the areas of love,
> land and health fuse in the nurturance motif with its twin
> themes of 'growing up' of people and land and the maintenance
> of harmonious relations between people and country. (21)

So Bell's research suggests that a whole anthropological tradition has
read preliterate women's sons with literate men's eyes, importing the literal
and theoretical framework of women's oppression and lack of value from a
well-inculcated Western model and imposing it on their readings of Aboriginal women's lives. The suggestion is that because what they sing
about is insignificant to the values attendant to a public rhetoric, women's
songs are devalued, and so, in effect, they are perceived not to sing at all.
Along with Chatwin, male anthropologists have been denied access to
women's secrets, but they have also failed to see much that was available to
them, and misread what they have been allowed to see. Among other

things, for example, none comments on the appropriative nature of male initiation and increase rites, a clear signal of how powerful women must be viewed to be if men seek that power so aggressively.

It appears then that, in this preliterate culture, literate testimony about women's silence (and perhaps also about their relative power in the culture) is the result of misreading. Can the same be said of testimony regarding women's song in the West?

Despite the dispossession of vernacular literatures that marked the rise of intellectual culture and the academic enterprise, has there always remained—literally—a (m)other tongue? Can the long tradition claiming women's silence "re-cant" its understanding of song so that the existence of their melodies may be reaffirmed and understood? We now know that, like Emily Dickinson, many women recognized the difference from the public rhetoric—an often unacceptable difference—of the songs they chose to sing. Evidence of women's ongoing claim to song has emerged in feminist study of preliterate people. It can also be read in the multiple personal narrative forms of postliterate women, and in their fiction. This chapter argues that without these songs, what has been viewed as the public rhetoric—a rhetoric that misreads and therefore so often disenchants and disenfranchises them—remains genuinely incomprehensible because it remains his-story without hers.

Orality and Literacy

There is not yet enough evidence to say who is correct in the war of anthropological interpretation. There is probably some truth in both interpretations, and Bell clearly documents concern among women about men's threat to their ritual integrity and their autonomy. All the same, these women sing. The kind of songs they sing, and the uses to which their songs are put, can help us in significant ways to revalue the idea of song itself. There are a number of ways to further explicate the implicit argument of this chapter: first, that because literate women's affinities remain with a kind of primal (primary, primitive) orality, their songs are, to all intents and purposes, simply silence for the larger culture in which they live; and second, that because they *do* sing in spite of this, there are finally *two* kinds of song in human culture. One is validated by a largely male audience as the language of power, defined as appropriate to public rhetoric and separate from the domestic sphere. The other affirms the connection between the body and the body politic. It is modeled on the oral tradition like that expressed by Aboriginal culture in Bell's citation above, a tradition in which home, land, self, and community interpenetrate. How can we attend to the importance of this second kind of song?

The first answer might be called "sociolinguistic," for want of a better category. This work has been done by numerous scholars in many disciplines, but it is best articulated by Walter Ong in *Orality and Literacy* and (less satisfyingly) in *Fighting for Life*. The feminist literary-critical position, the province of numerous scholars whose names will appear throughout these chapters, may be best represented by Margaret Homans's *Bearing the Word*. Aside from the sophisticated clarity of her theory, Homans's work summarizes and synthesizes the psychoanalytic work of Jacques Lacan[8] and French feminist theory as well as the psychoanalytic and sociological work of Nancy Chodorow,[9] and that of other American feminist thinkers.

Ong's thesis is that regardless of the extent to which cultures interiorize what he calls "alphabetic literacy," a sense of orality remains fundamental to conscious and unconscious thought. Homans points out the usual identification of women (nature/the material) with the literal—with the thing itself—and of men (culture/the abstract) with the figurative.[10] Thus, to make rational meaning is to "*figure something out*"; "configurations" become the shape of complex theory at an increasing remove from its "thingness" and its "ground." It is this rational act that makes culture and language what they are—constructs or representations, Lacan's symbolic order privileging and privileged by the phallus, within which those who hold power claim all experience occurs. Because of their literality and their Otherness in a phallocentric world, women must inevitably remain outside of this cultural space.

In this cultural model, belief in our access to a world of things—to the literal—is an illusion, necessary to the representative act, at least in the arts; but it is an illusion. While it is understood to offer the comfort of "at-homeness," the familiar, its very familiarity, its familialness, can also block not only the process of individuation but also the development of distance, of objectivity (making the thing an object available for examination) that has been prized in both scientific and much aesthetic theory from Aristotle to the present day. In short, in this false definition of symbol, the trivialization of the literal (women, nature) is imperative lest it threaten the very act of constructing meaning in the phallocentric universe.

Western literary history makes explicit women's claim to the power of song, the cultural fear of these claims, and the need to trivialize and silence both claim and song. The long tradition of women's exclusion from public rhetoric represented in the mythic songs of their culture takes the form not only of repeated demands for women's silence as appropriate to their place and duty, but also of pointed portraits of women's potential for evil, violence, and destruction of the social order when they claim access to certain kinds of song. When Penelope pleads with "the wise Telemachus" to silence those bards who sing of her long-lost husband, Odysseus, he reminds her that to *men* falls responsibility for songs, and to women "the loom and the distaff," the work of the household. She returns to her chamber "amaze[d]," "lay[ing] up the wise saying of her son in her heart" (Butcher and Lang, *The Odyssey of Homer*, 18). It is by the literality of the song's evocation of things that the enchantress holds her audience spellbound (O. E. *spel*, story, fable), and it is no accident that script will not do, but that the power of the word rests in its oral delivery. The Sirens' songs proffer Penelope's wandering husband rest, but also the abdication of his responsibilities as king and commander, though apparently not his responsibilities as husband, since he evidently had none. Once in possession of Merlin's charms, a snake-like Vivien—a not inconsiderable rhetorician herself—speaks them to imprison him for eternity in his own oak domain, where he is impotent to influence the future affairs of state.[11] Liberating themselves from loom, shuttle, and husband for the song, the dance, and finally the hunt, the women of Thebes, through their own private Dionysian rites, violate laws governing the secular and religious order and conventional prescriptions about acceptable sex-role divisions.[12]

But the clearest terror for men in women's songs involves their relationship to female sexuality: the very nature of the enchantress's power lies in the terror and the allure of her sexuality itself. Not only are these songs a call away from the power, prestige, and privilege of a world governed by public rhetoric and the access to fame its publicly sanctioned mythos may offer; more, attention to women threatens the carefully defined separation of the private and public worlds that education—understood as the initiation and immersion into the language of the public rhetoric, into discourse (and the reality constructed by it)—has so carefully sought to define. Finally, at its most profound psychological level, attention to these songs threatens the radical redefinition of woman as (m)other that in Lacan's cultural myth is the basis for separation, individuation, identity, and the formation of language itself.[13] Only the strongest man—an Odysseus, for example—could survive attention to this siren song.

Virginia Woolf's *To the Lighthouse* and the Problem of Access

Like their Aboriginal counterparts, many modern women also insisted upon their right to sing. The Aboriginal Walkabout is a part of the journey archetype that haunts the human imagination. Employing it in their own song, women writers in particular recognize that theirs is a journey not only through space, time, and spirit, but through language, as well. Their song-making involves exploring the ways the language of song itself can be remade. Virginia Woolf is among the most daring of these explorers.

Woolf identifies *To the Lighthouse* as an elegy for her dead parents.[14] Like many of her novels, its completion occasioned a severe emotional breakdown, but, by her own testimony, writing this novel was her final act in the long grieving of their loss. It is also an exquisitely balanced study of the descriptive and evocative qualities of language when traditional prosaic constraints are ignored. Modeled upon her parents, the protagonists Mr. and Mrs. Ramsay represent two ways of knowing and being in the world—and two ways of speaking about that experience—that Woolf clearly identifies as gendered. The tyrannical quality of her philosopher-father's demands for attention and her mother's relentless arranging of heterosexual relationships to yield marriage are the dialectical tensions that swirl around two of their five children, Cam and James. The novel focuses on their efforts to choose between these two worldviews and the kinds of language that represent them.

The novel begins with a plan to go to the lighthouse off the coast of St. Ives, Woolf's much-beloved summer home. Thwarted by Mr. Ramsay, the trip is finally completed only as the novel ends; chaos—Mrs. Ramsay's death and the First World War—has intervened. Lily Briscoe, an artist and surrogate daughter to Mrs. Ramsay, watches from the shore, painting, as she did when the initial proposal for the trip was made. The trip becomes for Cam and James, as well as for her, the opportunity to grieve Mrs. Ramsay's loss, to recover her song in their lives, and to explore the lyrical relations between language and the multiple realities it enforces and describes. In this sense, the novel is a literate articulation of the preliterate song tradition, and the journey is itself a kind of Walkabout. Woolf explores how women's songs have been suppressed in public discourse, the loss to consciousness when women remain *solely* (m)other, and the ways that their songs can offer reconnection to things and therefore to ourselves.

Sociolinguistics can help us better understand the nature and claims of women's songs; particularly, it can help us recognize how women maintain a connection both to the material and to the maternal that is actualized in the songs they sing in defiance of an imposed public silence. In short, there is another kind of song besides what is affirmed/confirmed by public rhetoric, and women—literate or not—sing it all the time.

Using Chodorow's work on object relations and Virginia Woolf's *To the Lighthouse,* feminist critic Margaret Homans argues that daughters remain, with their mothers, in the world of the literal; that is, that mothers (like Mrs. Ramsay) speak to their daughters differently from the way they may speak with their sons beyond a certain point in the child's development. These songs differ in content, and they differ in form, too. First, their emphasis is significantly oral/aural. "[W]ords matter as sounds . . . issuing from and returning to the body"; this nonsymbolic mother/daughter language is "a language of presence, in which the presence or absence of referents in the ordinary sense is quite unimportant" (*Bearing the Word*, 18). This nonsymbolic language is silenced and suppressed: it cannot be decoded by conventional principles governing symbolic signification. In other words, it is not easily subject to the question "What does it mean?" Nevertheless, Homans argues that it is not *repressed* in Woolf's texts. Without daughters but herself a daughter, Woolf sang through the voice of Julia Steven/Mrs. Ramsay the daughter's recollection of her mother's songs.

Without access to a patrilineage, their own inheritance written in the sand, women's matrilineage remains encoded in the memory of first songs, heard and sung at their mother's knees. "My mother always sang to her children," Eudora Welty writes. "[W]hen an Aboriginal mother notices the first stirrings of speech in her child, she lets it handle the 'things' of that particular country: leaves, fruits, insects and so forth. The child, at its mother's breast, will toy with the 'thing,' talk to it, test its teeth on it, learn its name, repeat its name—and finally chuck it aside" (Chatwin, *The Songlines*, 270). Woolf's novel demonstrates the extent to which, as they grow, children are increasingly caught between the claims of their mother's songs and their father's language.

The child's (and others') joy in the maternal voice, merging with other, nonhuman song, and the promise that these voices offer of a kind of rightness in the world—all are threaded throughout Woolf's text. " 'Yes, of course, if it's fine tomorrow,' said Mrs. Ramsay" of the journey to the lighthouse. " 'But you'll have to be up with the lark,' she added. To her son these words conveyed an extraordinary joy . . . endowed the picture of a refrigerator, as his mother spoke, with heavenly bliss. It was fringed with joy" (*To the Lighthouse*, 9).

Additionally, Woolf's text both inscribes and challenges the myth that privileges the phallus in the lives of men and in her son, James's life. James's trip to the lighthouse after his mother's death participates in the Wordsworthian assumption that certain kinds of language and loss are one experience. As his mother's emissary, he fulfills his mother's need for empathic caretaking ("Children don't forget, Children don't forget," she muses against the complementary threnody, "It will end, it will end . . . It will come, it will come" [97]); James, his father, and Cam go to the lighthouse on pilgrimage, bearing gifts she, now dead, has (metaphorically) chosen and packed. But at the same time, he is initiated into the phallocentric world of Lacan's symbolic language,[15] an initiation that Cam, along with Lily, witnesses (as a silent observer) and whose claims upon him she articulates mentally in a tone that expresses a cross between relief and contempt. "Well done!" pronounces their father, ostensibly approving James's sailing but figuring as well the entry of this new initiate into his language/world. "There! Cam thought, addressing herself silently to James. You've got it at last. For she knew that this was what James had been wanting . . . His father had praised him" (306).

Both Cam and Lily maintain a conspiratorial silence bound up with their roles (literal and surrogate) as daughters to Mr. and Mrs. Ramsay and with their consequent relationship to language. Cam faces powerful demands from both parents to take a position in relationship to language that signals her symbolic (and, in fact, literal) adherence to the role she will be asked to play as an adult woman. Like many mothers, unconsciously, Mrs. Ramsay has placed her daughter in this double bind. Speaking to her children an essentially subversive language, she nevertheless models a behavior signaling that the power of the adult world resides with the Father and his language.

Relentlessly, angrily, Cam resists. Even as a small child, she will not " 'give a flower to the gentleman,' as the nursemaid told her to do" (36). Her linguistic relationship to the phenomenal world has about it the alternate qualities of mesmerism and defiance. Told by her mother to inquire of their servant if Minta and Paul have returned from the walk during which Mrs. Ramsay knows that marriage will surely be proposed, Cam returns with the answer delivered in "a colourless singsong" (85). Both as child and as adult, she responds with a self-induced hypnosis that keeps her uncompliant even when obedience is called for: Words addressed to Cam, we are told, "seemed to be dropped into a well, where, if the waters were clear, they were also so extraordinarily distorting that, even as they descended, one saw them twisting about to make Heaven knows what pattern on the floor of the child's mind. What message would Cam give the cook? Mrs. Ramsay wondered" (84).

Cam erects that same hypnotic mesmerism as an adolescent/woman nearing adulthood, when she finds herself once again resisting her mother's efforts to gain her complicity in the plot to play the womanly/wifely role—to offer sympathy to men. Alone in the bow on the way to the lighthouse, Cam alternates between pity and outrage, "look[ing] down in the foam, into the sea with all its treasure in it. . . . thinking how all those paths and the lawn, thick and knotted with the lives they had lived there, were gone; were rubbed out; were past; were unreal, and now this was real; the boat and the sail with its patch; Macalister with his earrings; the noise of the waves—all this was real" (246, 248–49). "Exposed . . . to this pressure and division of feeling, this extraordinary temptation," Cam must take a position in relation to language that affirms the moment in which her reality is anchored and the objects to which she is attached; she must reject the temptation—the pressure of his symbolic language— to force compliance with her father's cloaked demand for sympathy (252–53). For Mr. Ramsay, language is a perpetual metaphor, things are never themselves but always bound in service to expressing his emotional demands. Her outrage at his repetition of Cowper's poem ("But I beneath a rougher sea/Was whelmed in deeper gulfs than he"), her indifference, despite his ridicule, to the points of the compass, and her refusal to "name the puppy" in response to this query are of a piece with her repetition of words that appear to have, for him, a reality and meaning very different from hers: "We perished, each alone" (249).

To be subject to Mr. Ramsay's demands is to become a sign in his self-constructed symbol system, inscribed in a silent space actualized only in his time and on his terms. It is to lose her place. It is death. This Cam must resist at all costs. She does this by maintaining relentlessly the connection between words and things. She writes her own stories, letting no one tell them for her.

Attached, as her mother was, to the sea, but without her mother's ominous vision of the meaning portended by the "fall of a wave," Cam's narrative is one of adventure and escape from the sinking ships of her daydream; she is safely entertained as long as her father reads his book and she can watch from the distance. Intuitively, Cam rejects the library as the canonical repository of kinds of knowing both foreign and inimical to her. It is not her mother's place, nor is it hers. While she is attracted to it as a place where "one could let whatever one thought expand here like a leaf in water; and if it did well here, among the old gentlemen smoking and *The Times* crackling then it was right," she can know the books only as phenomena; "small," "yellowish," "closely printed," they are valuable to Cam only because they keep her father—and the others—occupied and undemanding and in so doing guarantee her safety (and that of the Ramsay household) a point that, like Cam's indifference to their meaning, Woolf makes over and over again. "[W]hat might be written in the book which had rounded its edges off in his pocket, she did not know." And it mattered little, "for she was safe, while he sat there; safe, as she felt herself when she crept in from the garden, and took a book down, and the old gentleman, lowering the paper suddenly, said something very brief over the top of it about the character of Napoleon" (282, 283). Safe from men's knowledge, men's language, Cam is safe to observe, think, dream, be genuinely other, an otherness that Woolf suggests not as alien, but as detached and familiar at the same time.

Lily refuses sympathy to the men around her, painting despite the echoing rejoinder that "women can't paint." She takes Cam's indifference to men's language a step further, exploring its inadequacy as a descriptor or determiner of the lived experience that she and Mrs. Ramsay have known. "Little words that broke up the thought and dismembered it said nothing . . . Words fluttered sideways and struck the object inches too low," Lily reflects, gazing at the empty steps where Mrs. Ramsay had sat with James years before. "For how could one express in words these emotions of the body? express that emptiness there" (265). Language's failure to strike the mark is intensified by the multiple nature of vision itself: James remembers the lighthouse of his childhood ("then") embedded in a nostalgic recollection of life at his mother's knee, "a silvery, misty-looking tower with a yellow eye, that opened suddenly, and softly in the evening"; ("now") he sees it as a "tower, stark and straight . . . barred with black and white." His insight is that both the recollection and the present image are true, "For nothing was simply one thing" (276–77). But unlike Cam, for whom her father's immersion in the language of another world offers the safety to dream as her father reads, James's moment of the recollection holds neither joy nor permanence. He remembers his mother "stealthily, as if he were stealing downstairs on bare feet. . . . [He] listened to her talking. She talked to a servant, saying simply whatever came into her head. She alone spoke the truth; to her alone could he speak it. That was the source of her everlasting attraction for him, perhaps; she was a person to whom one could say what came into one's head" (278). Nevertheless, the pressure of Mr. Ramsay's presence and the language/thought to which his father is connected is a crushing one for James. "But all the time he thought of her, he was conscious of his father following his thought, surveying it, making it shiver and falter." Woolf's last comment has about it the quality of tragedy: "At last he ceased to think" (278)—one might add, "of her."

James's identification with his father involves simultaneously the loss of a mother and of the mother('s) tongue, and the adoption of a particular kind of discourse in which "words broke up the thought and dismembered it," in which, relentlessly and in spite of or despite them, R would follow Q, a world immersed in "ugly academic jargon" (22) utterly alien to Mrs. Ramsay or her own project with language, or Lily's, or Cam's. This substitution of discourse for language, essentially available to both children exclusive of gender, must be refused by Cam, for to exchange her mother's language for her father's discourse would necessitate the adoption of two mutually exclusive alternatives. The first would involve betraying one portion of her mother's legacy to her, the language itself. The second, learning as her mother did to give men what they needed without entering their discourse community, would involve betraying herself.

Thinking of Mrs. Ramsay, Lily's reflection proposes an important problem with language explored in Woolf's text: the relation of epistemology and ontology, and how that relation can be expressed. Sitting at Mrs. Ramsay's knees, as had James, Lily

> imagined how in the chambers of the mind and heart of the woman who was, physically, touching her, were stood, like the treasures in the tombs of kings, tablets bearing sacred inscriptions, which if one could spell them out, would teach one everything . . . What art was there, she wondered, known to love or cunning, by which one pressed through into those secret chambers? What device for becoming, like waters poured into one jar, inextricably the same, one with the object one adored? . . . for *it was not knowledge but unity that she desired,* not inscriptions on tablets, *nothing that could be written in any language known to men, but intimacy itself, which is knowledge,* she had thought, leaning her head on Mrs. Ramsay's knee. (79, italics mine)

Mr. Ramsay's knowledge—the knowledge of public discourse—and the language that expresses it—the language that James must learn, inevitably involves separation, "marking the channel out there in the floods alone" with its alphabetized reality (68). The kind of knowledge, intimacy, unity that Lily, Cam, Mrs. Ramsay have sought is not expressible "in any language known to men." Woolf's project, and Lily's, is recording the rhythmic experiences of merging and separating that loving relationship and identity formation are about. But it involves more profoundly the effort to articulate what appears to be essentially inarticulatable: to find language that expresses the experience of knowing the object/person by becoming it/him/her, the fusion of epistemology and ontology that gives way in Woolf's prose to ontology alone. Like the other enchantresses of Western literary history, Mrs. Ramsay puts "a spell on them all" by "talking about the skins of vegetables" (152). Like the others, she is also a Circe, both "frightening" and "irresistible." Nevertheless Mrs. Ramsay's real power resides in her silence, whose significance so impregnates Lily's memory of her that the pronoun referents in the passage are difficult to discern and the verb tenses fail to record the place of this scene in a long-finished past. One senses that she is not merely using the universal *we*.

> Mrs. Ramsay sat silent. She was glad, Lily thought, to rest in silence, uncommunicative; to rest in the extreme obscurity of human relationships. Who knows what we are, what we feel? Who knows even at the moment of intimacy, This is knowledge? Aren't things spoilt then, Mrs. Ramsay may have asked (it seemed to have happened so often, this silence by her side) by saying them? Aren't we more expressive thus? (255–56)

Woolf's great message is that this language—the language of connection to the literal—recognizes "that nothing was simply one thing" and that knowing and being are one. It becomes most evident in the world of "plain and ordinary things." In the section "Time Passes," Woolf evokes the figure of the cleaning woman, Mrs. McNab. "[T]earing the veil of silence with [her] hands" (196), she is herself a paradox in a prose poem of contradictions that distills the novel's multiple themes, images, and meanings. Mrs. McNab is "witless," but "she knew it"; her song, an old dance-hall tune, is "robbed of meaning," yet "like the voice of witlessness, humor, persistency itself, trodden down but springing up again . . . twined about her dirge" there is "some incorrigible hope." She is "bowed down with weariness," yet "visions of joy there must have been at the washtub—say with her children . . . at the public house, drinking; turning over scraps in her drawers" (196, 197). This great central prose poem in *To the Lighthouse* is Woolf's resounding catalog, her poetic argument for the relational primacy of things in our lives. Technological culture privileges language as an instrument; that very instrumentality demands that a thing lose its value as itself, that is, that it be valued only as it points to the outcome its use proffers. This is Mr. Ramsay's demand: his philosopher's tool, symbolic logic, will never get him past *Q*. Cam clings to a mode of knowing, to a kind of poetry, that his endless recitations will never allow her father to understand. Despite what she does, Mrs. Ramsay remains in Cam's mind through the agency of her song that evoked the things of Cam's childhood. This she will cling to at all costs. This an adult Lily will seek with a relentless honesty.

In his essay "Language," Martin Heidegger points out how far we have come in our understandings of song. He argues, in fact, that "Poetry proper is never merely a higher mode *(melos)* of everyday language. It is rather the reverse: everyday language is a forgotten and therefore used up poem from which there hardly resounds a call any longer" (*Poetry, Language, Thought,* 208). Later in the same essay collection he intones the poetry of Hölderlin: "Full of merit, yet poetically, man/ Dwells on this earth" (218) Earlier : "Language is—language, speech. Language speaks" (191). And earlier still:

> "Song is existence," says the third of the *Sonnets to Orpheus,* Part I. The word for existence, *Dasein,* is used here in the traditional sense of presence and as a synonym of Being. To sing, truly to say worldly existence, to say out of the haleness of the whole pure draft and to say only this, means: to belong to the precinct of beings themselves. This precinct, as the very nature of language, is Being itself. To sing the song means to be present in what is present itself. It means: *Dasein,* existence. (138)

Woolf's experiments with the prose poem seek to fulfill this Heidegerrian challenge. It is similar to the musical tone-poem in its efforts to evoke for listeners certain kinds of mood—emotional/psychological effects. At the same time, she addresses the problem of silence, a central one in any discussion of women's writing, and the necessity for the redefinition of song to re-sound certain kinds of calls that are central to women's experience with language.

First, her language (and the novel's structure) participate in the "corporate retrospection" that Ong notes as the mark of oral narrative (*Orality and Literacy,* 9). The point is less that her texts, *To the Lighthouse, The Waves,* and others, are the record of many voices, of many consciousness streams, but that their storytelling is collaborative in such a way that their reality can, must, be both the parts and the sum of the parts. ("Nothing," says James, "is only one thing.") The kinds of formulaic repetitions that mark the narrative's advance replicate both the recursive nature of memory and the thematic quality or "shape" of memory made song. Lily's painting and the threnody of the narrative return us to the now-empty window seat once occupied by James and Mrs. Ramsay, storytelling. Mrs. Ramsay and Lily function as chief storytellers of the novel's characters' lives; these narrative choices signal the power for Woolf of her remembered mother's song and of her own surrogacy as storyteller. They mark as well her recognition of the relation between language, love (or desire), and loss central to women's songs.

Orality and Literacy Revisited

Literate culture acts out the same exclusion of women's song as did some aspects of the preliterate tradition, but it has helped preserve those songs, too. The problem lies in how we read what is written. "Amnesia," Adrienne Rich writes, "is the silence of the unconscious" (*Blood, Bread, and Poetry*, 187). The complement to Schachtel's concept of childhood amnesia is the cultural amnesia that separates language from discourse—*materna lingua* from *patrius sermo* (*Orality and Literacy*, 26). Paraphrasing Saussure's argument that scholars persistently tend to think of *writing* as the basic form of language, Ong posits that, nevertheless, "the basic orality of language is permanent." *Orality and Literacy* traces that primary relationship between what are really two states of being-in-the-world, and the ways that the development of writing as a technology allowed discourse to be distilled and isolated from a culture's mother tongue. In a pivotal chapter on the ways that writing restructures consciousnessness, he notes that Learned Latin, Rabbinic Hebrew, Classical Arabic, Sanskrit, and Classical Chinese "were never first languages for any individual, were controlled exclusively by writing, were spoken by males only (with negligible exceptions . . .) and were spoken only by those who could write them" (114).[16] His discussion of Learned Latin is germane:

> Because of its base in academia, which was totally male—with exceptions so utterly rare as to be quite negligible . . . [f]or well over a thousand years, it was sex-linked, a language written and spoken only by males, learned outside the home in a tribal setting which was in effect a male puberty rite setting, complete with physical punishment [he comments here that violence disappears when women enter these schools] and other kinds of deliberately imposed hardships. It had no direct connection with anyone's unconscious of the sort that mother tongues, learned in infancy, always have. (113)

Writing's power for isolating discourse led, in Ong's view, to the restructuring of consciousness that made modern science possible, for it enabled the knower to be both separate and distant from the known: "by establishing knowledge in a medium insulated from the emotion-charged depths of one's mother tongue, thus reducing interference from the human lifeworld and making possible the exquisitely abstract world of medieval scholasticism and of the new mathematical modern science which followed on the scholastic experience" (114). The rhetoric of this world—"basically agonistic and formulaic" (110)—demonstrates, despite a gradual shift in emphasis from oral to chirographic understandings of its practice, the powerful link that remained between the rhetorical discourse of the various academies and their oral roots.

Nevertheless, there was one group whose literary style was untouched by academic rhetoric. These are female authors published from 1600 on, almost none of whom received academic training in rhetoric or Latin, and women from the seventeenth century onward whose education was undertaken in the newer, vernacular (therefore not Latin-based) schools. It follows then, according to Ong's logic, that, by virtue of a relationship to the technology of writing unmediated by the "agonistic and formulaic" nature of men's rhetorical education and experience with language, these women's relationship to language must have remained "unreconstructed," or at least was not structured in the same way as that of their male counterparts. And so, despite the fact that he sees women writers to be inevitably influenced by texts they read from that Latinate rhetorical tradition, "they themselves normally expressed themselves in a different, far less oratorical voice, which had a great deal to do with the rise of the novel" (112). I would argue that it also has a great deal to do with their skill as writers of the personal narrative form. This difference is connected to the relationship between orality and literacy.[17]

Nevertheless, a problem arises from Ong's definition of orality as "formulaic in design" and "agonistic in operation" (*Fighting for Life,* 123), a problem whose dimensions become clearer in his definition of women's writing as "less oratorical" in style and voice than that of their male counterparts.[18] Appropriately in pursuit of a relationship between orality and literacy, Ong has ended up primarily with a study of orality and rhetoric—with a relation between orality and a particular *kind* of literacy rooted in public performance that, by historical record, has belonged, as schools have, to men and (almost exclusively) to men alone: "All of the agonistic play activity from the ancient, medieval and modern world of the West . . . as making for the development of philosophy and of academic learning in general comes from the male agonistic milieu. . . . Far from considering the learning of such languages [might the better term here be *discourses?*] as attractive, women commonly shunned it as disabling" (*Fighting for Life,* 133–34). But the question becomes: *Is there another definition of orality, evolved from the experience of women's relationship to the "mother tongue" that is unmediated by the agonistic rhetoric of academic discourse? And if so, so how can this different understanding of orality be expressed?*

My own intuition as a scholar and a teacher is to begin by articulating a difference between language and discourse. As teachers, we use terms like *whole language skills* and continue in varying degrees to integrate the teaching the writing with literature in our writing classrooms and departmental curricula.[19] Yet in actuality we express our complaints about the impoverishment of students' writing in terms of their relationship not to language, but to the varying discourses of our subject areas. Witness the recent spate of books on "writing in the disciplines" or "writing in the arts and sciences." While we frequently begin our writing courses encouraging a connected and "personal" kind of writing, this notion of the importance of the personal voice fades rapidly as we move on to expository and argumentative modes that, despite the process orientation of the new-rhetorical tradition, mark the goals by which we must teach (if not live) if we are to serve the needs of students (and our faculty colleagues) across the disciplines. And the writing protocols that reflect the stylistic decorum of these disciplines inevitably reflect as well their understood relationship to epistemology and ontology—to the ways in which as scientist, mathematician, philosopher, and literary critic we know and are in the world.

If the gains acquired from literacy's making possible "the exquisitely abstract world of medieval scholasticism and the new mathematical modern science" are so obvious, less obvious are the losses imposed by "establishing knowledge in a medium insulated from the emotion-charged depths of one's mother tongue" (*Orality and Literacy*, 114). "The dialectical structure of deep truth," Ong writes, " . . . makes clear . . . why total explicitness, total clarity, total explanation is impossible" (*Fighting for Life*, 33). This is, of course, what Heidegger meant when he referred to the bankruptcy of everyday language. But what of the terms of the dialectic itself?

Describing orality as the production of the agnostic male voice whose higher volume naturally suited for oral performance, and canonizing "residually oral literatures" as those that "narrate stories of heroic model figures esteemed largely for their conspicuous external agonistic performance" (*Fighting for Life*, 187), we make the choices by which cultures define orality and its relationship to literacy and perpetuate their definitions. In the vast silence of one side of this dialectic there has been, all along, a kind of orality vested in language that our obsession with discourse and the power it accesses for us has caused us to ignore, to fear, and, often, to hate. Sanctioning and supporting this silence, we have canonized a relationship to our world that is objective, figurative, distant, disconnected from things; this disconnected "relationship" makes real compassion and therefore poetry, and in a real sense language itself, impossible.

Women's work suggests another kind of oral tradition, another kind of song maintained in response to their exclusion from the public rhetoric and often deliberately disruptive of it. Preliterate mothers and a literate twentieth-century journal-keeper and novelist demonstrate this tradition for us. Women have been silenced, but they are not silent.

Their experiments with personal narrative were many: lyric, not epic or dramatic; journal (not diary as a practitioner like Samuel Pepys understood it); autobiographical fragment (more rarely, autobiography itself);[20] forms frequently cyclic and formulaic rather than linear; literal and concrete rather than figurative and abstract. In a period of recovery and revaluation of the oral forms—the songs—that underlie the texts canonized by contemporary culture, recognizing this second kind of orality underlying our understanding of literacy offers those intent on canon re-formation a theoretical foothold both to explain women's "silence," to affirm their affiliation with minority literatures, and to further the process of revaluing their work and our own. Alice Walker writes in *Living by the Word* of women's relationship to language as she perceived it through Celie's character in *The Color Purple:* "For it is language more than anything else that reveals and validates one's existence, and if the language we actually speak is denied us, then it is inevitable that the form we are permitted to assume historically will be one of caricature, reflecting someone else's literary or social fantasy" (58). Elsewhere, Walker has written of the experience of her foremothers—and ours: "It is not so much that you sang, as that you kept alive, in so many of our ancestors, *the notion of song*" (*In Search of Our Mothers' Gardens*, 237).

It is of the nature of an oppressed people's life that much of their story resides in an oral tradition that, unlike the epic of the dominant culture, rarely comes to be written down as a text of itself, but emerges ultimately, if at all, as a fragment in a larger text—a poem, a journal, a piece of prose that has shouldered its way, by hook or by crook, toward literacy. Henry Louis Gates,[21] Mary Helen Washington,[22] and others have discovered/recovered an enormous oral tradition in African-American literature that made its way into hymnbooks and newspapers and obscure anthologies. Out of this tradition, and from its same impulse to identify, to name, and thus to utter and to preserve, comes also women's first and ongoing literate experiments with personal narrative forms—forms that remember the things on which we "tested our teeth" at our mothers' breasts. "[N]o song or poem will bear my mother's name," Walker writes. "Only recently did I fully realize this: that through years of listening to my mother's stories of her life, I have absorbed not only the stories themselves, but something of the manner in which she spoke, something of the urgency that involves the knowledge that her stories—like her life—must be recorded" (*In Search of Our Mothers' Gardens*, 240).

Walter Ong speaks about the basic orality of language and proceeds with a brilliant exegesis of its public manifestation as rhetoric—as discourse. But he has nevertheless told us only half the story—the story of what Heidegger recognized as the "poor imitation" of the long-forgotten poem. The other half resides in the stories women tell to their children about why the crow is black and why the emu cannot fly, "written" in pictures on the sand accompanying the mother's voice, and in the footmarks of their dancing. These are all the more valuable because when the images are wiped away, the embodied memory of its sounds remains—in the touch, taste, and smell of stones, plants, and other natural flotsam and jetsam that the child must know and remember if he or she is to survive in the microclimatic maze that is Australia. This is not to denigrate the powerful myth underlying the concept of the songline, or to lessen the significance of its power in culture. Nor is it to deny the significance of the discourses that have made disciplines of arts and sciences possible, nor the writing that has advanced our knowledge of them. Nevertheless, too often, categorizing language according to appropriateness of the performance situation is a controlling artifice that has served a specifically political end to maintain the power of the "haves" over the "have-nots." Reconsidering the relationship between orality and literacy offers the important reminder that before there is discourse there must be language, and before there is rhetoric—the public performance—there is poetry—the first voice.

Without the ability to imagine what Martin Buber[23] expressed as the relationship of I-Thou, without the capacity to become one with the object and therefore make it subject (not subject "to" or "of," but subject "with"), our students read no poems, write none, and frequently write poorly, if at all. Disconnected from things, they become disconnected from persons and from themselves. Our task is, quite simply, to teach them to "sing the world into existence" once again; what better models, then, than our mothers' songs, to show us how to try.

PART TWO

READING WRITING WOMEN:
VIRGINIA WOOLF, JOANNA FIELD,
AND ADRIENNE RICH

Campbell: The various Hebrew kings were sacrificing on the mountain-tops. And they did wrong in the sight of Yahweh. The Yahweh cult was a specific movement in the Hebrew community, which finally won. This was a pushing through of a certain temple-bound god against the nature cult, which was celebrated all over the place.

And this imperialistic thrust of a certain in-group culture is continued in the West. But it has got to open to the nature of things now. If it can open, all the possibilities are there.

Moyers: Of course we moderns are stripping the world of its natural revelations, of nature itself. I think of the pygmy legend of the little boy who finds the bird with the beautiful song in the forest and brings it home.

Campbell: He asks his father to bring food for the bird, and the father doesn't want to feed a mere bird, so he kills it. And the legend says the man killed the bird, and with the bird he killed the song, and with the song himself. He dropped dead, completely dead, and was dead forever. . . .

Moyers: And isn't mythology the story of the song?

Campbell: Mythology is the song. It is the song of the imagination inspired by the energies of the body. Once a Zen master stood up before his students and was about to deliver a sermon. And just as he was about to open his mouth, a bird sang. And he said, "The sermon has been delivered."

—Joseph Campbell, with Bill Moyers, The Power of Myth, *21–22*

III

Reclaiming the Garden Song:
Notes toward a Phenomenology of Intimacy

Australian Aboriginal Myth

Chapter 2 emphasized song, the rationale for male appropriation of women's songs as a means to appropriate their sexual potency and reproductivity, and the distortion this created in the stated relation between orality and literacy. Privileging the symbolic value of words enhanced by the technology of writing and the development of disciplinary discourses, men separated language from the things it named, and things themselves lost the actual value that a poetic language and consciousness express.

The separation of what Walter Ong calls *materna lingua* from *patrius sermo* led in turn to the privatization of the language by which women tell their stories, and to a sense that the stories themselves can have no collective significance or political impact. And so this chapter moves from the question of *language* to the question of *story*.

Asked whether the lack that prevented women from forming new lives was lack of language or of narrative, Carolyn Heilbrun comes down emphatically on the side of narrative (*Writing a Woman's Life*, 43). However, she goes on to say, "I do not believe that new stories will find their way into texts if they do not begin in oral exchanges among women in *groups* hearing and talking to one another. As long as women are isolated from one another, not allowed to offer other women the most personal accounts of their lives, they will not be part of any narrative of their own" (46).

In contrast, Heilbrun sees the consciousness-raising of the early feminist movement as essentially an effort to make the individual/private story hold collective/public significance. But it is this very collective enterprise that patriarchal culture most fears, for in collaborative work lies the deprivatization of knowledge, and in this kind of publicly collective knowledge there is power. "What became essential," Heilbrun writes, "was for women to see themselves collectively, not individually; not caught in some individual erotic and familial plot and, inevitably, found wanting. . . . There will be narratives of female lives only when women no longer live their lives isolated in the houses and stories of men" (46–47). To achieve this we must look first at the stories that men have told about women; these are the central stories of cultures, their myths.

"Children, say the Aranda, are 'deaf' and do not 'listen,' whereas initiated men 'speak wisely.' The latter understand the words of The Law and so indulge in real communication, unlike children, whose speech is not that of a 'thinking subject' . . . In Aranda terms, the language of desire is that of songs, whose words travel in death sentences to the centre of the heartlands" (Morton, "The Effectiveness of Totemism," 463). For women, the terms *desire* and *death* have a far different and more potent meaning than what Aranda men intend; they operate in the context of body, reproductivity, language, and, finally, story—all subject to male appropriation.

Examples of this appropriation abound. Male increase rituals, the controlling acts of "incestuous" males giving birth to themselves (becoming one with ancestral father nature in the guise of intercourse with mother), are understood as "the condition of future reproduction in the woman's realm" (Morton, "The Effectiveness of Totemism," 465). The symbols of ancestral male potency are sometimes handed over to women at the end of increase rites, reinforcing the exclusionary notion that her inheritance is the *symbol* but not the *song* (Spencer and Gillen, 153, cited by Morton, "The Effectiveness of Totemism," 465). The denial of women's reproductive power is enforced to the extent that in Aboriginal tribal tradition, child-spirits are generally directed to mothers—from whom they will be reborn—*by the father* or another patrilineal relative; someone else (generally the father), but not the woman herself, recognizes she is pregnant by interpreting an animal/natural phenomenon as the signal of the child-spirit's leap into her womb. While women occasionally perform rituals to induce pregnancy, these are generally considered dangerous, and *it is men* who claim the capacity to "sing" babies. (Ironically, enough, women's songs are more frequently directed to ways of *avoiding* the child-spirits and thus *avoiding* pregnancy (Merlan, "Australian Aboriginal Conception Beliefs Revisited," 475–76). Children are named from the *father's* song-cycle. Female sexual maturity (the onset of menstruation and development of secondary sex characteristics) is attributed to *the actions of men* who have intercourse with prepubescent girls and/or perform introcision rites preceding rituals of multiple intercourse.

Of equal or greater importance to gaining reproductive control are the sociopolitical rights gained by control of (vs. exclusive rights to) "the wife's and other female sexuality. Men make claims on the use of female sexuality as a means of creating ordered social relations" (Merlan, "Australian Aboriginal Conception Beliefs Revisited," 481). Women may be offered or exchanged to satisfy offenses between men or tribes, pregnancy is seen as a way to punish a woman who has had intercourse with "too many" partners, and those women who learn secrets of male rituals are beaten and/or must submit to intercourse with a number of men.[1] Denying a woman any claim to adult power over her own destiny, both preliterate and modern cultures effectively infantilize her—render her deaf, dumb, and without the capacity for rational thought or action. Essentially, they render her unable to tell her own story, substituting instead their stories *about* her, stories calculated to maintain her powerlessness. One of the most powerful among these stories is the Rainbow Serpent Myth.

In western Arnhem Land, pregnant or menstruating women or those carrying children are proscribed from going near other women lest floods be brought on by angering the Rainbow Snake of their central myth.[2] It goes this way.

At the beginning of time, two sisters were traveling across the landscape, conferring names on the features of a previously unnamed world. One carried a child, the other was pregnant. They had both committed incest in their own country, the country of the Wawilak. Carrying spears and other symbols of masculine power, they gathered food and hunted game animals, prophesying that everything they collected would soon become *marreiin* [sacred/taboo].

At last, having traversed many countries, they arrived at a waterhole in which, unknown to them, dwelt the great Rock Python or Rainbow Serpent, male in some versions (1, 3, 4), female in others (2). This Serpent was a kinsperson to the sisters. As the pregnant sister felt she was about to give birth, the other sister began to help her; they camped by the waterhole and lit a fire on which to cook their gathered food and game. But, in fulfillment of the prophecy, as they placed each item on the fire, it refused to cook, sprang to life and dived from the cooking-fire into the pool. This began to trouble and excite the snake.

As the sister, helped by her companion, began to give birth, afterbirth blood began flowing into the sacred pool, polluting it and arousing the Snake still more. A rain-cloud, lightening flashes and a rainbow (version 3) appeared in the sky, the Serpent was emerging in anger from its hole, unleashing the season of rain, floods and storms.

'Go away! Go Away!,' the sisters cried as they saw the immense Snake in the sky. Seized with fear, they sang 'menstrual blood'—the most taboo and potent of the songs known to them—and danced to make the Snake go away. But the dancing only brought on the second sister's menstrual flow, attracting the Serpent still more. The waterhole began overflowing, flooding the dry land all around.

Now filled with foreboding and despair, the sisters fled to the supposed safety of the little parturition hut/menstrual hut they had built. But at this point, inside the hut, they were both shedding blood and the angry Serpent thrust its nose into the hut and swallowed the women and their children alive. Then the victims, inside the serpent's belly, were carried to the sky. The snake became erect like a tree, its head stretching high into the clouds. Inside it, the sisters were still active and continued naming the countryside, speaking as the 'sacred knowledge' or thunder like 'voice' of the Snake itself (version 1). Snakes from neighboring countries joined in and all together inaugurated the great rituals which today bind in solidarity tribes from far and wide despite their linguistic differences.

The sisters and children now began an alternating movement between life and death, and between heaven and earth. The great Snake crashed to the ground when it had to admit to its companions the crime of having eaten its own kin. The ground was split open by the fall, creating the hollowed-out dance ground used in ritual today, and the sisters and children were 'killed,' their bones being smashed inside the Serpent's body as it fell. But the Snake then regurgitated its victims upon an ants' nest so that the ant-bites would resurrect them. The victims were swallowed again and then finally regurgitated to turn to stone—the form in which they can still be seen to this day.

Finally, men obtained from the spirits of the sisters the songs and dances necessary for them to perform the ceremonies on which their ritual power depends today. Some ancestral men (version 1) came upon the scene of the recent drama and collected and carefully preserved for their own use some of the sisters' blood. (Knight, "Lévi-Strauss and the Dragon," 22)

Women's birthing act is so powerful that throughout Aboriginal Australia, those giving birth are enforced to do so alone and without aid away from the village; they may return to the village only after the child is born (27). The fear of women's power revealed by this cultural practice culminates in the language of myth itself, and in the mythic deep structure which suggests that access to power and access to language (meaning) are one and the same. The Rainbow Serpent myth is one of the numerous dragon myths that mark the ascent of the hero as culture shifts from the primitive to the civilized. Anthropologist Chris Knight understands myth as providing markers and rationales for cultural shifts: "It seems that the essential function of myth is precisely to convey opposite messages to 'opposite' sections—unitiated and initiated—of society itself. . . . Everything in the myth is 'turned the other way around,' inverted with respect to its inside or secret meaning, because deception of the uninitiated [women and children] is essential to the maintenance of male ritual" (26). Part of the Wawilak sisters' power resided in their daring to name the world they walked. But the received interpretation of this, the Wawilak sisters' myth, replicates the story of Adam and Eve: it argues that to the man falls the task of bringing order from the chaos that wild women have wrought, vesting the control of language and law in rituals whose "forbidden sacred objects" women may see, but fail to recognize because they have been deliberately described in a way that offers them to sight but obfuscates meaning. Like children who are "deaf" in Aranda terms, women are "unable" to listen because they are proscribed from doing so and, at least overtly, embrace the proscription. Disabled from listening, they become unable to speak as well, and the appropriation of their primal power is complete.

The actual meaning of the Wawilak sisters' myth is a story of female closeness and reproductive power vested in the synchronicity of their menstrual cycles[3] and in the sacred/taboo act of blood-making itself. "[A]ll of the world's great patriarchal foundation-myths," says Knight, in fact express

a firm belief in the mysteriously potent and enviable connexions [sic]—'threads' and 'ropes' of life-blood and kinship—connecting menstrual forms of periodicity to lunar and other cosmic forms. Through the rituals which act out [replicate] their myths, men attempt to cut women's ropes—their Serpents and Dragons—in order to sustain their own cultural role. Men sever, as best they can, the bonds between women's periods and the wider rhythms of society and the cosmos, attempting to reconstitute these threads in their own hands. (43)

If "the men who perform the rituals know that they stole women's 'dance' or 'song' long, long ago in the mythological past" (45), women actually know it, too, yet they continue to collude in their dispossession. In western Arnhem Land, the Gunwinggu call both Rainbow Serpent and Mother the same "inside" name: *banagaga*. The image/power of the serpent and that of every woman's potentially bleeding womb are one and the same; men and women both know that the serpent woman came before any male ancestor from out of the ground at the beginning of time to form humankind. Yet in the tribe the rhetoric of inversion is maintained, denying this primary alliance and making women and the serpent inimical to each other. So the same fire that cooks men's meals and makes the purifying postpartum ash to clean mother and infant burns steadily in the menstrual hut where the first-menstruating girl must remain, kept away from others to avoid "harming" them by bringing on the anger of the Rainbow Serpent and its floods. "While men are allowed to combine their reproductive [blood] flows to engulf them in the Serpent's sanctifying power, women must carry on their reproductive activities isolated and alone. Women's *own power* is depicted to them as a force from which they [women] should bide in fear" (47).[4]

And so women teach their children to "name" their world, but do not name themselves; they allow their sons to be taught that to name (sing) themselves is to repudiate their mother's songs; they teach their daughters to submit to the Father's Law as they have themselves submitted.

Yet I have insisted that women sing.

How, then, do women maintain their legacy through song? By a mythmaking activity of their own. This activity involves a relationship to space and time expressed in picture *and* in song that both insist upon the return to the origins—to the things themselves—out of whose material substance male mythic inversions have been wrenched. By returning to their father's house and reinstating the claim of mothers—and their own claim—which is also a return to the body. By seeking behind the claims of Law the prior claims of Nature. By turning the inside out again. By imposing upon the linear narrative of his-cultural-story that powerful Romantic image of the snake biting its own tail: that is, by imposing the circle upon the line of time and experience. "They tried to make us believe that women were impotent, immobile, paralyzed," writes Xavière Gauthier. "That is because they tried to make women walk a straight line, in lock step, in goose step. In reality, they dance, they creep, they fly, they swim in every sea. They coil themselves up, they twist, they jump, they crouch, they leap."[5]

Gauthier's comments are well-illustrated by the Pilbara rock drawings of the Rainbow Serpent myth, which include a number of pairs of dancing women whose conjoined menstrual streams circle upward and around the figures in the shape of a snake or two-headed dragon (Knight, "Lévi-Strauss and the Dragon," 39). Furthermore, men's songs reveal that these dancing women are to be feared—and why. Aranda men sing of their female ancestors, *alknarintja*, "women who refuse men," whose ritual powers resides in their song and dance of blood:

> The alknarintja women cut their breasts
> On their breasts they make scars
> They slap their thighs . . .
> They are menstruating.
> Their flanks are wet with blood.
> *They talk to each other.*
> They make a bull-roarer . . .
> They are menstruating.
> The blood is perpetually flowing[6]

The terror is, then, not that one woman should sing, dance, bleed, but that many women will sing together. The terror, in other words, is that there should be a conjoining of these forces: song, dance, blood-women-serpent, knowledge attained by eating the fruit of the serpent's tree, by becoming one with the serpent's knowledge and so becoming the serpent (epistemology as ontology) controlling the controller of flood and rainbow, making the covenant and *therefore* making the Law, the power of the *sorcière* answered by mother-power. "Why witches?" writes Gauthier.

> *Because witches sing.* Can I hear this singing? It is the sound of another voice. They tried to make us believe that women did not know how to speak or write; that they were stutterers or mutes. That is because they tried to make women speak straightforwardly, logically, geometrically, in strict conformity. In reality, they croon lullabies, they howl, they gasp, they babble, they shout, they sigh. They are silent and even their silence can be heard. ("Pourquoi Sorcières?" 199)

There have been numerous attempts to explore the question of "difference" in women's writing. Among the French feminist theorists these descriptors of difference have been characterized by the terms "plural, continuous, interdependent, nonsensical, roundabout, a narrative of ruptures, gaps, wordplay, and *jouissance*" (Smith, *A Poetics of Women's Auto-biography*, 13). American theorists—Nancy Chodorow, Dorothy Dinnerstein, Jane Flax, and others—suggests that these narrative differences are emergent from the differing psychosexual development of men and women.[7] Citing Roland Barthes, Julia Kristeva represents their position in psycholinguistic terms that explore the difference of the writing woman's voice in this previously cited passage: "[S]tyle as a 'frame of reference is biological or biographical, not historical . . . a *sublanguage* elaborated where flesh and external reality come together' (*Writing Degree Zero*, p. 11); 'its secret is *recollection* locked within the body of a writer' " (*Desire in Language*, 111–12).

But in addition, Barthes's image, as Kristeva calls it to her own purposes, becomes a descriptor for the kind of mythmaking activity that women's writing entails: the act of personal and collective memory by which they call themselves and other women back to the place of origins, imposing upon the line of tribal history (the line of their dispossession), the circle of origin (their own and that of the tribe). The place where the ancestor "goes in" becomes the place out of which the Wawilak sisters, Eve, women, may come out again. The imposition of the circle on the line becomes both an act of exorcism—banishing the inverted myth, the false creation narrative by which they have been dispossessed from history, from language, from sexuality, from the law, from themselves—and an act of desire: "Let the priests tremble," writes Cixous, "we're going to show them our sexts!"[8]

To study this mythmaking activity in women's writing is to watch the evolution of a phenomenology of intimacy and to perceive language used in its service. If narrative is an expression of our relationship to space and time, then to study the nature of women's narrative, their storytelling, their mythmaking, is to study our relationship to space and time. Time in the garden has become a powerful image—and reality—in women's lives in many cultures. I believe these garden stories—expressing both a place and a time in women's lives—express as well a relationship marked by a particular kind of intimacy. I also believe that the recovery of the body (their own, others', their mothers'), the recovery of the garden, and the recovery or reconstruction of themselves become one and the same act. To borrow Kim Chernin's phrase, I believe that women's narrative begins in the garden, reinventing Eve.[9] To borrow Martin Heidegger's, I believe that women's narrative seeks expression in language understood as "the house of Being."[10] And borrowing a phrase from Gaston Bachelard (*The Poetics of Space*), I believe that in women's narrative, a genuine poetics of space is at the core of their phenomenology of intimacy. The next section of this text explores the relationships among these ideas.

Garden Myths in Some Western Narratives

For Western culture, the first Eucharist belonged to Eve and her foremothers: mythically (literally and metaphorically) eating of the flesh of the mother/goddess/tree, mother's and daughter's power conjoins like the menstrual streams of the women in the Pilbara rock drawings. In the garden, it is good to be hungry, and good to eat, good to be close to the earth, good to cultivate its fruits. The phenomenology of intimacy begins with the body, in a garden.

As Chernin suggests, it is not an accident that, in the Hebrew myth, Eve reached for knowledge (and therefore power) by an act of eating. Apple trees emerge in numerous mythic traditions associated with goddesses who dispensed their fruit to kings, heroes, and even other gods, plucking it from sacred trees in gardens protected by dragons, offering with it "both resurrection and immortality to those who ate them" (*Reinventing Eve,* xviii). The inverted myth leaves a woman threatened and betrayed by these mythic creatures, and needing the salvation of a conquering hero. In reality, the dragon and the snake have always belonged to her. So also have the fruits of the garden and their enjoyment. But the desperate irony of Western culture is that, like their proscription from access to language and power, women have believed themselves to be and *have been* forbidden the very fruit of the gardens that belong to them. They have literally and figuratively been starved, sometimes to death.

For years, male writers and poets have placed (fenced, locked) women into gardens that were alternately scenes for sentimental romance, seduction, or cold-blooded murder. In male eyes, these garden-bound women became visions of imprisoned sexuality; this first-plucked fruit was made all the more tantalizing by its forbidden nature, and by the voyeurism and the force that gaining entry required. What is more, not only were these women *in* gardens, but the language of male description ultimately made woman and garden one, displacing and exiling female subjectivity.

In *The Portrait of a Lady,* Henry James brings Isabel Archer from an old house in Albany to Gardencourt, the English country home in whose garden we see her first. In this garden she is met and watched alternately by three men, each of whom will proffer his love to her: a dying American expatriate, an English peer, a brash American naif. (In fact, there are four if we include the novelist himself). James's identification of Isabel with the garden, first a typical metaphor of American innocence, soon portends her less than happy fate.

> Her nature had, in her conceit, a certain garden-like quality, a suggestion of perfume and murmuring boughs, of shady bowers and lengthening vistas, which made her feel that introspection was, after all, an exercise in the open air, and that a visit to the recesses of one's spirit was harmless when

one returned from it with a lapful of roses. But she was often
reminded that there were other gardens in the world than
those of her remarkable soul, and that there were moreover a
great many places which were not gardens at all—only dusky,
pestiferous tracts, planted thick with ugliness and misery. (56)

In this same garden, as the novel closes, Isabel perceives that she has lost
love and all chance of happiness; from it, she returns with stoical endurance to a loveless marriage and a pathetically childlike stepdaughter named
Pansy.

The garden has been the backdrop of Isabel Archer's unhappiness
and her stoical endurance of the consequences of her fateful choice to
marry Gilbert Osmond. For Beatrice Rappaccini, her father's walled garden offers her a sweet poison—"the breath of life"—and death. Peering
down from his window upon Beatrice, enclosed within its walls,
Hawthorne's naive narrator speaks more than he knows:

Soon there emerged under a sculptured portal the figure of a
young girl, arrayed with as much richness of taste as the most
splendid of the flowers, beautiful as the day, and with a bloom
so deep and vivid that one shade more would have been too
much. She looked redundant with life, health, and energy; all
of which attributes were bound down and compressed, as it
were, and girdled tensely, in their luxuriance, by her virgin
zone . . . [T]he impression which the fair stranger made upon
him was is if here were another flower, the human sister of
those vegetable ones, as beautiful as they, more beautiful than
the richest of them, but still to be touched only with a glove,
nor to be approached without a mask.[11]

Isolated in her father's garden and wedded to his poison flower, which she
embraces with the ardor of a lover, Beatrice is, in her father's exultant
words, made "able to quell the mightiest with a breath" (Hawthorne,
"Rappaccini's Daughter," 1064). Drinking the antidote provided by
Rappaccini's enemy and offered by the hand of her unknowing lover,
Giovanni, Beatrice dies. She is not the only one of Hawthorne's women
who become the victims of man-made science (cf., for example, Georgiana
in "The Birthmark"), but her story is a dramatic example of yet another
creation myth gone awry as her parent-scientist, his enemy, and her unwit-
ting lover seek to assert control over women and nature at the same time.

Thomas Hardy places Tess d'Urberville in two kinds of gardens. One
is the product of Angel Clare's idealizing imagination, a garden in which she

is his Artemis and his Demeter, alternately an image of the unspoiled virgin who circles the Maypole in the novel's first scene and the luxuriously fertile milkmaid who blooms with the summer later on. The other is a far less romantic one, "at the outskirts . . . uncultivated for some years . . . now damp and rank with juicy grass which sent up mists of pollen at a touch; and with tall blooming weeds emitting offensive smells." Through this nightmarish garden, "She went stealthily as a cat . . . gathering cuckoo-spittle on her skirts, cracking snails that were underfoot, staining her hands with thistle-milk and slug-slime, and rubbing off upon her naked arms sticky blights which, though snow-white on the apple-tree trunks, made madder stains on her skin" (*Tess of the d'Urbervilles*, 104). Identified powerfully with Edenic worlds and Edenic worlds gone bad, Tess's rape by Alec d'Urberville and her rejection as a "Fallen Woman" by Angel are yet other male expressions of women's identification with the earth in a nineteenth-century world that first brings the machine to the garden—to control and to destroy—all in the name of progress.

Finally, D. H. Lawrence is less subtle in making the sexual connection between woman and garden. Connie Chatterley makes orgasmic love to her husband's inarticulate gardener, Mellors, in his hut deep in the woods of her crippled husband's estate. The novel ends with a letter to her composed by an improbably voluble Mellors: "My soul softly flaps in the little pentecost flame with you, like the peace of fucking. We fucked a flame into being. Even the flowers are fucked into being between the sun and the earth" (*Lady Chatterley's Lover*, 327–28).

In contrast to this masculine horticulture, when women place themselves, or children, or other women, in gardens, the stories they tell differ radically from male narratives. In their stories, women are not the betrayers of Eden but its keepers, not the harbingers of chaos but artists whose hands move lovingly to mediate creative chaos and formal order. In their own stories, too, women (and children) become the gardens in which they work or play, but they do not take the stance of protection or defense; in fact, they freely invite people in, and give portions of the garden away. Often, as is the case with Eve and other mythic goddesses, their relationship to the garden is intimately connected with their relationship to mothers. And often, house and garden are interpenetrating worlds. Alice Walker writes:

[M]y mother adorned with flowers whatever shabby house we were forced to live in. . . .

Whatever she planted grew as if by magic, and her fame as a grower of flowers spread over three counties. Because of her creativity with her flowers, even my memories of poverty are seen through a screen of blooms—sunflowers, petunias, roses, dahlias, forsythia, spirea, delphiniums, verbena. . . .

I notice that it is only when my mother is working in her flowers that she is radiant, almost to the point of being invisible—except as Creator: hand and eye. She is involved in work her soul must have. Ordering the universe in the image of her personal conception of Beauty.

Her face, as she prepares the Art that is her gift, is a legacy of respect she leaves to me, for all that illuminates and cherishes life. She has handed down respect for the possibilities—and the will to grasp them. (*In Search of Our Mothers' Gardens*, 241–42)

"Flowers and plants," writes May Sarton, "are silent presences; they nourish every sense except the ear. . . . What a pleasure it is to touch the hairy bud of a poppy, or to pick up the velvety fallen petal of a rose, or to get a wave of sharp sweetness from the peony bed as one goes past! . . . Like any grand passion, my garden has been nourished by memory as well as by desire, and is a meeting place, an intersection where remembered joys can be re-created" (*Plant Dreaming Deep*, 124–25). And later, "My mother is most with me as a living presence when I go out to weed" (127). *Journal of a Solitude* blooms with the realities of Sarton's gardens, inside and out, as entry after entry begins with her connection to the garden outdoors. Sarton's houses are never separate from her gardens, but of a piece. The houses arrange themselves around vases of cut flowers: "On my desk small pink roses. . . . On the mantle, in the Japanese jar, two sprays of white lilies, recurved, maroon pollen on the stamens, and a branch of peony leaves turned a strange pinkish-brown. . . . When I am alone the flowers are really seen; I can pay attention to them. They are felt as presences. Without them I would die . . . I am floated on their moments" (11). And the garden's colors flow inside: "My mother tasted color as it if were food, and when I get that shiver of delight at a band of sun on the yellow floor in the big room, or put an olive-green pillow onto a dark-emerald corduroy couch, I am not so much thinking of her as being as she was" (*Plant Dreaming Deep*, 184). In the novels, the sounds of houses are inevitably a duet of human and natural. *Mrs. Stevens Hears the Mermaids Singing* opens as Hilary Stevens is "forced awake by the twice-repeated piercing notes of an oriole in the flowering plum just outside her windows. At the same moment the French clock cut through the spontaneous song with its rigid intervals" (11–12).

"—'I begin: the first memory,' " writes Virginia Woolf.

This was of red and purple flowers on a black ground—my mother's dress; and she was sitting either in a train or in an omnibus, and I was on her lap. I therefore saw the flowers she was wearing very close; and can still see purple and red and blue, I think, against the black; they must have been anemones, I suppose. (*Moments of Being*, 64)

My mother would come out onto her balcony in a white dressing gown. There were passion flowers growing on the wall; they were great starry blossoms, with purple streaks, and large green buds, part empty, part full. (66)

The gardens gave off a murmur of bees; the apples were red and gold; there were also pink flowers; and grey and silver leaves. The buzz, the croon, the smell, all seemed to press voluptuously against some membrance; not to burst it; but to hum round one such a complete rapture of pleasure that I stopped, smelt; looked. But again I cannot describe that rapture. It was rapture rather than ecstasy. (66)

I see it—the past—as an avenue lying behind; a long ribbon of scenes, emotions. There at the end of the avenue still, are the garden and the nursery. Instead of remembering here a scene and there a sound, I shall fit a plug into the wall; and listen in to the past. I shall turn up August 1890. I feel that strong emotion must leave its trace; and it is only a question of discovering how we can get ourselves again attached to it, so that we shall be able to live our lives through from the start. (67)

In *The Waves,* each chapter begins with a lyric interval, a kind of ode to sea, garden, and house, the garden the world "between." The garden is the place where children play the hide-and-seek games that become for Woolf a metaphor of identity-making:

"Now they are all gone," said Louis. "I am all alone. . . . It is very early, before lessons. Flower after flower is specked on the depths of green. The petals are harlequins. Stalks rise from the black hollows beneath. The flowers swim like fish made of light upon the dark, green waters. I hold a stalk in my hand. I am the stalk. My roots go down to the depths of the world, through earth dry with brick, and damp earth, through veins of lead and silver. I am all fibre. All tremors shake me, and the weight of the earth is pressed to my ribs." (182)

It is the place of song, overheard by an omnisicent narrator who invests the sound and movement with a playful, childlike anthropomorphism, but who remains at the same time at a noninterfering distance:

> In the garden the birds that had sung erratically and spasmodically in the dawn on that tree, on that bush, now sang together in chorus, shrill and sharp; now together, as if conscious of companionship, now alone as if to the pale blue sky. They swerved all in one flight, when the black cat moved among the bushes, when the cook threw cinders on the ash heap and startled them. Fear was in their song, and apprehension of pain, and joy to be snatched quickly now at this instant. Also they sang emulously in the clear morning air, swerving high over the elm tree, singing together as they chased each other, escaping, pursuing, pecking each other as they turned high in the air. And then tiring of pursuit and flight, lovelily they came descending, delicately declining, dropped down and sat silent on the tree, on the wall, with their bright eyes glancing, and their heads turned this way, that way; aware, awake; intensely conscious. (225–26)

It is the place between childhood and adulthood, between the sea's utter chaos and the order of the house, between death and life. The garden is women's particular ritual space. Dispossessed from it by the power of "Genesis," another inverted myth, women work assiduously in their narratives to reclaim and cultivate it for themselves.

Definitions toward a Phenomenology of Intimacy

There are a number of ways to explicate the term *phenomenology of intimacy*. Some of these are implicit in the ways that women I have referred to in this chapter have written of gardens. The first and most obvious emerges from the **quality of these women's relationship to the earth.** This relationship echoes themes of earlier chapters. The refusal to privilege knowing over being or culture over nature leads to the rejection of hierarchies and the embracing of dialectical ways of knowing and being in the world. We come to know the thing by entering its experience through what Bachelard calls the act of "material imagination," a return to *"direct images of matter,"* images in which "the form is deeply sunk *in* a substance" (*The Poetics of Space,* ix). The implications of Bachelard's work on a poetics of space and of Woolf's work on the emergence of character through a controlled stream-of-consciousness narrative reinvoke the terms of yet another previous theme: the collapsing of the boundaries between epistemology and ontology, that is, the affirmation that we know the thing by becoming it, that we are genuinely *engagés*, as only the French can render it, not merely sympathetic but empathic. Contradicting Descartes: "I know because I am."

"I feel sometimes," Sarton writes, "like a house with no walls" (*Journal of a Solitude*, 114). Yet her greatest anguish, when neither the process of writing nor the process of living is working, is being "unable to become what I see" (12). Echoing Heidegger's reflection on the quality of poetic language,[12] Bachelard affirms Sarton's intuition about her own life as a writer: "Poets will help us to discover within ourselves such joy in looking that sometimes, in the presence of a perfectly familiar object, we experience an extension of our intimate space" (Bachelard, *The Poetics of Space*, 199).

Besides our relationship to the earth, a phenomenology of intimacy takes up as well this **relationship to the familiar, to "plain and ordinary things."** Like our relationship to the earth, this relationship is also marked by paradox, by the refusal of hierarchies and the exchange of dualism for dialectic, by an intensity of vision and a concomitant intensity of consciousness. Modifying Descartes: "I see, therefore I am."

As illustrated in the works of Sarton and Joanna Field, this intensity of vision/consciousness is a central theme in women's writing and an important part of a phenomenology of intimacy.[13] Sarton's journals evoke houses and gardens literally bathed in light that reaches toward metaphor but retains, with tenacity, its thingness, its materiality. "[I]n a supreme moment of light," quotes Sarton from a friend's letter, "one becomes aware of the 'sacred' " (*Journal of a Solitude*, 117). The lights of inner and outer worlds (enlightenment and physical light) are not separate. Still, while each contributes to maintaining the other's identity, the metaphysical is never privileged over the literal. "It is poetry" that "lights up the house" (115). "[T]he great autumn light begins, a time of change in the inner world" (206), but it moves over zinnias, cosmos, autumn crocuses and asters, and finally, "upward from the flower borders to the leaves overhead—saffron yellow of the beeches, vermilion and orange of the maples, wave on wave of massed translucent color, the stained-glass days against a brilliant blue sky" (206). The sacred remains rooted in the ordinary: this is the very nature of its sacredness. The form remains but the shape of content, nothing without its connection to the thing itself.

Implicit in both the relationship to the earth and to things is a third dimension of a phenomenology of intimacy, a recognition of what Joanna Field calls *"the texture of experience"* (*A Life of One's Own*, 94).

The characteristics of this awareness involve affirming a relationship to things that is not instrumental,[14] but allows them to be qualitatively what they are without demanding that they serve some overweening purpose. It is an awareness that uses "texture" to "contextualize," a goal worthy of any curriculum and a project without which good writing seems impossible. For example, she writes of "a lump coal on the hearth": "From having been aware of it simply as something to burn I began to feel its blackness as a quite new sensation, to feel its 'thingness' and the thrust of its shape, to feel after its past in forests of giant vegetation, in upheavings of the land passing to aeons of stillness, and then little men tunneling, the silence and cleanliness of forests going to make up London's noisy filth" (95). It is a kind of vision—or perhaps revision—whose emphasis is qualitative versus quantitative, a version of what Coleridge termed the "suspension of disbelief."[15] It is an attitude of mind, one that allowed Field to perceive even "the squares and angles of the outhouse from [her window]" as "comforting" (*A Life of One's Own*, 94) and one that allowed her to suspend the kind of restless instrumentality that in fact prevented rather than enhanced genuine awareness:

> It seemed then that my purpose in life was to get the most out of life. And because I was not capable of more than very muddled thinking, I still assumed that the way to this was to strive to do more and more things; and this, in spite of my intuition about the need for surrender. Here then was a deadlock. I wanted to get the most out of life, but the more I tried to grasp, the more I felt that I was ever outside, missing things. At that time I could not understand at all that my real purpose might be to learn to have no purposes. (92)

While it may seem easy to understand Field's concept of the texture of experience in relationship to objects smaller than ourselves, or those subject in some way to our control, Bachelard's poetics offers the concept of "intimate immensity," the additional connection between the vast and the intimate that is imperative to an understanding of Woolf's relationship to the sea and of human connections with other vast geographies that are collectively described as "earth." "[I]mmensity in the intimate domain," he writes, "is intensity, an intensity of being, the intensity of a being evolving in a vast perspective of intimate immensity" (*The Poetics of Space*, 193). In Woolf's text, human consciousness is not privileged over animal or even plant, but all participate in a steady stream of consciousness that for Woolf is life itself—a life punctuated by "moments of being" during which that consciousness is at its most intense. Woolf emphasizes the contextual nature of these moments over and over again. "Life," she writes in "Modern Fiction," "is not a series of gig-lamps symmetrically arranged; life is a luminous halo, a semi-transparent envelope surrounding us from the beginning of consciousness to the end. Is it not the task of the novelist to convey this varying, this unknown and uncircumscribed spirit, whatever aberration or complexity it may display . . . ?" (*Collected Essays*, 2:106).

Fourth, the evolving feeling for the materiality of things becomes inextricably interwoven with both **maternality and memory:** through memory the material as (m)other is recovered and reclaimed. This involves in turn a recovery and reclamation from the sentimentalized Victorian fusion of mother and home that Adrienne Rich rightly condemns when it is articulated as the slogan of racism, sexism, or classism. In other words, this reclamation causes us to ask what the phrase *woman is the embodied home* (Rich, *Of Woman Born*, 42) might genuinely signify if it were not spoken by the "racist southern historian" Rich cites.

Sarton says that without her gardens, "nourished by memory as well as by desire" she "would die." In these gardens her mother is with her "as living presence." In Woolf's memory of her mother, garden imagery mixes with the imagery of passion and desire. Red and purple flowers riot on the black ground of her mother's dress. Passion flowers, "great starry blossoms, with purple streaks, and large green buds, part empty, part full" climb the wall by the balcony on which her white-gowned mother stands, virgin, "she who is unto herself." Despite her perception that she was never able to do so,[16] Woolf writes the language of the body through the power of her style: the language of the cradle-song becomes the language of orgasm. "The buzz, the croon, the smell, all seemed to press voluptuously against some membrane; not to burst it; but to hum round one such a complete rapture of pleasure that I stopped, smelt; looked . . . It was rapture rather than ecstasy" (*Moments of Being*, 66). The garden and the nursery, she says, are at the end (the beginning) of the avenue that is the past. Memory involved "attachment" to it, "so that we shall be able to live our lives through from the start." And this is what women's mythmaking is about: the recovery of the garden, of the material, of maternality, so that we can reconstruct, so that we can "live our lives through from the start" and "recant" them—re-sing them, rewrite them. It is perpetually a process of completing circles.

Finally, reclaiming the garden and the nursery is **a repossession of two contiguous, neighboring "territories"—knowledge and sexuality.** In some mythic geographies, these acts of reclamation are represented as the claims of the periphery upon the center, the claims of the

"Other" upon "us," of the "outside" upon the "inside," or of nature/
chaos upon culture/law. Many festivals and cultural rituals exemplify
these claims, frequently represented in ecstatic dance and song.

   For example, variously named "the great loosener," the "god of
blossoms," and the one who "turned things inside out," Dionysus,[17]
whose rites were primarily observed by women and slaves ("groups at the
periphery"), at festival time was rolled through the riotous streets of
Athens on a ship cart that symbolized the chaos of the no-man's-land,
the lawless sea, overcoming order, the land's Law (Duerr, *Dreamtime*,
24). Like the Pilbara Rock dancers, "[W]hen herbs and flowers awake to
new life" the Couroi and Couretes of Dionysus (closely related to the
maenads of Zagreus-Dionysus that Euripedes writes of in *The Bacchae*)
"swarmed *(thyein)* and danced over the meadows and the fields in the
retinue of the 'Great Mother,' nurturing the animals of the wilderness"
(24). Women and wildness/wilderness are firmly connected to each other.
For example, the rites of the virgin Artemis and of Dionysus are virtually
indistinguishable, as are their respective followers, the Erinyes
("enrapturers") and the Bacchae. They are tree deities whose nymphs
(*numphai*, buds) and maenads offer their breast milk to human and
animal alike (196, n. 59). In their ecstatic rites the kinship of blood is
replaced by the kinship of milk. Like the *alknarintja*, these women
refuse men and so refuse them the carnal "knowing" that has been male
privilege. The knowledge of the body liberated by women's ritual dance
replaces the knowledge of law; men will never "know" women, but
women will know themselves. As those who have been "known" claim
knowledge for themselves, the narrative comes full circle at the behest of
revisionary consciousness.

   Finally, it is important to understand this space/time connection in
relationship to the narratives of conventional history, a relationship that
can go a long way toward explaining women's silence in the larger
cultural story. Alice Jardine, among others, has written extensively about
the traditional association of women and space, men and time. Briefly,
she begins *Gynesis* by citing the work of Jean-Joseph Goux. Goux postu-
lates that "Moses' anger at the worship of the golden calf, a female
deity—*mater*—and the Jews' ensuing departure from Egypt with its female icons and hieroglyphic imagination" emerges through Plato and the
Judeo-Christian tradition as "*the* founding fantasy: the active negation of
the Mother." Thus, "Since the beginning of Western patriarchal history,
'woman' has been but the passive matter to which 'Man' could give form
through the ever-increasing spiral of abstract universals: God, Money,
Phallus—the infinity of substitution" (*Gynesis*, 32). Nevertheless, Goux's

argument culminates in the recognition that in the twentieth century, the end points of both Marxism and Freudianism are remarkably similar. Following the separation of man from nature and the conflict between the two, Marxism culminates in "the interaction of Man with *another* nature (historical materialism)." Following the separation from mother and the conflict of man versus woman, Freudianism ends with "reunion with *another* Woman." Both systems, then, end with "a reuniting of form with matter—*mate*rialism (but only after a long period of *pate*rialism) and a new relationship to the feminine (but only after castration)." Jardine summarize these returns:

> For Goux, history has been the history of Man and men, but now we are entering a new historicity. The End of History, the Death of Man: a true *jouissance* as we move beyond the fear of falling back into the original maternal abyss and move toward a 'new access to the feminine.' This (re)union with the feminine is the end point of History—u-topia
>
> . . . . .
>
> We might say that what is generally referred to as modernity is precisely this acutely interior, unabasedly incestuous exploration of these new female spaces: the perhaps historically unprecedented exploration of the female, differently maternal body. (*Gynesis*, 33–34)

Certainly any phenomenology of intimacy that will allow reading Woman must involve the recognition that the inside is turned out. But the exploration Jardine describes is men's, not women's, nor is the exploration "historically unprecedented." In fact, the "new access to the feminine" Goux describes, and the "new female spaces" to which Jardine refers seem to have very ancient roots indeed, among them the "transvestitism" that Page DuBois describes as "consistent with a pattern of the Greek male's fascination with and gradual appropriation of the socially suppressed female other" (*Sowing the Body*, 177).

Historical records are indeed rich with the conception of woman as the place "inside" that men have sought. For the Greeks she is the furrow laid open by the plow, a "vessel" in which seed can be hidden, from which grain is offered, from which nourishment is obtained, and within which the dead are buried. She is a vase made of earth and water holding "the goods of life" and "the bones and ashes of the dead" (DuBois, *Sowing the Body*, 132); erect nipples *(mastoi)* protrude from the shoulders of the vase. She is the stone treasury, the Erechtheion guarded by Athena's caryatids, and the temple. She is the oven. She is "the tablet folded up on itself, the papyrus that must be unfolded to be deciphered" (47). She is, in all cases, inscribed by men.

Narratives of Resistance and Reappropriation

A phenomenology of intimacy seeks to reappropriate this interiority and reinscribe it. Just as I have insisted that, despite their apparent exclusion from the public rhetoric of the tribe, women have sung, so also do I insist that, despite their inscription by men, women like the Erinyes and the Bacchae have always been engaged in the reappropriation of their experience, of their bodies, and of the songs that inscribe them. And their engagement has been aimed not solely at resisting male inscription, but in large part at inscribing themselves. Modern perhaps, but an age-old problem as well.

Both resistance and self-inscription occur in a return to the past by opening the closed door of memory, an act both mythic and personal in its activity and intent. The choice of the journal form is one way women do this. Narrative style is another. For example, Woolf's ultimate reappropriative act is the orgasmic quality of her style, embodying a narrative stance that, in novels like *To the Lighthouse* and *The Waves*, is somewhere "between" the two poles (sexual positions), omniscience and stream-of-consciousness. As is the case for many women, there are many men's hands from which Woolf must seize the past—and her self.[18]

Interestingly enough, fictional characters do the same—and they need not necessarily be created by women writers. Tess d'Urberville, for example, never has her own house in Hardy's novel; the houses and temples built by men in which she stops are places in which she becomes their victim, finally quite literally on the altar of sacrifice, as is illustrated by the final scene at Stonehenge where she too will be sacrificed to the demands of patriarchal practice. Nevertheless, she responds to Angel Clare's naming her out of the culturally appropriated myths of Artemis and Demeter with the words "Call me Tess." Thus does Hardy (albeit quite likely unwittingly, since his novel concludes with Tess as "victim once again") create a character who lays claim to her interiority despite male inscription of her red lips and tongue and mouth—and womb.

There are numerous other examples. Reappropriating interiority, from Kim Chernin's perspective, involves reappropriating the goddess and her power. To do so one enters an underworld of consciousness in which "time does not exist" and "[w]hat we call years are stacked like the floors of a house, all sorts of stairways going up and down to give one access to them" (*Reinventing Eve,* 107). Ice-age prototypes of Artemis with enormous breasts and open vagina with swollen labia are found in hearth pits at the center of communal dwellings and near the fire pits of cult caves. In cultures all over the world, caves more or less explicitly defined as vaginas of the earth or belonging to the "Great Goddess" were/are entered by initiates who seek "death" in order to be "born" again. On the day of the "Great Mother," tribes who celebrated her would lift the incest rule (Duerr, *Dreamtime,* 25); in some cultures, the cave gave way to the temple, the Goddess to her "prostitutes" (16). But the power of women's association with the place inside—the cave, the home, as well as the temple and the womb—is far greater than any sentimental Victorian fantasy might lead us to believe. Woman's association is not with domestic space solely because that is the experience to which she has found herself relegated. It is the space she has chosen, inevitably outside of historical time because her time is the circle, not the line; in that circle is the reproductive space out of which we must come and to which we must return, recursively, reentering the multiple incarnations that involve identity-making. With this conception of "inside," Rich's earlier notion of "woman as embodied home" takes on a whole new meaning.

A good part of sentimentality involves imposing and accepting the inevitable. But the connection of women and home need not be a sentimental one. Home need not be the only space to which women can belong. In the following case it is, in fact, no sentimental place at all. In Charlotte Bronte's *Jane Eyre,* a recalcitrant Jane is locked into the blood-red bedroom in which her guardian's husband has died. Bronte describes it in this way:

> A bed supported on massive pillars of mahogany, hung with curtains of deep red damask, stood out like a tabernacle in the centre, the two large windows, with their blinds always drawn down, were half shrouded in festoons and falls of similar drapery; the carpet was red; the table at the foot of the bed was covered with a crimson cloth; the walls were a soft fawn colour, with a blush of pink in it; the wardrobe, the toilet-table, the chairs, were of darkly-polished old mahogany. Out of these deep surrounding shades rose high, and glared white, the piled-up mattresses and pillows of the bed. (7)

Gazing at herself in the mirror, the adult narrator, Jane, reflects that in this room without a fire, "All looked colder and darker in that visionary hollow than in reality: and the strange little figure there gazing at me with a white face and arms specking the gloom . . . had the effect of a real spirit . . . like one of the tiny phantoms, half fairy, half imp . . . coming out of lone, ferny dells in moors, and appearing before the eyes of belated travelers" (8). Bleeding from a blow to the head struck by her guardian's bully son, exhausted by defiance and a growing despair, "oppressed, suffocated," Jane swoons before her aunt's shouted demand for silence and the remonstrance that "it is only on condition of perfect submission and stillness" (11) that she might receive her liberty.

From the red room in which the child Jane has been immolated on the altar of sacrifice, a very different Jane emerges. From the erotic space of love and death, this second womb, she is returned to the nursery and its hearth with the sense that everything familiar has become alien to her: a favorite china plate, a cherished volume of *Gulliver's Travels,* her nurse-maid Bessie's favorite song—all are reminders of her existentially orphaned state. But she returns as well with a fixed sense of her own identity as different (of herself as other), which allows her to affirm of her stepfamily: "They are not fit to associate with me!" (20). This same sense will later allow her to reject Rochester's efforts to make her his doll-wife, to reject St. John's efforts at making her the ministering angel of his ministerial household, and to become Rochester's wife very much on her own terms.

"I could not answer the ceaseless inward question—*why* I thus suffered; now, at the distance of—I will not say how many years—I see it clearly" (9). The intrusions of the adult Jane's narrative voice upon the apparent present tense of the scene she details is startling, but not a mark of Bronte's insufficiency as a narrator. Rather, it signals the collapse of time and space that occurs through the intensity of memory and desire. That it occurs without explanation or apology is a function of what Bachelard called "intimate immensity"—the intensity of consciousness that skips over vast gaps of years and makes the past now. The narrative circle of space closes, as well, as Jane returns again to the houses—Rochester's and her aunt's—from which flight was at first a necessity if she were to grow. Her refusal to name the years is more than the narrative artifice of matronly coyness. Linear time here simply is a matter of indifference except as its span suggests how intense the memory has remained, and how powerful Jane's (and Bronte's) writing must be to effect integration of the pain and thus of the person.

This fictional journey is recapitulated in the American experience. Women have journeyed frequently across the vast spaces whose potential for "intimate intensity" Bachelard has suggested. A rich body of diary literature (recently collected and in the process of interpretation) records their transoceanic hardships and their settlements in the first American Puritan colonies.[19] Their diaries and personal narratives of the trans-Mississippi West (1840–80) record their struggle to define community (and thus relationship) in a century when the privatization of value had intensified, the sphere of domestic responsibility was increasingly relegated to women, and its values were viewed as alien to those of the public world in which men largely lived and worked.[20]

Nineteenth-century slave narratives record the relentless journey north from equatorial Africa to abolitionist New England (c.f. especially Washington, *Invented Lives*). These stories, too, participate in the epic tradition of the heroic journey toward identity, although they are rarely recognized as such. Their mythic acts are miniaturized in the hands that move from basin to forehead, soaking, wringing out, and applying cooling compresses to reduce the fevers of New World disease, in the journeys to the well for water, to the stream or river to wash the clothes, to the field, bit in mouth, to till, plant, cultivate, and harvest the white man's cash crop, to the bedroom of the mistress and the bed of the master, to the nursery, to the cemetery to bury the dead. In fact, their narratives reproduce women's participation in this paradoxical geography—so vast and so intimate—that marks their phenomenology. "It would seem, then," writes Bachelard, "that it is through their 'immensity' that these two kinds of space—the space of intimacy and world space—blend. When human solitude deepens, then the two immensities touch and become identical" (*The Poetics of Space*, 203).

A Reading of *A Worn Path*

In a superb short story by Eudora Welty, "A Worn Path," all that I have written of women's mythmaking, of the phenomenology of intimacy that I believe women's writing seeks, comes together. This is how Welty begins:

> It was December—a bright frozen day in the early morning. Far out in the country there was an old Negro woman with her head tied in a red rag, coming along a path through the pinewoods. Her name was Phoenix Jackson. She was very old and small and she walked slowly in the dark pine shadows, moving a little from side to side in her steps, with the balanced heaviness and lightness of a pendulum in a grandfather clock. She carried a thin, small cane made from an umbrella, and

with this she kept tapping at the frozen earth in front of her. This made a grave and persistent noise in the still air, that seemed meditative like the chirping of a solitary little bird. (*Collected Stories*, 142)

Phoenix Jackson is a mother, a grandmother, a former slave, a witch, a goddess, Eve and the Tree at once. "Her skin had a pattern all its own of numberless branching wrinkles and as though a whole little tree stood in the middle of her forehead, but a golden color ran underneath, and the two knobs of her cheeks were illumined by a yellow burning under the dark" (142). She is a Jesus whose geographic journey is to Memphis and, in Welty's rewriting of it, whose mythic Christmas journey is to the cross. She is a gritty traveler ("she looked straight ahead"), a comic heroine in a "long apron of bleached sugar sacks, with a full pocket" (142) whose success is unthreatened by the shoelaces dragging from her unlaced shoes. She makes her own fire, and in this her dying time she will arise from it. Her pendular association with time is not linear but circular (mythic), grandmother's time expressed but not finally measurable by a grandfather's clock. In this rhythm is her dance. She has made this journey to Natchez many times before, seeking medicine for a grandson (who has swallowed lye) whose actual existence in linear time remains uncertain, but whose existence in memory is sure; the journey of love is a circle undertaken in love's name and as such it is paradoxically purposeless. Hers is Bergson's *durée reelle*[21] its significance intensified by her very real endurance and her triumph.

Other male heroes have gone to the woods before her. Spenser's Red Cross Knight rushed willynilly pellmell through the wood of Error toward his own folly, hacking away at a dragon as he went. A terrorized Dante struggled in "a gloomy wood," "savage wild," "astray/Gone from the path direct" (*Inferno*, 1, 2–4). Panther, lion, and she-wolf ("So bad and so accursed in her kind/That never sated is her ravenous will," *Inferno*, 1, 93–94) were inimical to him, and he awaited the aid of Virgil as his mentor and his guide. Yet in a pinewoods where "sun made the pine needles almost too bright to look at" Phoenix is a conjuror with grandmotherly voice: " 'Out of my way, all you foxes, owls, beetles, jack rabbits, coons and wild animals! . . . Keep out from under these feet, little bob-whites. . . . Keep the big wild hogs out of my path" (Welty, "A Worn Path," 142). She is the Greek Artemis, the "lioness of women," a goddess of trees. She is the Roman Diana, a goddess of wild animals, the mistress of Dante's wolves, affiliated with "all those who live outside the social order: outlaws and strangers" (Duerr, *Dreamtime*, 12, 13)—and those whose throat is closed, that is, those who have no recognizable language or no voice to speak for themselves. " 'Don't let none of those come running my direction,' she calls out. 'I got a long way' " (Welty, "A Worn Path," 142). For her in this place the only fear is delay, the only temptation the sweet sleep of death, the quiet pleading of the grave, of rest: "The path ran up a hill. 'Seem like there is chains about my feet, time I get this far,' she said, in a voice of argument old people keep to use with themselves. 'Something always take a hold of me on this hill— pleads I should stay' " (143). Men's time, Phoenix knows, is "getting all gone here," but her time is her own, and she walks on (143). In the Christian myth, Jesus' crown of thorns is an instrument of his degradation. In Welty's retelling of it, Phoenix perceives the thorn, catching her skirt, as a "pretty little green bush," "doing [its] appointed work. Never want to let folks pass, no sir" she muses. (Later, it will be metamorphosed as an old barbed wire fence).

Crossing over water like the epic heroes of old takes the form, for the comic Phoenix, of a balancing act across a creek spanned by a log bridge. Resting under a "cloud of mistletoe," daytime and dreamtime melt into one another; grace comes not in the form of a lover's kiss, but in the hand of a little boy holding a slice of marble cake (143). Buzzards brood, and Phoenix scolds, "Who you watching?" (144). The field of dead corn is a maze to be threaded through, its garden scarecrow a ghost to be danced with. Past silvered slave cabins "all like old women under a spell sitting there," time is memory: "I walking in their sleep," she reflects (144). Her drink is neither wine nor the traditional waters of Lethe but the sweet water of an ageless well "here when I was born" (144). The devil appears not as the snake, but as the archetypal black Cerberus. Despite the fact that he knocks her into a ditch, she looks at him with "admiration" because "He ain't scared of nobody" (144). The fiercest enemy is the white man, the hunter with gun in hand, pointing it at her with a bravado that intensifies when he sees her unafraid. Out of his pouch hangs the claw of a dead bobolink, "its beak hooked bitterly to show that it was dead" (145). The power of the gun, Welty makes clear, is very different from the power of the conjuror. Her journey does not end in Golgatha, but at the place "where her feet knew to stop"—the physician's office where (although she momentarily forgets what she has come for), with "a fixed and ceremonial stiffness," she will receive her grandson's medicine (147).

Phoenix's forgetfulness of why and for whom she has come expresses the paradoxes of love, sight, and time that are characteristics of the phenomenology of intimacy of which I have spoken in this chapter.

Suddenly jarred by the nurse's questions about her grandson's health, she insists that the child remains alive: "We is the only two left in the world. He suffer and it don't seem to put him back at all. He got a sweet look. He going to last. He wear a little patch quilt and peep out holding his mouth open like a little bird. I remembers so plain now. I not going to forget him again, no, the whole enduring time. I could tell him from all the others in creation" (148). Welty has made frequent mention of Phoenix's failing eyesight throughout the text: her feet find the physician's office as effectively as they have traced and retraced the worn path of her journey to Natchez and her journey through life. Yet her relationship to the earth and to "plain and ordinary things" is marked by an intensity of vision and of consciousness appropriate to the ritual nature of her acts.

Phoenix lives in enduring time, a place of love and memory where all acts are ritualized by the nature of their repetition and the consequent quality of celebration that marks them. The world through which she walks "with the balanced heaviness and lightness of a pendulum in a grandfather's clock," singing and dancing as she goes, has about it the quality of a cosmic garden, spellbound by her tapping cane and chanting, old woman's voice: it is an intimate space and a universe at the same time. All of its bird songs are one song—the tapping cane, the bobolink, the buzzard, her grandson's, and Phoenix's own—because they are inextricably linked to a felt texture of experience that marks Welty's narrative description and her character's being-in-the-world. Her return with medicine, like the dream of proffered marble cake, is Eucharist.

In her comic rewriting of the Christian myth, Welty's heroine sings a story that no nation will make its epic, no literary high priest will canonize. But she sings it just the same.

Before the nineteenth century literature took almost solely the form of soliloquy, not of dialogue. The garrulous sex, against common repute, is not the female but the male; in all the libraries of the world the man is to be heard talking to himself and for the most part about himself. It is true that women afford ground for much speculation and are frequently represented; but it is becoming daily more evident that Lady MacBeth, Cordelia, Ophelia, Clarissa, Dora, Diana, Helen and the rest are by no means what they pretend to be. Some are plainly men in disguise; others represent what men would like to be, or are conscious of not being; or again they embody that dissatisfaction and despair which afflict most people when they reflect upon the sorry condition of the human race. To cast out and incorporate in a person of the opposite sex all that we miss in ourselves and desire in the universe and detest in humanity is a deep and universal instinct on the part both of men and of women. But though it affords relief, it does not lead to understanding.

—*Virginia Woolf,* Men and Women

Virginia Woolf
and the
Problematic of Intimacy

Claiming the Disclaimed

If Virginia Woolf has a single subject paramount above all others, it is the subject of intimacy. She explores this subject in numerous essays, pieces of fiction, and autobiographical fragments as well as innumerable letters and diary entries. Her novel *Between the Acts* was written shortly before her death by suicide in 1941 and published, after final editorial revisions, by Leonard Woolf. It is set in the house and garden of Pointz Hall where the Oliver family and the citizenry of a tiny English village gather in the ominous time of June 1939 for the annual pageant of scenes from English history. It can be read as a culminating statement of Woolf's interests in the role of song in the novel and in our lives, and of its ritual power to invoke both memory and desire, should we render ourselves able to listen and respond to what we hear. Like dance, song can be a vital means of connecting ourselves to the images of our lives. Consequently, both song and dance are prominent in ritual activity. *Between the Acts* is an experiment in using song to do just that; as such, it is a novel that explores the role of ritual in our lives. Looking at these and other issues related to ritual experience, I will refer to this work along with other fiction and essay writing by Woolf that precedes it, as well as some selected essays by Martin Heidegger.

It is not an accident that Virginia Woolf expresses profound hesitancy and inadequacy around the subject of intimacy, nor is it an accident that she expresses the same hesitancy and inadequacy when she (and her characters) speak about their ability to make language do what they want it to do. One senses that for Woolf **intimacy is not about how one uses one's body, but about how one uses words to express the infinite relationships that the body has with persons and with the world.** To make one's words do all they they are capable of doing in the situation is to establish an intimate relationship. To fail at this language-making activity is to fail *utterly* in its truest etymological sense—to fail to "outer" oneself, to fail to establish identity. For only in intimate relationship can identity be conceived and sustained.[1]

When she thinks of "something about the body, about the passions which it was unfitting for . . . a woman to say" ("Professions for Women," 61), she is wordless. And so when Woolf says that while she has successfully "killed the [Victorian] Angel in the House," she has not solved the problem of "telling the truth about my own experiences as a body," she is expressing a failure of intimacy. But this is the simpler expression of the problem. Its increasing complexity emerges in a single sentence she cites in her essay "Men and Women," a review of Leonie Villard's *La Femme Anglais au XIXème Siècle et son Évolution d'après le Roman Anglais Contemporain* (*TLS* 18 March 1920): " 'I have the feelings of a woman,' says Bathsheba in *Far From the Madding Crowd*, 'but I have only the language of men' " ("Professions for Women," 67).

Recent research about human emotions (and Darwinian theory before it) suggests that experiencing particular emotions may in part be caused by adopting the facial expression typically thought of, not as the *cause,* but as the *effect* of, the experienced emotion. In other words, not having access to the expression might mean not having access to the feeling. Analogously, Woolf suggests that having access only to men's (i.e., to an oppressor's) language blunts the expression of women's feelings and, finally, blunts the feelings themselves. This is a problem for women students and women faculty—in the writing classroom and in other places too—and it is one that cannot be ignored.

Additionally, Woolf's intensifying exploration of the problem of intimacy suggests that it has **something to do with orality and aurality, with a music** that is "inner" and "outer" at the same time, evocative, for those who can hear and so see, of a particular kind of vision.[2] In *Between the Acts,* the pageant audience is called back to its seats by an overture that Bartholomew Oliver, in his sense of separateness, hears only as "sugared, insipid" and "[in] the minor key" (118). Yet for the others, Woolf's narrator tells us, the music is magical, because it offers the language of intimacy. The broken is made whole, the hierarchical relationship between human, animal, and vegetable is leveled, and a Biblical rhythm appropriate to sacred narrative is appropriated **to sing the relationship of "plain and ordinary things":**

> For I hear music, they were saying. Music wakes us. Music makes us see the hidden, *join the broken*. Look and listen. See the flowers, how they ray their redness, whiteness, silverness and blue. And the trees with their many-tongued much syllabling,

their green and yellow leaves hustle us and shuffle us, and bid us, like the starlings, and the rooks, come together, crowd together, to chatter and make merry while the red cow moves forward and the black cow stands still. (120, emphasis added)

Woolf often problematizes her struggle with language when she reviews other writers' work, and through the reflections of characters in her novels. She also does this in letters, like this one to Vita Sackville-West regarding *To the Lighthouse* (which is a variant on the previous passage from *Between the Acts*)—a letter about au/orality:

> . . . it is all rhythm. Once you get that, you can't use the wrong words. But on the other hand here am I sitting after half the morning, crammed with ideas and visions, and so on, and can't dislodge them, for lack of the right rhythm. Now this is very profound, what rhythm is, and goes far deeper than words. A sight, an emotion creates this wave in the mind, long before it makes words to fit it; and in writing [such is my present belief] one has to recapture this, and set this working [which has nothing apparently to do with words] and then, as it breaks and tumbles in the mind, it makes words to fit it.[3]

This question of intimacy is related to Lily's desire to get "that very jar on the nerves, the thing itself before it has been made anything" (*To the Lighthouse*, 287). And it is expressed in Woolf's desire to write a novel that was a process tracing a process, art made alive by capturing the kind of life that "has in it the essence of reality" (*A Writer's Diary*, 100) and by seizing upon the "integrity of one's thoughts . . . hot and sudden as they rise in the mind" (*A Writer's Diary*, 93). "Why is there not a discovery in life?" she writes.

> Something one can lay hands on and say "This is it"? . . . What is it? And shall I die before I find it? . . . I have a great and astonishing sense of something there, which is "it." It is not exactly beauty that I mean. It is that the thing is in itself enough: satisfactory; achieved . . . [O]n this showing which is true, I think, I do fairly frequently come upon this "it"; and then I feel quite at rest. (*A Writer's Diary*, 85)

And the question of intimacy once again returns this material sense of "it" upon which we seek to "lay our hands," to the maternal. Over and over again, Woolf places her characters in gardens, retelling an original creation myth, reinventing Eve. Conceiving *To the Light-house*, she writes, occurred

> in a great, apparently involuntary, rush. One thing burst into another. Blowing bubbles out of a pipe gives the feeling of the rapid crowd of ideas and scenes which blew out of my mind, so that my lips seemed syllabling of their own accord as I walked. What blew the bubbles? Why then? I have no notion. But I wrote the book very quickly; *and when it was written, I ceased to be obsessed by my mother.*[4]

With these few examples as a beginning, this chapter looks at Woolf's work in terms of her mythmaking, of her phenomenology of intimacy, and of its relationship to orality as Ong (and others and I) have sought to define this relationship. If learning to write is about the discovery of one's own voice, making the transition from objects to a theory about them occurs through the ritualizing medium of language as the *spel*-caster learns to use it.

Reading and Writing As Ritual Acts

What does the word *ritual* mean in this context? I have found help in exploring its meaning and significance, in relationship to the writing process, in Dolores LaChapelle's book *Sacred Land, Sacred Sex, Rapture of the Deep*, the best and most lucid compilation of cross-cultural thinking on ritual I have found.

In general, ritual is any pattern repeated in time and space. While there are many kinds of rituals, both human and animal, their common purpose is communication, a far more complex statement than we might first think. Sometimes, for example, we have information of which the conscious mind is simply unaware. LaChapelle cites the work of Anthony Stevens on Jung's transcendent function to explore the implications of this statement for "sacred" ritual, ritual that for LaChapelle negates any duality of "us" and "them" and expresses radical, ongoing relationship (including us but not caused by us). "[T]he word we give, the label we give to our recognition of what is always going on, or on-going, always, is 'the sacred' " (*Sacred Land*, 128). Later, she expands this basic definition:

> Sacred ritual takes us out of this narrow, artificial human world and opens us up to the vast unlimited world of nature—both outside in our non-human environment and inside, in

our own deeper layers of the older brains and cellular body knowledge. For us in modern times, one of the most important, immediate effects of ritual is that it reduces the more or less continuous inhibition, which the left hemisphere of the neo-cortex exerts over all the rest of the brain. Thus there is increased communication between both hemispheres of the neo-cortex and between that more recent part of the brain and the "older" brains. Jung gave this activity the label of the "transcendent function" because it transcends the narrow limits of the ego. (153)[5]

In his study of animal ritual, whose shared pattern our anthropocentrism often causes us to forget or ignore, Konrad Lorenz speaks about ritual as allowing the discharge of aggression without hurting others. He argues that ritual ceremonies not only express our bonding with each other, but "they themselves constitute it" (LaChapelle, *Sacred Land,* 153). Further, they may create new motivations to influence social relations. Ritual is connected to what Bergson (and Rappaport) call "enduring" time; that is, the ceremonies "make reference to processes or entities outside the ritual in words or acts that have . . . been spoken or performed before."[6] Consequently, ritual is intimately connected to the land, the ritual site where participants gather. This stability of place is the most obvious expression of the ongoing nature of ritual activity.

Elsewhere in this text, I have spoken of the relationship between space and place, and have drawn an analogy with the page as a space that the writer claims for his or her (sacred) place. Writing, like ritual, mediates between the conscious and unconscious aspects of the human psyche. Like Paleolithic humans who "transformed" their caves by writing on them, we can use the blank page as a ritual space where an ongoing relationship can be articulated and celebrated. But what relationship are we celebrating there? Connecting childhood play and adult ritual, LaChapelle calls on Erickson, Jung, and a number of modern and contemporary anthropologists to answer this question.

All mammals play, including humans; the basis for play resides in the "daily rituals of nurturance and greeting" between mother and child (cited by LaChapelle in *Sacred Land,* 152). Erickson claims, in fact, that this first mammalian greeting ritual involves all the aspects that give us our sense of the sacred. In these daily rituals, demonstrably necessary to life itself, Erickson claims that we experience both "separateness transcended" and "distinctiveness confirmed." Further research into childrens' experience of "place" demonstrates that a child's bonding with its mother is followed by its bonding with the earth. The necessity—the power—of both these experiences, is reflected in Erickson's summary definition of ritual:

> Ritualization is grounded [in the life of those involved] and yet permeated with the spontaneity of surprise; it is an unexpected renewal of a recognizable order in potential chaos. . . .
>
> It minds instinctual energy into a pattern of mutuality, which bestows convincing simplicity on dangerously complex matters. . . .
>
> Thus the decay or perversion of ritual does not create an indifferent emptiness, but a void with explosive possibilities.
> (cited by LaChapelle in *Sacred Land*, 151)

In the first chapter of this book, I argued that our students are "broken" writers because their writing represents the brokenness of their experience. In subsequent chapters I traced that brokenness to the splitting off of our relationship to the material and the maternal expressed in the appropriation and silencing of women's songs in the culture. The third connection, from song to story, occurs through the agency of mythmaking. Here, all of the themes of previous chapters combine. While myth fulfills the "cognitive imperative" to explain the apparently unexplainable, ritual "which comes out of the myth applies a solution on the action level" (LaChapelle, *Sacred Land*, 156). Myth is important, crucial in fact, but it is not enough, because cognitive understanding alone is not enough. On the neurophysiological level, ritual action enables the stimulation of both brain hemispheres, enabling "solutions" to logical paradoxes that are irresolvable by rational thinking alone. Appropriately undertaken, ritual should remind us of the radical relationship we share with the natural world and our own multifaceted selves. A sense of the sacred is rooted in this "deep ecology."[7]

Writing is, or can be, a ritual opportunity for mythmaking. The "ontological value," the "communitas" (LaChapelle, *Sacred Land*, 159) that Victor Turner ascribes to successful ritual can attend to writing processes as well. And writing can be a potent entree to "communication" and "community" as they involve the communicative act. "Communication is a celebration of 'community or participation in a social group whose members communicate with one another by means of shared images, words, and concepts . . . ' It can also provide emotional interaction that is largely preverbal or subverbal . . . and such interaction, too, is communication. The chief characteristic of this second kind of communion—and communication—is mutuality" (161).

Writing and reading as ritual acts involve recognizing ways of using and hearing language that are other than instrumental and abstracting. They involve attention to the things words describe, to sound as it resonates with the "thinking of the body" (161) about our experiences of connecting feeling to meaning. Both of these tasks are more problematic, from LaChapelle's point of view, because Greek is the only written language that did not develop out of the spoken language; consequently, the connection between meaning and sound was broken. As a consequence of this inheritance, our language remains unlike the Chinese pictograph, where meaning is expressed in a pictorial relationship among things and ideas about them. There, words stay connected to things in a relationship that our language makes impossible for us to maintain. Consequently things lack value for us. Things have meaning only because we give meaning to them. Thus the anthropocentrism and instrumentality of the Western relationship to nature is expressed in our relationship to the word itself.

> In all European languages, locked as they are into the Greek grammar, we have a subject (that which does the action), the verb (what is done), and the object (that which it is done to). Since for the newly literate Greek, there was no longer any implicit meaning in each letter or syllable of the sentence, he, himself, the writer or reader, *gave* the meaning. . . . From this it is only a short step to the illusion that man gives meaning to the rest of the world. Without the knower, (the reader or writer) the rest of the world has no meaning. (25).

What, then, can we learn from Virginia Woolf? Her work is a lesson not in how meaning is given, but in how it is found—how we get close to it.[8] Writing, as Woolf understands it, involves ritualizing the object. Through this ritual, Bachelard's intimate immensity—and intimate intensity—are achieved. Woolf's task, the writer's task, and the writing teacher's task, is to render us, reader and writer, *spelbound* in order that we might be freed for the act of our own discovery. Ritualizing the object, Woolf offers us a theory for our own process. But she also proffers a warning, a response to this problem of language we have just explored, that encapsulates in a few short phrases both the essence of reader-response theory and an essential explication of the problem of authority in the contemporary writing classroom; "never . . . desert Mrs. Brown." Woolf's reference is, of course, to the hypothetical companion in the reader's railway carriage who becomes in her essay a figure for "the spirit we live by, life itself." In so becoming, Mrs. Brown is a figure for the kind of vision that a phenomenology of intimacy enjoins us to cultivate. Charging her audience with "the duties and responsibilities that are [theirs] as partners in this business in writing books," she reminds them:

> In the course of your daily life this past week you have had far stranger and more interesting experiences than the one I have tried to describe. . . . In one day thousands of ideas have coursed through your brains; thousands of emotions have met, collided, and disappeared in astonishing disorder. Nevertheless, you allow the writers to palm off upon you a version of all this, an image of Mrs. Brown, which has no likeness to that surprising apparition whatsoever. In your modesty you seem to consider that writers are of different blood and bone from yourselves; that they know more of Mrs. Brown than you do. Never was there a more fatal mistake. It is this division between reader and writer, this humility on your part, these professional airs and graces on ours, that corrupt and emasculate the books which should be the healthy offspring of a close and equal alliance between us. . . . But the things she says and the things she does and her eyes and her nose and her speech and her silence have an overwhelming fascination. ("Mr. Bennett and Mrs. Brown," *Collected Essays*, 1:336–37)

The Heideggerian version of this commitment to Mrs. Brown might be that ritualizing the object evokes its being related to Being. Like Turner, Heidegger is interested in the "ontological value" of ritual. For Woolf, the act of writing, itself a ritual act, establishes this relationship, but does so without the loss of the thing's 'thingness.' In fact, establishing the relationship *affirms* (confirms) that thingness. So to say that Woolf's topic is intimacy and that her work proposes for her readers a phenomenology of intimacy is to suggest that, like Heidegger, she laments the loss of "nearness" in modern culture, and that both of them recognize this loss as vested in our problematic relationship with the thing.

To explore these two problems—the loss of nearness and our relationship with things—is to explore human experience of space and time and, inevitably, to explore narrative, our stories about this experience of space and time. I suspect that Woolf's notions of thingness, of Being, and of relationship, while different from Heidegger's, are nevertheless approximate enough that the work of the two writers, philosopher and poet, can illuminate each other.

Woolf seeks in poetry what Heidegger sought in a philosophy of poetry/language. Their dual search suggests the intensity of the experience of brokenness each must have felt in that "modern" period between the wars when Romanticism's failure to make connection and the transcendence of separateness a permanent reality became so evident to anyone paying attention—and even to those who were not. When Woolf writes that "on or about December, 1910, human character changed," in fact, that "[a]ll human relations have shifted" and with them "religion, conduct, politics and literature" ("Mr. Bennett and Mrs. Brown," *Collected Essays,* 1:320, 321), she prefigures Heidegger's remarks about the postmodern abolition of distance that has forever distorted spatial and temporal relationships and, in consequence, relationship itself. Like Woolf, Heidegger perceives this change to be dramatic. In fact, he says of our atomic terror that it prevents our seeing "the atom bomb and its explosion [as] the mere final emission of what has long since taken place." So *great* is our terror, in fact, that we have come to place "everything outside [our] own nature"—we have become desperately and essentially alienated from everything to which we might stand in relationship. "What is it that unsettles and thus terrifies? It shows itself in the *way* in which everything presences, namely, in the fact that despite all conquest of distances the nearness of things remains absent" (Heidegger, "The Thing," in *Poetry, Language, Thought,* 166).

The many forces that have worked the change in human character and human relationship have inevitably worked on the relationships among writer, reader, and text. Woolf's call to pledge again our fidelity to Mrs. Brown is the beginning of the modern writer's reeducation; the philosophical underpinnings Heidegger offers enrich the possible ways that we can, not only live, but "dwell," in the profound sense in which he conceives it. His goal in the series of essays surrounding "The Thing" is "building dwelling thinking," so that we might genuinely know how "poetically man dwells." This must be the writing teacher's goal, too. For without the ability to be in some way intimate with the object, without an essential faithfulness to Mrs. Brown, no authentic act of writing is possible.

A Reading of *Between the Acts*

Heidegger begins "The Thing" (1950) with the reflection that "all distances in time and space are shrinking." "Yet," he continues, "the frantic abolition of all distances brings no nearness; for nearness does not consist in shortness of distance" ("The Thing," 165). *Between the Acts,* in fact, explores the confusion of these two principles: what is far seems near, what is near, far. Out of the dialectic of nearness and farness intimacy comes. This paradox is true of persons, of things, and of time.

Family and friends gather on a summer's evening of 1939 in the big room of Pointz Hall overlooking the garden, conversing about the town's failure to build a cesspool. The setting is apparently intimate (they are near to each other), but each remains enclosed in the world of his or her own memory. A cow coughing reminds Mrs. Haines of a childhood incident in which a cart-horse brushes her face and she becomes forever terrified of horses. Mr. Oliver remembers his mother's locked tea caddy and the copy of Byron she handed him "in that very room." Isa Oliver fantasizes herself a swan, floating in one of two "perfect rings" down stream with Rupert Haines, but his breast is "circled with a tangle of dirty duckweed" (his wife, one might suppose) and Isa's webbed feet are "entangled, by her husband, the stockbroker" (*Between the Acts,* 5).

Like a butterfly impaled on an avid collector's mat, present time in the novel is held captive and captivated by the past. The Olivers' ancestral past is a mere century in comparison with other owners of their land, "the old families who had intermarried and lay in their deaths intertwisted, like the ivy roots, beneath the churchyard wall" (7). Their own time is ringed by more and more concentric centuries—an immensity of time and so of space, too. In the dining room is "a watch that had stopped a bullet on the field of Waterloo" (7). Surrounding Pointz Hall is a landscape that, seen from the air, is scarred by generations of conquerors: Britons, Romans, Elizabethans, and by the plough. Mrs. Swithin's "favourite reading" is an "Outline of History" that evokes the continent's Paleolithic past, a past into which her descent is so complete that "It took her five seconds in actual time, in mind time ever so much longer, to separate Grace herself, with blue china on a tray, from the leather-covered grunting monster who was about, as the door opened, to demolish a whole tree in the green steaming undergrowth of the primeval forest" (9). And there is, of course, the annual pageant itself, a half-comical history of England that ends with its audience on the main stage, reflected (to their discomfort) in mirrors held up by actors representing "the present moment" in England.

The neighbors of Pointz Hall, good English citizenry that they are, have come to the pageant to celebrate their joint nearness to each other and to their common history. It doesn't work. The gramophone blares the repeated refrain "Dispersed are we . . . Dispersed are we . . . " (198) and as the Rev. Mr. Streatfield interprets the play's invitation to unity ("One spirit animates the whole . . . "), the drone of twelve (war)planes flying overhead in ominous formation makes his conclusion inaudible. *"That,"* the narrator says, "was the music" (193). The audience, cringing from its fragmented reflection in the stage-held mirrors, scatters with the question: "And if we're left asking questions, isn't it a failure, as a play?" (200). It hasn't worked—or has it? In the pause between the acts, the narrator asks us to explore if, how, and why. In so doing, she asks us to listen to numerous voices in the novel, but especially to the single "inner voice" that will guide our response to this question.

In "The Function of Criticism," T. S. Eliot had written with mistrustful scorn that "The possessors of the inner voice ride ten in a compartment to a football match at Swansea, listening to the inner voice, which breathes the eternal message of vanity, fear and lust" (*Selected Essays*, 16). Woolf sees it far otherwise. In *Between the Acts* she calls the inner voice the all-important "other voice," that opposes itself to the chatter and nonsense that marked the conventional nineteenth-century novel whose stuffy constraints she fled for freer air. This voice does not merely "[give] us a house in the hope that we might deduce the human beings who live there" ("Mr. Bennet and Mrs. Brown," in *Collected Essays*, 1:332), but it gives us the people, too. Amidst the cacophony of voices that mark modern life,

> the inner voice, the other voice was saying: How can we deny that this brave music, wafted from the bushes, is expressive of some inner harmony? "When we wake" (some were thinking) "the day breaks us with its hard mallet blows." "The office" (some were thinking) "compels disparity. Scattered, shattered, hither thither summoned by the bell. 'Ping-ping-ping' that's the phone. 'Forward!' 'Serving!'—that's the shop." So we answer to the infernal, agelong and eternal order issued from on high. And obey. "Working, serving, pushing, striving, earning wages—to be spent—here? Oh dear no. Now? No, by and by. When ears are deaf and the heart is dry." (*Between the Acts*, 119)

It is the voice heard "between the acts." It is the voice that the writing classroom seeks to put students in touch with, too, because it is the voice that allows the connection to things.

In her novel of the same title, Woolf's characters await for a second time the annihilation of which Heidegger spoke, but their ears are full of music and many hearts overflow. How does Woolf achieve this? More than one person—Isa, Lucy Swithin, William Dodge—listens to the inner voice. To listen to this voice is to "attend" to things in a particular way which Heidegger will elsewhere identify as a way of "building dwelling thinking."[9] "Nearness, it seems," Heidegger writes, "cannot be encountered directly. We succeed in reaching it rather by attending to what is near. Near to us are what we usually call things" ("The Thing," 166). Woolf achieves this sense of nearness by placing her characters (and her readers) in intimate proximity to things. Her answer to Sartre's nausea at phenomena[10] is to luxuriate in things through the agency of language's ritualizing power.

One early passage in *Between the Acts* echoes an autobiographical fragment from *Moments of Being*.[11]

> The flower blazed between the angles of the roots. Membrane after membrane was torn. It blazed a soft yellow, a lambent light under a film of velvet; it filled the caverns behind the eyes with light. All that inner darkness became a hall, leaf smelling, earth smelling, of yellow light. And the tree was beyond the flower; the grass, the flower and the tree were entire. (*Between the Acts*, 11)

Like Heidegger, making her characters attend to nearby things allows Woolf to ask the question "What is nearness?" Like him, answering that question, she explores "thingness" (in its etymological sense) as "a gathering" that involves deliberation on a matter or "presence" pertinent to persons.[12] In other words, it involves a kind of ritual engagement yielding "communitas" and "mutuality."

At the pageant of *Between the Acts*—but mostly between the pageant's acts—persons come together, exploring the "thingness of things," to use Heidegger's phrase. And in finding the thingness of things, the nature of nearness—intimacy—is discovered. We find the thingness of things not by means of any instrumental human act, but by accessing a quality of awareness or consciousness akin to Bachelard's intimate intensity. This awareness is "a step back from the thinking that merely represents—that is, explains—to the thinking that responds and recalls" ("The Thing," 181).[13] Heidegger warns that this is "no mere shift of attitude," but that it is a step back from one kind of thinking (the "representational") to another kind that "takes up its residence in a co-responding which, appealed to in the world's being by the world's being, answers within itself to that appeal" ("The Thing," 181–82). Heidegger's term, *co-responding*, emphasizes the dialectical nature of the activity: Citing Meister Eckhart, he clarifies his meaning: "*diu minne ist der natur, daz si den menschen wandelt in die dinc, di er minnet*—love is of such a nature that it changes man into the things he loves" (176).

How does Woolf use words in the ritualization of the thing, evoking therefore its nearness? First, she says, words "ring" experience—they evoke context through their appeal to image and the memory that at-

tends (is recalled by) it. In *Between the Acts*, this ritualizing act is rein-
forced by characters' preoccupation with rhyme: words signify less than
the memories and feelings that they can evoke. Once again, recollection
begins first in the garden, with song. Once again, the maternal relationship is evoked. Roused from her reverie of the primeval forest, Lucy
Swithin hears the birds in their garden:

> The window was open now; the birds certainly were singing.
> An obliging thrush hopped across the lawn; a coil of pinkish
> rubber twisted in its beak. Tempted by the sight to continue
> her imaginative reconstruction of the past, Mrs. Swithin paused;
> she was given to increasing the bounds of the moment by
> flights into past or future; or sidelong down corridors and
> alleys; but she remembered her mother—her mother in that
> very room rebuking her. (9)

"All writing," Woolf writes to Ethel Smyth, "is nothing but putting
words on the backs of rhythm. If they fall off the rhythm one's done."
(*Letters*, 4:303). Isa Oliver plays out this postulate throughout the novel.
As is always the case in Woolf's work, the poetic and the mundane
interpenetrate. Isa's rhyming conjures the kind of thinking that Heidegger
says, "responds and recalls." In the looking glass, Isa sees her own reflection but slips into a romantic fantasy that hangs on the image of a
spinning aeroplane propeller:

> . . . she groped, in the depths of the looking-glass, for a word
> to fit the infinitely quick vibrations of the aeroplane propeller
> that she had seen once at dawn at Croydon. Faster, faster,
> faster, it whizzed, whirred, buzzed, till all the flails became
> one flail and up soared the plane away and away. . . .
> "Where we know not, where we go not, neither know nor
> care," she hummed. "Flying, rushing through the ambient,
> incandescent, summer silent . . . "
> The rhyme was "air." She put down her brush. She took
> up the telephone. . . .
> "Three, four, eight Pyecombe," she said.
> "Mrs. Oliver speaking. . . . What fish have you this morning?
> Cod? Halibut? Sole? Plaice?"
> "There to lose what binds us here," she murmured. "Soles.
> Filletted. In time for lunch please," she said aloud. "With a
> feather, a blue feather . . . flying mounting through the
> air . . . there to lose what binds us here." (*Between the Acts*, 15)

The dialectic of flight and boundedness haunts Isa, haunts this novel, and like the wave that is her most typical imagistic expression of it, this dialectic is a primary category set in Woolf's exploration of the problem of intimacy. Its variant is another dialectic: permanence and change. The things that "bind us here" are the very things that, when we genuinely dwell with them, to use Heidegger's term, offer us the experience of being's connection to Being, and so of our own felt connection to life itself. How we experience the relationship—as bondage or as opportunity—depends upon how authentically we render ourselves available to the experience, and how clearly we recognize that any understanding of a larger, transcendent imaginative ground must remain rooted in the figure against which it is seen and known. Isa makes poems in the midst of ordering the fish for lunch. But in labeling herself "abortive," and in scorning to write them down in the account book she uses to hide this poetry-making from her husband Giles, she disowns herself in the way many modern writing students do. Domestic politics aside, Isa abandons herself just as effectively as Woolf's readers have abandoned Mrs. Brown. She fails to learn the lesson Lucy Swithin will insist upon: that the best poems are made in the midst of ordering the fish. In fact, ordering the fish can be, itself, a poetry-making act.

The journey of this text for Isa, Woolf's would-be poet, our student of writing, is her discovery of this. Moving her toward the recognition that we are not, indeed, called to fly away from what "binds us here," Woolf places Isa in the stable yard and with great specificity establishes her relationship to things. Her narrative's rhythmic style ritualizes the experience, and establishes as well the "hard green pear" as a kind of totem that will carry Isa to this second step in her preparatory understanding. From an imaginary romantic fantasy land where "[c]hange is not; nor the mutable and lovable" Woolf brings a still unwilling Isa

> into the stable yard where the dogs were chained; where the buckets stood; where the great pear tree spread its ladder of branches against the wall. The tree, whose roots went beneath the flags, was weighted with hard green pears. Fingering one of them she murmured: "How am I burdened with what they drew from the earth; memories; possessions. This is the burden that the past laid on me, last little donkey in the long caravans crossing the desert. 'Kneel down,' said the past. 'Fill your pannier from our tree. Rise up, donkey. Go your way till your heels blister and your hoofs crack.'
>
> The pear was hard as stone. She looked down at the cracked flags beneath which the roots spread. "That was the burden,"

she mused, "laid on me in the cradle; murmured by the waves; breathed by restless elm trees; crooned by singing women; what we must remember; what we would forget." (155)

As Isa's reflections make clear, a relationship to space is inevitably tied to a relationship with time. In Woolf's novels, the dialectic of linear and mythic time plays itself out in the structure of plot itself. "[P]eople write what they call 'lives' of other people; that is, they collect a number of events, and leave the person to whom it happened unknown," Woolf had written in *Moments of Being* (69).

Writing students do this often.

Like this evocative world, the writing classroom, a theater of inquiry,[14] becomes the place where all pretense and its civilized veneer are stripped away so that we can indeed "catch ourselves in the act." The chorus has encouraged the pageant audience to do this, and the writing teacher encourages her students to do the same. The opportunity to construct a "new plot" is an opportunity to establish a new relationship with the persons and things in our world and with ourselves; like Mrs. Swithin's offer to William Dodge, it is the opportunity to tell our story— perhaps for the first time—to name ourselves and in so doing, to begin to be healed. The paradox expressed in Woolf's novel of recognizing our brokenness—"orts and fragments"—in order that we might be made whole, obtains in the writing classroom, too.

In her essay "Feminist Criticism," Elaine Showalter has argued that "women's fiction can be read as double-voiced discourse, containing a "dominant" and a "muted" story.[15] Showalter and other feminist critics, Sandra Gilbert and Susan Gubar among them, have named as their task the search for a cultural model of women's writing—"thick description," they term it in Clifford Geertz's words (Showalter, "Feminist Criticism," 35)—that will help us to read women's texts. We also need a cultural model that will enable us to *write* women's texts, and we need to use that model to teach both men and women new kinds of access to textuality, to writing, itself. In the now-acknowledged relationship between sexuality and textuality may lie a rich model for reading and for writing, too.

So what of Isa, our writing student? What exists for her in the world of Woolf's novel, in the muted story, that we may learn about as well?

First, that student writers need mentors, that women students in particular need women mentors. Also, sadly, that oftentimes the dominant story has been told so loudly and for so long in their lives that they cannot recognize either the muted story or its storyteller. Part of the muted story of Woolf's text is the bittersweet tale of Lucy Swithin's marginalization; it is, after all, no accident that the homosexual William

Dodge is the audience who recognizes her gift. And so, *first,* our work is to validate the wisdom of the Lucy Swithins of our world so that the Isas of this world will be able to hear their voices underneath the (albeit often symphonic) din of the dominant Western canon. Next, our work is to ritualize (or reritualize) the writing classroom in such a way that we interrupt the distorted environments and relationships drawn from the rituals of our heritage in the common school movement.[16] As Madeleine Grumet's description makes clear, this heritage suggests yet another angle in the sexuality/textuality relationship. Women, she writes, were invited into schools to bring maternal nurturance; they accepted the invitation seeking paternal approval—with devastating consequences for themselves and their students.[17]

> The father/daughter relation of the department head, principal, or superintendent to the teacher functioned to deny their eroticism and extend her infantilization. The cult of maternal nurturance ignored female sexuality, oblivious to the erotic gratifications of maternity and the sensual and sexual life of the young women it kept under constant surveillance. The teacher was expected to banish sensuality from the classroom and from her life. The repudiation of the body was a blight that fell upon the curriculum as well, severing mind from body and draining the curriculum of the body's contribution to cognition, aesthetics, and community as realized through its capacity for sensuality, for movement and for work. (*Bitter Milk,* 53)

To reritualize the classroom is to invite—to rewrite—the body back into experience. If this is a tricky task for male students, it is even more a tricky task for women, for all of the reasons that Woolf suggests when she speaks of her own struggle to write the body. It is tricky for the teacher, too. Once the body returns to the classroom, everything changes—everything. Like the family gathered in the Olivers' parlor and the village citizenry come to the annual pageant, students come to the writing classroom with a varying but firm sense of themselves as audience. Like the villagers' anxious response to the village idiot, they have a well-defined sense of the decorum, resisting unacceptable intimacies (the vast majority are unacceptable) and preferring to remain firmly offstage. Some are lured to accept acting roles, but only if the bait is permission to remain firmly costumed and masked, speaking in voices they have learned to mimic only too well, reciting inevitably other people's lines. The writing teacher experiences all of Miss LaTrobe, the pageant director's, anguish and more. Miss LaTrobe waits breathlessly for each member to fulfill her or his charge, but she struggles as well with the necessity to maintain the illusion of the drama lest the audience "slip the noose," be "split up into scraps and fragments" (*Between the Acts*, 122).

Conducting the classroom ritual, the writing teacher, too, waits for her students to learn and recite their lines: the politics of her situation is such that all of the academic world will judge whether her coaching has been a success or a failure, and so she, too, must be concerned with maintaining the multifaceted (and multidisciplinary) illusions that reflect what that world defines as competency. In the face of this politic, what I argue for as the desired experience of the writing classroom may seem alternately a neo-romantic, sentimental, and insufficient one indeed. It is nevertheless the thesis of this book that we cannot fix broken writers without fixing what is broken in their relationship to things and to each other. Grumet suggests that this brokenness, which I have defined through literary texts, and she through educational history and theory, is so pervasive that it has infused and "blighted" the curriculum itself. The politics of the writing classroom is an integral part of this larger curricular politic that Grumet seeks to name and revise through the lens of feminist theory. For my own part, I turn back to the literature to begin the process of sorting how revision and reconstruction in the writing classroom's curriculum can begin.

Like her character Lucy Swithin, Woolf concludes that in order to *make known* the persons to whom events happen, an appeal to mythic time is inevitable. That is, in addition to the discrete moments that mark life's events, if we are genuinely connected to Being, and if we want to talk about *that* connection, we must recognize and talk about the other lives and lifetimes in which, by virtue of our "dwelling" with "things" we are inevitably implicated.

Nevertheless, some people see this, and others don't. Linear time is inexorable, but in the dialectic of unity and separation played out in her novel, Woolf marks some as "unifiers" and others as "separatists." Bartholomew Oliver is a self-confessed separatist; his sister Lucy Swithin is, he says, a unifier. The faith that drives Lucy's fascination for the "Outline of History" is a felt connection to another kind of (nonlinear) time, another relationship to things. An old woman, tired and breathless from the stairs and heat, Lucy brings the stranger William Dodge to the room where she was born, completing the circle of her consciousness of time. Sinking down on the bed, she offers him that faith: "But we have other lives, I think, I hope. . . . We live in others. . . . We live in things" (70). Words cooperate in establishing and expressing this relationship by the ways they allow things to be named by the persons who use them. "The nursery," Lucy says, taking Dodge across the hall. Woolf's cinematic eye pans with her, walking across to the room where the baby's cot is empty and a Newfoundland dog in the Christmas annual is pinned to the wall. In her mouth, "Words raised themselves and became symbolical. 'The cradle of our race,' she seemed to say" (71). Longing to kneel before her who has become the mother goddess in his eyes, William can say silently of himself to this reinvented Eve: "I'm a half-man, Mrs. Swithin; a flickering mind-divided little snake in the grass, Mrs. Swithin; as Giles saw; but you've healed me" (73). But—and perhaps more importantly—in the intimacy of the moment, he can say aloud to her, "I'm William" (72). In Woolf's inversion of the myth, the snake, not the woman, comes seeking.

Lucy Swithin appeals to mythic time through the agency of plain and ordinary things, become "symbolical" but remaining still themselves. By returning time to its beginnings, she invites Dodge to return to his own beginnings, as well, as she has done to hers. For him, the return is a kind of exorcism, as is most personal narrative: "At school they held me under a bucket of dirty water, Mrs. Swithin; when I looked up the world was dirty, Mrs. Swithin; so I married; but my child's not my child, Mrs. Swithin . . . but you've healed me" (73). Her name is Dodge's charm, its rhythmic repetition a reminder that "Lucy's within," the light's within, the light's within. And his ability to name himself—"I'm William"— signals the ritual's healing moment.

The primary task of the writing classroom's teacher is to make available to students a particular relationship with things, a particular relationship with space and time, a particular relationship with words mediated by sound (rhythm and rhyme) and consequently a particular kind of vision. Students must be invited not only to tell their own stories but also to overhear what they tell of themselves. Woolf is writing about what Madeleine Grumet calls, in a paper on classroom pedagogy, a "theater of inquiry," a theater that Grumet says "gives us a chance to catch ourselves in the act" ("Phenomenology and Pedagogy," 86). That is what Lucy Swithin has given William Dodge, and it is what she has offered to Isa Oliver, although it is less certain what of herself, even after this offering, Isa will ultimately affirm. In short, the writing teacher offers to her students a phenomenology of intimacy: she teaches them how to be close to things and consequently how to be close to themselves and to each other.

Structure and *organization* are often the bywords that describe the strategic goals of learning how to write. The more process-focused models pay lip service to creative chaos in the name of discovery, but the drive is toward the heuristics that will provide patterns (for utility's sake) into which this chaos can rapidly fit itself. Lucy Swithin's vision is that in order to side with the one, to be a unifier, an establisher of relationship, to discover the single voice, an appreciation of chaos must precede this singular vision. In fact, more than appreciation, engagement is requisite—the very engagement, fraught with risk, that so many of our students resist. The audience is always resistant to becoming a part of the play, especially in this ritual theater of inquiry that is the writing classroom. They fear, like Miss LaTrobe, the failure of illusion that the authoritative models of education have taught them the classroom should be about. And the failure of illusion, she moans, is "death, death, death" (*Between the Acts*, 180) to a particular vision of oneself. As the pageant's actors turn their mirrors upon them, the audience cringes, moves to leave, reflecting incredulously on the cruelty "[t]o snap us as we are, before we've had time to assume. . . . And only, too, in parts" (184). They "shifted, preened, minced" (186), listening to the actors' abjuration to suspend all long-cherished beliefs:

> [L]et's talk in words of one syllable, without larding, stuffing or cant. Let's break the rhythm and forget the rhyme. And calmly consider ourselves. Ourselves . . . Don't hide among the rags, Or let our cloth protect us. Or for the matter of that book learning; or skilful *[sic]* practice on pianos; or laying on of paint. Or presume there's innocency in childhood. Consider the sheep. Or faith in love. Consider the dogs. Or virtue in those that have grown white hairs. Consider the gun slayers, bomb droppers here or there. They do openly what we do slyly. . . . Look at ourselves, ladies and gentlemen! Then at the wall; and ask how's this wall, the great wall, which we call, perhaps miscall, civilization, to be built by . . . orts, scraps and fragments like ourselves? (187–88)

To genuinely engage this process is to give up, for a time, along with cherished poses of the self, the kind of thinking that insists upon representation, and, with Woolf's characters, to give up a cherished relationship to language that holds the fragments of the disordered self at bay. It is to wander in a song world of language, singing with Isa's uncle, a clergyman with a skullcap who never did anything (even preach) but walk in his garden, saying his made-up poems aloud. The "loftier strain" to which Miss LaTrobe's chorus shifts is not the music of epic pronouncement, but a song of "our kindness to the cat," of "the impulse which leads us—mark you—when no one's looking—to the window to smell the bean." It is the song "of the resolute refusal of some pimpled little scrub in sandals to sell his soul." Animal, vegetable, human—the connection to plain and ordinary things. And to genuinely engage this process is to wait. *"You can't descry it? All you can see of yourself is scraps, orts and fragments?"* the chorus asks of its shifting, puzzling, cringing audience. *"Well then listen to the gramophone affirming"* (188). "Wait," says the writing teacher, "wait."

About the role of song Woolf has a great deal to say, and Heidegger does, too. Music might be perpetually an agent of unity, but it is subject to the hearer's interpretation. So too, always, are words. William Dodge hears Lucy Swithin name things that make him feel connected to Being for the first time in his life. More importantly, he hears her invite him to name things, too. But for an angry Giles, "Words this afternoon ceased to lie flat in the sentence. They rose, became menacing and shook their fists at you" (59). Isa's faith is in rhyme—and one senses that her faith expresses Woolf's, as well. "Why judge each other?" Isa reflects on Giles's contempt for William's homosexuality. "Do we know each other? Not here, not now. But somewhere, this cloud, this crust, this doubt, this dust—She waited for a rhyme, it failed her; but somewhere surely one sun would shine and all without a doubt would be clear" (61). For words to "work," Woolf seems to say, they must be connected to song, which is connected to feeling, which is connected to memory, to another kind of time, which is connected to things, to which, if we are genuinely connected, says Heidegger, we will be genuinely near (being as Being). To be so connected (I would argue) is to be intimate.

Linear time is inexorable, but to be connected to things, to be near to them, to be intimate with them is to escape its inexorability. Images of flight record the escape. Gazing excitedly at the swallows that circle the barn, the trees, and her heart, Lucy Swithin reflects on yet another variation of mythic time: "Across Africa, across France they had come to nest here. Year after year they came. Before there was the channel, when the earth, upon which the Windsor chair was planted, was a riot of rhododendrons, and humming birds quivered at the mouths of scarlet trumpets, as she has read that morning in her Outline of History, they had come" (108). "You don't believe in history," William Dodge remarks to her. Later in the text, her brother Bartholomew intones this, Lucy's totem, with a weary irony: "What's the use, what's the use . . . O sister swallow, O sister swallow, of singing your song?" (116). From out of the garden, separate notes become words, phrases, "a simple tune, another voice speaking, a waltz" and the answer to Bartolomew's question comes: "As they listened and looked—out into the garden—the trees tossing and the birds swirling seemed called out of their private lives, out of their separate avocations, and made to take part" (117).

Sometimes, this being "called out" occurs through song that is without words altogether: pure sound, so pure feeling and pure thought. " 'We haven't the word—we haven't the words,' Mrs. Swithin protested. 'Behind the eyes; not on the lips; that's all.' 'Thoughts without words,' her brother mused. 'Can that be?' " (55). Yes, answers Woolf, if we are genuinely near to things. Oftentimes, the "inner voice" is purely that: thoughts without words—the record of the kind of attending that does not merely represent, but co-responds.

In *Poetry, Language, Thought*, Heidegger's definition of what it means to be near becomes a fulcrum for all that Woolf is trying to say in this novel, drawing together image, theme, ideas about words and the aurality/orality that is part of her consideration of song. Very early in her novel, a short passage about two paintings hanging in the dining room ends with this lyric: "Empty, empty, empty; silent, silent, silent. The room was a shell, singing of what was before time was; a vase stood in the heart of the house, alabaster, smooth, cold, holding the still, distilled essence of emptiness, silence" (36–37). Heidegger's essay "The Thing" is constructed around a jug, the discovery of whose nature as a thing, he says, allows us "to catch sight of the nature of nearness" (177). In its thingness, the jug both holds and gives—pours out. "Even the empty jug retains its nature by virtue of the poured gift" (172). In its outpouring gush, the rest of the universe is implicated:

> The spring stays on in the water of the gift. In the spring the rock dwells, and in the rock dwells the dark slumber of the earth, which receives the rain and dew of the sky. In the water of the spring dwells the marriage of sky and earth. It stays in the wine given by the fruit of the vine, the fruit in which the earth's nourishment and the sky's sun are betrothed to one another. In the gift of water, in the gift of wine, sky and earth dwell. But the gift of ourpouring is what makes the jug a jug. In the jugness of the jug, sky and earth dwell. (172)

Recalling that etymologically "gush" means to offer in sacrifice, so Heidegger reminds us that "In the gift of the outpouring earth and sky, divinities and mortals dwell *together all at once*" (173). And so finally, what is nearness?

> The thing things. In thinging, it stays earth and sky, divinities and mortals. Staying, the thing brings the four, in their remoteness, near to one another. This bringing-near is nearing.

Nearing is the presencing of nearness. Nearness brings near—
draws nigh to one another—the far and, indeed, *as* the far.
Nearness preserves farness. Preserving farness, nearness
presences nearness in nearing that farness. Bringing near in
this way, nearness conceals its own self, and remains, in its
own way, nearest of all. (177–78)

In their own ways, Lucy Swithin, Miss LaTrobe, the pageant's
producer/director, and Woolf's narrator of the events "between the acts"
go about the project of evoking the kind of "nearness" that "preserves
farness." The text is threaded with the songs that they make, hear and
imagine in the advance of this project. In this project human and animal
are one; the cow's bellow is as "functional" as the gramophone and the
chorus's human recitation. When the stage is empty, Miss LaTrobe recognizes that "the only thing to continue the emotion was the song."
When human words become inaudible, a cow who had lost her calf
"lifted her great moon-eyed head and bellowed. . . . It was the primeval
voice sounding loud in the ear of the present moment. Then the whole
herd caught the infection. Lashing their tails, blobbed like pokers, they
tossed their heads high, plunged and bellowed, as if Eros had planted his
dart in their flanks and goaded them to fury. The cows annihilated the
gap; bridged the distance; filled the emptiness and continued the emotion" (*Between the Acts,* 140–41). Among Bartholomew Oliver's trees
the swallows dart as in "an open-air cathedral," seeming "to make a
pattern, dancing, like the Russians, only not to music, but to the un-
heard rhythm of their own wild hearts" (65).

One of the songs of this text is the plot itself. Certainly, there must
be a plot. But plot lives largely in linear time. And as Isa recognizes, plot
is not the point: begetting the requisite emotions is (90). In fact, so
erratic is the role of plot—the series of events in our lives—in helping us
name the human experience (and thus become characters in the drama)
that Lucy Swithin can ask of Isa, "Did you feel . . . we act different parts
but are the same?" Isa's reply reflects the difficulty in human time of the
act of naming that William Dodge has struggled to achieve: " 'Yes,' Isa
answered. 'No,' she added. It was yes, No. Yes, yes, yes, the tide rushed
out embracing. No, no, no, it contracted" (215). The expanding and
contracting of her vision of identity is the ultimate dialectic in the tension of unity and dispersion, permanence and change, inner visions and
outer, inner voices and outer, that mark the novel's movement. The
question becomes deciding who to listen to, what thing to attend. Imagining the music that will trumpet the end of the world, "the day we are

stripped naked," Isa reflects on the corruption of the voices that surround her. Her own struggle is to listen to the voices that will feed her own imagination, becoming the "inner voice."

> " . . . none speaks with a single voice. None with a voice free from the old vibrations. Always I hear corrupt murmurs; the chink of gold and metal. Mad music. . . . " . . . "On, little donkey, patiently stumble. Hear not the frantic cries of the leaders who in that they seek to lead desert us. Nor the clatter of china faces glazed and hard. Hear rather the shepherd, coughing by the farmyard wall; the withered tree that sighs when the Rider gallops; the brawl in the barrack room when they stripped her naked; or the cry which in London when I thrust the window open someone cries . . . " (156)

Lucy Swithin comes down decidedly on the side of the one versus the many, much to the amusement of her companions, including Isa. But like that of numerous other dotty old Edwardian dowagers (the lurching Mrs. McNab in *To the Lighthouse,* and Forster's enigmatic Mrs. Moore in *A Passage to India,* for example), Lucy Swithin's vision is infused with a mystical quality; despite the apparent sentimentality of Lucy's faith, Woolf clearly means us not to discount it. It is Heidegger's vision of being "thinking and speaking about Being, the differing being of different beings and the onefoldness of their identity in and with all their differences" (*Poetry, Language, Thought,* xi).

> She was off, they guessed, on a circular tour of the imagination— one-making. Sheep, cows, grass, trees, ourselves—all are one. If discordant, producing harmony—if not to us, to a gigantic ear attached to a gigantic head. And thus—she was smiling benignly— the agony of the particular sheep, cow, or human being is necessary; and so—she was beaming seraphically at the gilt vane in the distance—we reach the conclusion that *all* is harmony, could we hear it. And we shall. (*Between the Acts,* 175)

"A vision imparted was relief from agony . . . for one moment . . . one moment" (98) reflects Miss LaTrobe in a voice closest to Woolf's own. Isa seems to glimpse it. William Dodge clearly experiences it. The other men, however, remain largely inconsolable. Bartholomew Oliver, his heart by his own confession " 'condemned in life's infernal mine, condemned in solitude to pine' " (115), deep in shadow, "leafless, spectral," stalks off to bed alone. Giles, who has foundered throughout the text in a sea of words he cannot understand, feeling himself "not in his perfect mind," will seek consolation, apparently, through his sexual connection with Isa. Along with Lucy, only William Dodge, in fact, seems genuinely to have had his moment.

Isa herself, our writing student, remains a puzzle. If the goal is to discover the voice and thus, *spelbound,* to heal oneself, Isa seems at least on the brink of that new place. Mrs. Swithin's legacy has been the glimpse of a "new plot" for which Isa so longs, a plot that can emerge because the inexorability of linear time has been mitigated through imaginative effort expressed as rhyme. As the old people withdraw, leaving their relational space to Isa and Giles, Isa repeats the phrase that negates linear time: "This year, last near, next year, never" (214, 217). Civilized time and space fall away: their sexual embrace will be preceded with a fight "as the dog fox fights with the vixen, in the heart of darkness, in the fields of the night." As the house "lost its shelter," it becomes "night before roads were made, or houses . . . the night that dwellers in caves had watched from some high place among rocks" (219). Where Isa will go with her glimpse it is hard to say. For here, Woolf says, on the brink of what we do not know, the play genuinely begins.

Classrooms As Erotic Spaces

What then can we learn from *Between the Acts?* Walter Ong has argued that the rhetorical tradition as it developed in the academy, in flight from the mother tongue, values the objectivity and distance that are in turn the values of the science its discourse would articulate and serve. A classroom that belies these values, I have argued, is an intimate one. But what does "intimacy" as a classroom experience mean? First, an intimate classroom is one in which students are encouraged to reestablish a relationship with things. This involves time and space and memory. Models for exploring these dimensions of experience have been suggested by aboriginal peoples and by oral poets, by journal writers and by those writers (often women) working within this long personal narrative tradition. Heidegger, Woolf, and Welty have identified an intimacy with things as the cultivation of a kind of attention whose hallmark is its contextuality. This kind of attention involves affirming and celebrating the interpenetration of the poetic and the mundane. It complements recollection and representation with active response, one expression of which is learning to employ a kind of language that reveals what Alice Walker means when she speaks of "living by the word." It means, in phenomenologist Gabriel Marcel's terms, being available and being engaged.[18] It means, in all of their terms, moving from ego-centeredness to person-centeredness, from Buber's I-it relationship to that of I-thou.

Despite the "de-mythologized" state of the modern world (now well commented upon by numerous persons in numerous fields), at least one world has, up until very recently, retained the degree of homogeneity that has allowed its rituals to remain largely intact: the American classroom. The ingredients of ritual as they are evoked by this classroom theater of inquiry, to use Grumet's term once again, are universal ingredients adhering to any kind of theatrical ritual activity.[19] For example, Richard Schechner identifies them simply as gathering, performing, and dispersing.[20] Yet they are marked by the particularity of the classroom as the ritual site and by the classroom's *own* contextuality in the history of American education.

In this world, one obvious way of helping students place themselves near to things is to place them *near* to each other. Many attempts have been made to rearrange classroom space—circles, small groups, seminar tables, and so on—to facilitate student interaction. Yet the long-ingrained spatial relations of this ritual site continue to instantiate and replicate the feelings and psyche of the original classroom site, one in which the classroom teacher is surrogate priest and the students her still, forwardly intent, and expectant congregation.[21] (I mean by this not only "forward-facing" but also "without an obvious sense of the present"). The writing classroom is invariably presented as a utilitarian place whose value is founded on where it can take them in the future rather than upon the gift it offers in a perpetual present of self-discovery lived out as "now." For many students the classroom remains the place where salvation still hangs in the balance, where the predestined quality adhering to discovering one's "calling," arduous and individual as that discovery is, overwhelms any other "call" for genuine collaborative work.

In this discourse world, largely (and designedly) without taste, touch, smell, or feel, a world in which sight is only forward, focused on the word and not the thing, only the teacher's voice is validated as authentic. Calls to read aloud are not infrequently received with a discomfort that is intensified when the text to be read is a student's own. Small-group work all too often deteriorates into opportunities for gossip. While students may have a good sense of themselves as a social group of conspirators against the very process in which they are engaged, they have little sense of themselves as a community of knowers and "be-ers" mutually engaged in the process of enhancing their own, and others', competence. And so this process of inviting students to be near to each other is a complex one, indeed.

The traditional ritual act of engagement often involves the offering or exchange of things, the joining of hands, the collective movement of feet in dance or of voices in song. The stories sung and danced, the food or drink or object exchanged, are part of a larger mythic narrative that celebrates the ongoing life of the community, regardless of whether its stated purpose is overtly this (initiation, marriage, harvest ceremonies), or whether it is overtly to propitiate, to exorcise, or to grieve. Mythmaking in its ritual expression seeks the harmony of minds and bodies gone awry; this supports us through developmental and temporal crises of our lives. Mythmaking begins when we recognize the reality of death in the world, when the sense of separateness this defines for us causes us to seek connection with the ongoing life of the community to which we belong (Campbell, *Myths to Live By*, 70, 72).

As Grumet makes clear, shaping the classroom as the place where this kind of ritual behavior occurs is both a deconstructive and a reconstructive act. There are first all of the old myths to come to terms with: that objective knowledge and value-free expression are more appropriate than subjective knowledge and value-laden expression;[22] that to be disciplined is to do your own work independently in someone else's time frame to meet someone else's deadline; that the sensory, the sensuous, the intimate (the material, the maternal)—in short one's personal past drenched in memory (and desire)—has no place in a genuinely scholarly search for our place in the collective history of the West. Exposing this is deconstructive activity—an activity that I would argue all of women's reading and writing is about.

The reconstructive activity, inviting into this classroom space the elements of personal time, of subjectivity, of the body—the sensory, the sensuous, the material, and the maternal—reproductive values into an otherwise productively defined world—carries with it great risk. It is little wonder that many teachers (and writing teachers are among the boldest) extend this invitation with reservation and trepidation. And it is little wonder that they have traditionally had great difficulty in describing to their colleagues in the disciplines exactly what they do. To invite the past with its materiality and maternality into the classroom these days is to risk the invitation to a great deal of pain, to risk having stories told that we would prefer not to hear, hearing and overhearing feelings to which we would prefer not to respond, to which, in fact, we have been trained to believe that we are not supposed to respond. It risks transference, too. I have become more and more convinced that the "demythologized" nature of contemporary knowledge and experience, that students' apparent indifference to the past, may well be a reflection of the pain of their own personal histories. Perhaps one among the many reasons their texts are so bleached of the sensory and the sensual is that the act of memory itself, once engaged, risks the opening of their own personal Pandora's box—that exploring the once-valued Arnoldian "free play of the mind on all subjects which it touches" ("The Function of Criticism," *Complete Prose Works*, 3:270) is now too great a chance to take.

More mundanely, our once-homogeneous classrooms have become explosively heterogeneous in the last twenty-five years, in ways, and with consequences, that we have yet to fully understand. To invite the past into these classrooms, or the present, for that matter, may invite much in the way of values, life choices, language, and experience foreign to our own tradition and a challenge to the authority with which we have presided over word and idea. Rituals in these classrooms must genuinely look back to those of a pre-Puritan America, before the minister and his carefully arranged rows of pews, to worlds where song and dance were the skeleton invitations to a controlled but nevertheless ecstatic experience, where it was understood that individuals might name their experience but remain, nevertheless, integral to the community of believers in whose context their search for knowledge had led them to be placed, or to place themselves. The classroom as experience is not therapy, but we are sadly mistaken if we do not recognize that it is often a relentlessly therapeutic place, and take responsibility for our participation in that process.

The therapeutae (fr. *therapeutai*) were "attendants" or "worshipers," ascetics of both sexes who lived near Alexandria whom Philo described as "devoted to contemplation and meditation." Interestingly enough, the Greek root *-ther* means "wild beast," the Sanskrit *thera*, "elder," comes from *sthavira*, "stout, old, venerable"; and it provides the name for a class of spiders, *(Thera-phosidae)* and an order of upright reptiles from which mammals descend *(Therap-sida)* (*Webster's Third New International Dictionary*, 2372). Obviously, the ultimate issue of therapy lies in treatment, but its etymological roots reinforce the notion of attention to things, the kind of awareness that is enhanced by any meditative practice, including what writing theory calls "incubation" and invention. It reinforces as well the extent to which Lucy Swithin's all-inclusive vision was truly the wise one. Form is a significant organizational principle in our lives, and chaos would result in its absence, but we need to cultivate as well the kind of vision that reminds us of our intimate connection to the things of our world beyond and behind form. Ritualized, this kind of attention is worship. Mediating this attention is a task that offers a new way to identify the connection between teacher, therapist, and priest. It is this, I believe, that Woolf implies in the midst of her essay

"Moments of Being." To make words is to make an experience "whole"; it is an act of "rapture," "making a scene come together; making a character come together. From this," she writes

> I reach what I might call a philosophy; at any rate it is a constant idea of mine; that behind the cotton wool is hidden a pattern; that we—I mean all human beings—are connected with this; that the whole world is a work of art; that we are parts of the work of art. *Hamlet* or a Beethoven quartet is the truth about this vast mass that we call the world. But there is no Shakespeare, there is no Beethoven; certainly and emphatically there is no God; we are the words; we are the music; we are the thing itself. (*Moments of Being,* 72)

Inviting students to say, like Dodge, "I'm William" is part of the larger invitation to name the things and persons of their world in myths of their own making, returning them to their origins like the Aboriginal Australians return to the place where the ancestor has "gone back in." The contextual nature of this return is defined in the same way that Isa defines it when she orders the fish, the way Wordsworth did when he spoke of the "miracle of the ordinary": memory is drenched with the mundane, with the "cotton wool" of everyday experience if only we can be taught to value and to validate it. Moments of insight are found here if they are to be found anywhere at all.

The frequency with which even more sophisticated students skip from unadulterated summary to indiscriminate symbol-searching in the literature that they read suggests the extent to which the ordinary has lost its spell in our lives. Helping them to recover this life context is helping them to recover a lifeline to their own experience, a variant upon giving them access to a totem that can become an ever-present, and therefore sacred, presence in the story of their lives.

To help students have this kind of access to space is also to help them gain access to Bergson's *durée reelle,* an "enduring" time in which every thing is "near" because in this understanding of time, "nothing is 'far away' " (Kern, *The Culture of Time and Space,* 44). And it is to put them in touch once again with yet another understanding of song. The act of memory, Husserl argued along with Bergson and James, involves retention of a near experience and recollection of one that is "far" away. "[I]n listening to a melody, if the past sound were entirely to disappear, one would hear only unconnected notes and not be able to make out the melody. But in order for the past to integrate with the present, it must

diminish in intensity from its original form; otherwise the crescendo of
sounds in a melody would soon become a hopeless jumble. The past
must remain in consciousness but in changed form" (Kern, *The Culture
of Time and Space*, 44). That changed form is the material of myth.[23]

The writing classroom may finally be the most intimate space of any
that students occupy during their educational careers, an erotic space, in
fact. The term *erotic* applied to curriculum and instruction has become a
popular one in postmodern theory. Richard Rorty, for example, claims
the implications of eroticism for the postmodern classroom, conceiving
of general education classes as spaces in which a knowing faculty member
seduces students to love what he loves among the general studies of a
core curriculum. He sees pedagogy in the last year of high school and
the first year of college as "more like seduction than instruction" (cited
by Nicholson 200). Elsewhere, the word *erotic* appears in theories that
bring together sexuality and textuality; Roland Barthes, for example,
makes the connection explicit in his book *A Lover's Discourse*.[24]

But it is Anne Carson's ingenious connection of eros, breath, and
song that makes this claim for the erotic in the contemporary writing
classroom most clear. Considering classical poetry as the followers of
Sappho practice it, her work returns this text to its first premise about the
lessons oral people can offer contemporary writing teachers, and the
lessons literate cultures may learn about the extent to which they have
sold their birthright. "[A] longing for love," Archilochus writes, "filch[es]
out of my chest the soft lungs" (cited by Carson in *Eros the Bittersweet*,
46). But to lose our breath in this way is to lose far more, for "The eyes
and tongue and ears and intelligence of a/quick-witted man/grow in the
middle of his chest" (Theognis, cited by Carson in *Eros the Bittersweet*,
49). Object-relations theory is about a child's discovery of boundaries, of
separations, and thus about the child's experience of loss and desire. It
studies how language is made (literally) *in other words*, in a world suddenly discovered to have edges. It studies in miniature what it must have
been like for a people first struggling to *come to terms* with the impact of
literacy coming into their lives, an experience in miniature of a world in
which relationships could no longer be taken for granted, but were
suddenly negotiable, in fact *demanded* to be negotiated. In a postliterate
world, our sense of "the edge"—our "edginess," if you will—is intensified by the very language-making act in which we postliterate peoples
engage: "Literacy desensorializes words and reader. A reader must disconnect himself from the influx of sense impressions transmitted by nose,
ear, tongue, and skin if he is to concentrate upon his reading. A written
text separates words from one another [a task that Carson notes is learned

only with great difficulty], separates words from the environment, separates words from the reader (or writer) and separates the reader (or writer) from his environment. Separation is painful" (Carson, *Eros the Bittersweet*, 50).

In an oral world, Carson says, "there are no edges" like those that separate the text of the written word, for there "breath is everywhere." "The breath of desire is Eros," and in this world the very universe and all it contains breathes this desire—the desire to overcome separation and loss—to penetrate and so to disarm the edges of things.

> Inescapable as the environment itself, with his wings [Eros] moves love in and out of all creatures at will. The individual's total vulnerability to erotic influence is symbolized by those wings with their multi-sensual power to permeate and take control of a lover at any moment. Wings and breath transport Eros as wings and breath convey words: an ancient analogy between language and love is here apparent. The same irresistible sensual charm, called *peitho* in Greek, is the mechanism of seduction in love and of persuasion in words; the same goddess (Peitho) attends upon seducer and poet. (*Eros the Bittersweet*, 49–50)

Becoming literate, we gradually lost lungs, lost breath, lost song, lost the multifaceted nature of our sensual connection to the breathing universe, lost the continuity of time present in a world without edges, were forced to invent history to manage this discontinuous temporal experience and to perform the tasks that song once did. Students cannot articulate a longing for what they do not know, and of the absence of this kind of song in their lives they know little if anything. And so while Rorty seeks the seduction of the subject matter, I seek the seduction of breath, of sound, of song, in a classroom whose eroticism is defined by the ways that we teach our students to breathe again and so to be connected again—in a rich sense, to love again. I do not, clearly, propose the impossible return to a preliterate (or pre-Oedipal) world without edges. Instead, I propose a new relationship to the alphabet, and so to literacy, that the writing classroom is uniquely suited to forge. "[E]ros is vitally alert to the edges of things and makes them felt by lovers. As eros insists upon the edges of human beings and of the spaces between them, the written consonant imposes edge on the sounds of hu-man speech and insists on the reality of that edge, although it has its origin in the reading and writing imagination" (Carson, *Eros the Bittersweet*, 55).

Breaks interrupt time and change its data. . . . Breaks make a person think. When I contemplate the physical spaces that articulate the letters "I love you' in a written text, I may be led to think about other spaces, for example the space that lies between 'you' in the text and you in my life. Both of these kinds of space come into being by an act of symbolization. Both require the mind to reach out from what is present and actual to something else, something glimpsed in the imagination. In letters as in love, to imagine is to address oneself to what is not. To write words I put a symbol in place of an absent sound. To write the words 'I love you' requires a further, analogous replacement, one that is much more painful in its implication. Your absence from the syntax of my life is not a fact to be changed by written words. And it is the single fact that makes a difference to the lover, the fact that you and I are not one. (*Eros the Bittersweet*, 52)

To recognize this reality in our lives is to recognize—and embrace—a new kind of brokenness different from that created by an evolving technology and the loss of the Romantic vision that accompanied it. We confront this new (or rather old) kind of brokenness with every breath we take, not because it is a new and startling experience, but because in a postliterate universe the pain of our separateness is intensified by all of the other discontinuities that come with text and technology. Text has decontextualized our experience. Still, we must find a new way to use text in order to recover that lost context.

As an erotic place, the writing classroom can make no claim to resolve permanently the problem of separateness, distance, absence, brokenness. But eros expresses the *longing* for connection, and imagination, if it reaches out for "something else," must reach from the present, from a space that is here and now. To reach out from the here and now, we must first recognize our own edges, and then believe in the possibility that we can extend ourselves beyond them. In rhetorical terms, both self and audience must have a rich texture if the subject matter is to follow suit. When Dodge says, "I'm William," to Lucy Swithin, he has not only affirmed his edge, but confirmed the imaginative leap that began with pretext (a tour to view the house's rooms and things) and ended with context (the stories of both their lives).

Nancy Miller argues with regard to the questions of difference in women's writing that these questions must be answered "in the body of her writing and not [in] the writing of her body."[25] Yet in her quest for intimacy and a phenomenology to express it, Woolf's insistent reverse anthropomorphizing of both men's and women's bodies suggests that her effort is, indeed, to "write the body"—that the body of her writing *is* the writing of her body. The metaphors of body as they emerge in *The Waves*, for example, reveal an enormous amount regarding Woolf's ideas about intimacy. In a sense, like the passages cited above from *Between the Acts*, Woolf's text demonstrates the appropriation of the body by the earth rather than the traditional appropriation of the earth (and thus of the female body) that has marked practice (and thus textuality) in the West. In this sense, at the level of metaphor, at least, she acts out her claim to a body that she believes language (except at the level of song and style) does not yet allow her to name—a body genuinely intimate with the earth and all the forces that attend that intimacy. And in this sense, now beyond the level of metaphor, we call women who make text to recognize the nature of both kinds of appropriation: of the earth as well as of the men who colonize (decontextualize) them. If, as Cixous writes, *"in the beginning was the end of her story,"* the writing teacher's task must be always to return women students to their origins, to help them reinvert the inverted myth that Chernin, Woolf, and Gilligan[26] have explored.

At the beginning of *Reinventing Eve,* Chernin climbs a spiral staircase from the underworld, carrying, among other things, a lump of mud from the garden out of which every woman comes and to which every woman must inevitably return—twice. The first time, we return, as Chernin does, to get the lump of earth that will be worked, to make, as she does, our first "mudpie woman." The second time we return to learn to tell the story of the body, eventually, to allow it to tell its own *in other words,* as it will do even in spite of us. The first time we return to *find* the story. The second time, to *tell* it. About this feminist heuristic there will be yet more to come.

The aspect of things that are most important for us are hidden because of their simplicity and familiarity. (One is unable to notice something because it is always before one's eyes.) The real foundations of his enquiry do not strike a man at all.

—Ludwig Wittgenstein

Sometimes the meaning of an experience would only begin to dawn on me years afterwards, and even then I often had to go over the same ground again and again, with intervals of years between. In fact, I came to the conclusion that the growth of understanding follows an ascending spiral rather than a straight line.

—Joanna Field

V

Rituals of Happiness: Joanna Field's Method of Following the Image

The Bacchae, a Narrative of Denied Access

In the fifth century B.C. the playwright Euripedes recorded the story of an unholy trinity. Semele (in spirit), Autonoe, and Agave led the women of Thebes out of the city into a land that, at the touch of their ivy-twined wands, flowed with milk and honey. Here they suckled wild animals at their breasts, they sang songs to celebrate the coming of a god twice-born of woman and of man, by repute and appearance (as the myth would have it) both human and divine. And most of all, they danced. Outraged by the defection of their women from loom, hearth, and marriage bed, the men of Thebes struck back, using the testimony of a herdsman cum voyeur in an attempt to substantiate the most serious defection of all: contamination of the paternal seed by promiscuous sexual practice. The women of Thebes, claimed Pentheus, the Theban ruler, were having an unholy orgy outside of the city in the wilderness world to which they had been called by Dionysus and that, at his behest, they had claimed as their own.

Driven by the exigencies of the mythic story underlying the play, its outcome is a familiar one: the men attack, and the aftermath is violence and tragedy. Pentheus's fearful effeminacy leads him to transvestite parody as he, too, becomes voyeur, peeping down upon the women from the height of a phallic pine. In the ritual violence that follows, the women swarm over Pentheus's erect perch, which bends low under the pressure of their grasping hands, and he is torn to pieces by his own mother, a blood sacrifice offered to appease a wrathful god whose madness is said to inspire the Bacchic frenzy.

The domestic has been pitted against the political, nature against culture, wilderness against civilization, the Dionysian against the Apollonian, and the latter category privileged by custom and law. So also will the customary silence prevail, marking the ascendancy of *his*-story over hers. After a lengthy, interpolated passage written to replace "the great lacunae," a repentant and guilt-ridden Agave takes her shame into exile from Thebes with her father's admonition: "Farewell, poor daughter—if you can fare well." The other women (one can only presume) return to hearth and loom and bed. Duped again by the belief that, like men, they too might participate in the divine dimension of their humanity through the liberation of body, and so the liberation of the spirit and of its voice in song and dance, these women are sent back, paradoxically, *inside* as a reminder of their permanent status as Outsider(s), as Other(s). The foreign god, it seems, has taken his revenge, so the myth goes, on *everyone*. Or has he?

Euripides' play can be read as the paradigmatic story of women's lives in societies where the nomadic life has been abandoned for enclosure that marks off a domesticated order and defines a wilderness. Men relegate women's bodies to the first world, but fear that their spirits remain with the latter—with the wilderness. Confronting daily women's embodied sexuality, they must restrict women's physical space and denigrate their emotional, intellectual, and spiritual lives. In short, they denigrate the feminine principle as active agent in culture, and in themselves.

The masturbatory quality of Pentheus's voyeurism, along with the voyeuristic and ultimately violent activity of the herdsmen, reveal both the men's fear and their desire, their need and its inadmissible grip on them. Part of Dionysus's foreignness is his femininity; part of the need to project and to blame is reflected in the powerful grip he (his femininity) and the women hold upon male imagination. "We are at the mercy of what we bury," Carl Jung had written in the context of analyzing the ways we privilege the sensory and rational functions of consciousness at the expense of the sensual and the intuitive. The violence of the outcome, the men's (and perhaps Euripides') conception of Dionysus, the central scapegoating ritual itself, with Pentheus in bad drag, a parody of a parody, is a mark of how profound the resistance to the feminine had become. *The Bacchae* makes clear that to resist the feminine is to resist ways of knowing and being in the world that are contrary to the dominant (male) culture's understanding and practice. Thus, access to knowledge, and a concomitant question of the *kind* of knowledge validated in a culture, are the archetypal problems raised by the play.

The story of denied access is a classic one, readily recognizable generally in feminist paradigms and implicit to the actions and values informing this play and the culture it records. First, complex mythic stories are disconnected from the subtleties of their early significance and their truths are gradually inverted by selection, omission, or deliberate distortion that expresses itself in half-truths or outright lies. Kim Chernin gives an example of this process in her work with the myth of Eve *(Reinventing Eve)*, which is expressed as "re"-invention because it represents a recovery of past connection between the goddess and the snake that is distorted in the Hebrew version of Eden, emerging as it does from the larger political aim to smash the goddess religions and institute a single patriarchal god (and a single patriarchal state) in their place.[1] In *The Bacchae*, this distortion and inversion is revealed in a number of ways: in Theban culture's sneering emphasis upon the effeminacy of Dionysus, whose bisexuality is in fact a sign of the completeness of his knowledge and thus of his power; in the rejection of women's efforts to resacralize *orgia*, originally understood as integral to religious ritual and as celebratory of the ecstatic dimensions of worship that is rooted in yet transcends the body;[2] in the enfeebling of Tireseus's voice and insight that ignores his own bisexual history and connects him to the corrupt pragmatism of Cadmus; in Pentheus's effort to cloak a base political aim—maintaining personal (patriarchal) control of Thebes and resisting change that might destabilize that control—through actions falsely defined as emerging from religious practice and natural law. In Pentheus's terms, Dionysus is a false god and the women of Thebes are performing unnatural acts in their worship of him. Effectively, he projects guilt and blame for his own repressive regime and his own sexual fears upon external sources inherently feminine in nature. The moral of Pentheus's story can consequently become "Great harm comes to those who fail to recognize and honor the power of the gods," a poor substitute for Jung's overarching wisdom about the dangers of repression: "What we repress—persons and parts of ourselves—will inevitably rise up in fury and violence and get us in the end."

Finally, there is the conflict upon which all tragedy turns: the basely human—both male and female—cower before a magnificent and all-powerful divinity. In *The Bacchae*, this conflict can be played out only by the suppression of a vital portion of the Dionysian mythic stories. When the Titans, the kidnappers of Dionysus, are incinerated by the thunderbolt of a jealous Hera, angered because Dionysus is the bastard product of Zeus's intercourse with the mortal Semele, the human race rises out of these Titanic ashes. As humans, we are *both* mortal and divine: the dualism of body and soul or spirit, or Earth and heaven, is thus expressed as an opportunity to claim our birthright and therefore, as Heidegger recognized in the concept of Dasein,[3] no dualism at all.

This casts a far different light on the purposive activity of the Theban women, on the nature of their dance, long recognized in many non-Western traditions as the ecstatic, ritual liberation of spirit or soul, and on the wisdom with which they take to the hills to engage themselves in this ritual act. In summary, then, the truths emergent from this myth are inverted to reaffirm the power of patriarchy, which suppresses, represses, silences, and exiles the voices that offer another way.

In this book I have argued that, despite an apparent public silence, there is a long tradition of narrative through which women both explore and express their experience of being and knowing in the world. It is particularly a tradition that records a discomfort with accepted models—men's models—and seeks in the attachment to plain and ordinary things an alternative epistemology and an alternative praxis. These narratives tell the other half of the story that falls silent when Agave goes into exile, interpreting her experience as singer and dancer while *affirming* the experience of "otherness," a wilderness experience out of which both song and dance emerge.

The systematization of these narratives' themes is beginning to emerge in the writing of developmental and cognitive psychologists and philosophers working in the context of feminist paradigms. First, they have argued that, against traditional developmental theory, "premised on separation and told as a narrative of failed relationship," women's stories of adolescent self-absorption, interpreted in the Freudian model as a deepening and problematic narcissism, can be read instead as a deepening self-knowledge so that care and connection can be maintained and enriched" (Gilligan, *In a Different Voice*, 39).[4] The notion that separation is uncomfortable and can in fact be downright dangerous is acted out in the violence that informs *The Bacchae*. The radical dis-integrity and dis-ease of Theban society founded on the primary separation of nature and culture allows all of the mayhem that follows to occur: women's lives are separate from men's, mothers from sons, the human from the divine, the country from the city, the ruler from the ruled, the old from the young.

Secondly, the narratives argue a morality of care predicated not on impersonal or universal concepts of justice but upon caring and careful actions whose justice can only emerge from the "web of connection" within which individual rights and interpersonal needs must be mediated.

> If aggression is tied, as women perceive, to the fracture of human connection, then the activities of care, as their fantasies suggest, are the activities that make the social world safe, by avoiding isolation and preventing aggression rather than by seeking rules [Pentheus's activity in a nutshell] to limit its extent. From this perspective, the prevalence of violence in men's fantasies, denoting a world where danger is everywhere seen, signifies a problem in making connection, causing relationships to erupt and turning separation into a dangerous isolation. Reversing the usual mode of interpretation, in which the absence of aggression in women is tied to a problem with separation,

makes it possible to see the prevalence of violence in men's stories, its odd location in the context of intimate relationships, and its association with betrayal and deceit as indicative of a problem with connection that leads relationships to become dangerous and safety to appear in separation [an apt description of Pentheus's fears]. Then rule-bound competitive achievement situations, which for women threaten the web of connection, for men provide a mode of connection that establishes clear boundaries and limits aggression and thus appears comparatively safe. (Gilligan, *In a Different Voice*, 43)

But *appears* is the operative word here. For real life is not a game, and, as *The Bacchae* amply demonstrates, healthy human relationships are rarely sustainable in rigidly rule-bound systems, despite the prevalence of powerful rules in the most common of these systems, the modern family. Confronting this reality is a complex task. Often, as is the case in this play, we act out roles in these systems that have virtually unbearable consequences. Despite (perhaps because of) our own responsibility for our actions, we project both blame and shame on our gods. Agave and Cadmus are not exceptions to this act of projection. Agave laments: "This brutal onslaught Dionysus made/on all your children is a monstrous thing" (Sutherland, *The Bacchae of Euripides*, 69). In the surface structure of the narrative, the god-centered, universalist ethic of justice essential to tragedy appears to prevail: "if there be/a man whose intellect dare scorn the powers,/let him see this man's death, and admit the gods!" (63). So goes Cadmus's admonition, and the choric voices follow suit. Dionysus, we are told, has claimed an eye for an eye, and Agave's complaint is drowned out in a vast chorus affirming divine justice:

> Many the forms of the divine.
> Many an unforeseen event
> comes on us by the gods' design.
> We plan. They do not bring about
> what we expect, and they find out
> ways for the ends we never meant.
> Such was the way this matter went. (70)

The greatest tragedy, if there can be a question of degree, is that Agave believes her own story. Exiled, her silencing is complete. But at the center of the play, the narrative of women's journey outside of the rule-bound patriarchal law into a land of milk and honey, a land in which they can both sing and dance, must not be forgotten. This narrative within a narrative is told by a herdsman who returns to Pentheus describing the wonders he has seen along with the guilty account of his own involvement in the ensuing violence. Significantly, Agave must be *told* about her experience; "divinely induced" amnesia renders her unable to remember it herself. This is the story of many women in patriarchal culture.

Joanna Field's Narrative Models of Reappropriation

Nevertheless, some women have attempted the difficult task of *themselves* creating a narrative within the larger patriarchal story that tells them about themselves. Contemporary epistemologists and psychologists working within feminist paradigms do this. Many women students in writing classes do it, too.

In the first decades of the century, it was also the attempt of biologist-turned-psychoanalyst Marian Milner, who wrote under the name Joanna Field. The first of her books, *A Life of One's Own* (1936), is a self-conscious response to Virginia Woolf, a mental journey constructed in part from her study of her own journals that complemented the sociopolitical journey Woolf offers in *A Room of One's Own*. In one sense, Field's book is a "how-to" manual that describes what to do when that elusive room is finally the writer's own. It is also a model writing text, demonstrating for students how to learn to record and trust their own experience, how to free-write and focus that free writing, how to record the protocols of their invention process, how to make the kinds of judgments about that writing that allow them to push beyond the blocks of the critical voices they have internalized from their personal and educational lives and to write more.

The second book, *An Experiment in Leisure* (1937), aims to extend the fruits of the initial explorations of *A Life of One's Own*. The last book, *On Not Being Able to Paint* (1957), theorizes anger brilliantly using a Freudian model—an extraordinary achievement for its day—this time with her own drawings as well as journal material as the subject of her commentary. I want to look closely at these three texts, both because they inform the writing classroom's praxis, and because they offer some fit answers to the dilemma of otherness and its bitter costs that *The Bacchae* proposed as the lot of those women who dared to sing and dance their own difference some twenty-five centuries before. Given the opportunity, and often in spite of it, women in writing classrooms will consistently produce narratives within narratives, using them as a means of coming to moments of insight about the inverted myths whose themes they have inadvertently lived, and about the way that these myths can be agents in reinventing not only Eve but themselves.

Field's design self-consciously attempts to exploit this activity: her books are narratives of her own experiences as a painter, analyst, and journal keeper, self-conscious commentaries on journal entries that range from controlled, conventional diary-keeping to genuine experiments in free-writing that upon later examination yield remarkable insights about her own writing/thinking process and the struggle for identity it both reveals and becomes. Out of the question "What makes me happy?" comes a text whose themes prefigure the formal issues of feminist theory by some fifty years: silence, shame, relationship, intimacy, voice, and many more. "[U]nless I wrote about it," Field reflects in a telling early passage, "I [was convinced that] I would lose my way. Yet for years I hesitated, not knowing in what form to tell it. . . . What helped me most was the gradually growing conviction that silence might be the privilege of the strong but it was certainly a danger to the weak. For the things I was prompted to keep silent about were nearly always the things I was ashamed of which would have been far better aired and exposed . . . I knew then that though my decision to write in direct personal terms would lead me on to dangerous ground, yet it was the very core of my enterprise" (*A Life of One's Own*, 30).

Early on, Field's language reveals the two voices that reflect the two kinds of consciousness accessible to her exploration: these are the voices of the scientist and the poet, or, in the terms of one psychologist, the voices of the logico-scientific and the narrative modes of cognition (Polkinghorne, *Narrative Knowing and the Human Sciences,* 17). Her work begins with the gradually dawning sense of her own brokenness, "the feeling of being cut off from other people, separate, shut away from whatever might be real in living" (*A Life of One's Own,* 20). These scribblings on the back of envelopes, early prewriting experiences, lead to the method of observation and experiment that marks Field's scientific training. But it quickly becomes the method of Field the poet, too, the kind of observation that allows one to find oneself by losing oneself in gradually more acute, Wordsworthian "spots of time." *"I want to let go, to lose myself, my soul. . . . I want all the life of the universe flowing through me"* (22, 23). Yet while her first attempt is a rational one, "consideration of all the things I seemed to be aiming at" (24), she continues, "Since I was suspicious of my own power of reasoning, I decided it was no good trying to answer these questions by sitting down and thinking them out" (25). And in the midst of her reflections about the limited utility of reason comes the insight that is the thesis of this book: "But might there not perhaps be a private reality, a reality of feeling rather than of knowing, which I could not afford to ignore?" (29).

Her search for this "reality of feeling," involving a relentless commitment to the method of observation, leads inevitably to the world of "plain and ordinary things" and, just as inevitably, to shocks of awareness much like Woolf's intensely felt "moments of being." In a "moment of absentmindedness," she writes, "I looked up from my desk and found myself gazing at grey roofs and chimneys, a view typical from a million of London's top-floor windows. I do not remember exactly what I saw but only the shock of delight in just looking" (35). Later: *"I walked on a dark country road with glimmers of sunset under a hail-storm sky, and wind and Orion clear in a light patch of sky, and laughed until the tears came just at being alive"* (44). And still later, *"the grass, sodden with winter rains, the squelch of mud under foot . . . the splash of water, a mist of green buds . . . things . . . familiar and intimate"* (46).

In search of the "still small voice" speaking "after the wind" (41) that can express that joy of pure awareness, Field's reflection is equally close to Woolf's: *" 'They' assume that what happens is what matters, where you go, what you do, things that happen, the good time that you have. But often I believe it's none of these things, it's the times between, the long days when nothing happens, the odd moments, perhaps when you open a letter, or sit alone in a restaurant, or exchange the time of day with a stranger"* (43).[5] Her method, her insistence on a genuine seeing as the prerequisite of insight, is expressed as an "interest gradually shifting from what to do with my life to how to look at it" (44). The interpenetration of coming to awareness and claiming her voice are reflected in a shifting series of visual and oral metaphors: *"The thing that matters, that you are looking for, is like the roots of plants, hidden and happening in the gaps of your knowledge"* (44). There is *"Some serenity and a sense of not being 'outside of life'—but of 'being life'—one's hopes and fears and strivings"* (45), and at a Schubert concert, after *"ceasing all striving to understand the music, partly by driving off intruding thoughts, partly feeling the music coming up inside me,"* there is *"myself a hollow vessel filled with sound"* (45).

Coleridge's credo was the Romantic "suspension of disbelief"; Field's is the suspension of both rational consciousness and a socially imposed *self*-consciousness, both of which have inevitably blocked a genuine connection to things. In pursuit of this connection, her free-writing becomes at once more systematic and more boldly experimental. By allowing the suspension of syntactic order and a genuinely associative play with the words she writes, she creates in her journals the kinds of semantic networks[6] that emerge from current experiments on writers' composing processes. Like the typical naive writer first introduced to brainstorming as a concept for generating text, Field begins first with lists—"things I hate" and "things I like"—but graduates rapidly to writing "whatever came into my head," reflecting on the familiar difficulty of being "obsessed by the feeling that it was no use, that if I did not guide my thought it was just waste of time" (59). The kind of "plunge into memory" this work evokes offers yet another insight: "It seemed," she writes, "that I was normally only aware of the ripples on the surface of my mind, but the act of writing a thought was a plunge which at once took me into a different element where the past was intensely alive" (60). What is more, her intuitive recognition of the "danger" of this ground is affirmed. The power of the painful and fearful memories evoked by this writing process should be well noted by writing teachers who, with all good intentions, extend these experimental invitations to their students, and thus must inevitably bear some responsibility for what emerges from students' texts. So too should be recognized the frequency with which, as for Field, they can recover "childhood affairs and echoes of intense emotional urgency" (62), powerful factors in any learning process. What is more, we have no reason to assume that students do not, like Field, intuit the danger they may face if a writing process is genuinely engaged, and all of this may well explain the reluctance of our students to write, even about the most apparently indifferent subject, for the act itself seems a potent opportunity to unwittingly open the Pandora's box of their own experience. One of Field's journal entries offers a rich example of this:

> *I remember telling a lie at school when I'd cheated with my poetrybook under the desk and a girl saw it. I remember making excuses to Miss B. for bad work—why did I lie?—to escape something? —what?—punishment?—what sort?—hole in corner—Death?—why death?—what does death mean?—End—anger—hate—father—cruel—homecoming—futile—foolish—who?—me?—because stupid . . . (and so on, ending up with): crying when I went to bed at B. because I was missing things—out of it—outcast—dead—?—?—crying at getting lost at B.—emptiness—not knowing where to turn—crying at the Tinder Box cat—fear of the white-faced Miss W. who did the ghost in the play—fear of thunder—apprehension—the before-sleeping sensations—of what? immense bigness.* (61)

Gradually, as Field identifies the emergence of an "automatic self" whose narratives complement those of the "deliberate" one, she experiments with a guided free-writing that yields a significant result: the longing for a kind of embodied thinking that can complement the typi-cally cerebral way "things" and our relationship to them are examined and explored. As the body-rejecting values emergent from her not-un-common experience with patriarchal religious practice reveal, part of the problem with human connection to things is that there must be body as well as mind to engage itself in the connection.

> SEA . . . mother—perhaps derived from "mer"—feeling ashamed when they laughed at Miss R.'s and they said I'd painted the sea blue—why did I feel such accusations always unjust, a hot fighting to deny and escape—to bathe in the sea. What does it mean? Deep cool green water to dive into, but often no bathing-dress and people watching—?—God—is that what the sea means?—lose myself—this is just maundering—fear of the sea at B.—fear to go in farther than up to my ankles. . . .

> GOD . . . happiness—wrong—damnation—those who do not believe shall be damned—as soon as you are happy, enjoying yourself, something hunts you on—the hounds of heaven—you think you'll be lost—damned, if you are caught—so never stop—God is wicked, cruel . . . miserable sinners—shall we never escape from the body of his death—grow old along with me, the best—they said you'd be raped by tramps on the grassy hills . . . glorious sun—adoration—I love you more than God, the God of my learning—trees, grass, wind and sea—"I give thanks and adore thee, God of the open air"—crawling worms and mud,—blind sea worms—white worms—intestinal worms—enemas—beastly, hateful—menstruation—the hellish smell of blood—the end of everything—prison—prison—skirts . . . —jokes—nasty—dirty—foul smells—sweaty bodies—a man's healthy body—shirt open—P—vigor and happiness—freedom—damn the God of your Fathers—blasphemy—my God is better than . . . (63, 64–65)

Dancing unconsciously on the edge of the goddess tradition, Field's experimental free-writing brings together a nexus of issues that are par-ticular to, if not exclusive to, women's writing. She calls the chapter that describes this work "The Coming and Going of Delight." Here, personal narrative work as the work of identity making becomes yet another thread added to the fabric of issues that include shame, silence, voice, and relationship, a part of her ongoing struggle to do what Woolf calls writ-ing "as if the body thought." And she offers yet another relational paradox, that of insideness to outsideness, that has been understood—or embraced in practice—by many meditative traditions.

Both separate from and enmeshed with mother, longing for both experiences and fearing both of them, it can be as difficult for many women in writing classrooms to be open to their experiences—to speak heart and mind—as it is to engage in the kinds of distanced and distancing analysis called for in most academic settings. The sense that writing is a way both of getting reconnected to what is separate and separating from what binds us, and the confusion between connection and being inappropriately merged, highlighted by William Perry's schema for moral development,[7] is probably a tension in both men's and women's writing. But traditional schemas still emphasize separation as an ultimate value—witness the whole notion of justice argued by both Perry and Euripides—a value that allows genuine, objective assessment of right and wrong without the emotional confusion of values that genuine connection will inevitably bring. So what is a women to do? And particular to our purposes here, what is a woman in the writing classroom to do? "Become aware," Field writes, and her three books are a blueprint for her own process that models how.

Field's effort to widen and deepen her awareness is variously described in this chapter as "putting [this center of awareness] out into different parts of my body or even outside myself altogether" (71), as "putting myself out of myself" (73), as "stand[ing] aside" (74) to let the body engage in whatever activity is at hand. By this means, Buber's I-Thou becomes real for her: "I remembered to spread the arms of my awareness towards the trees, letting myself flow round them and feed on the delicacy of their patterns till their intricacies became part of my being and I had no more need to capture them on paper" (76). But this activity of "pressing [her] awareness out of the limits of [her] body" is not without its accompanying terror—a terror she identifies as "a fear of losing myself, of being overtaken by something," a kind of "panic ecstasy" (79). The address to the panic comes in the form of an "incantation," the song of plain and ordinary things. "I was lonely and filled with a sense of inadequacy, I longed to do something, to act, as an alternative to the ceaseless chatter of my worrying thoughts . . . I sat down and remembered how I had sometimes found changes of mood follow when I tried to describe in words what I was looking at. So I said, 'I see a white house with red geraniums and I hear a child crooning.' And this most simple incantation seemed to open a door between me and the world" (80).

While the scientist's understanding begins Field's quest, enabling her to separate and label categories of perception (wide-focused and narrow-focused) and thought (blind thinking and "sightful" thinking), the conduct of her investigation turns inevitably to the artist/poet's often unconscious wisdom, a broader and more encompassing realization of how the body's experience can be engaged and named. The incantatory quality of the language that names things so simple as the white cottage and red geranium, a lump of coal and a tin cup, lies in its ability to bridge the gap between "inside and outside," between the knowing subject and that subject's often-fearful ideas about things and the facts of the things themselves. This genuine engagement marks wide attention: attention to things as a whole without expectation either of failure or of delight, attention informed, in other words, by a detachment and disinterest that is paradoxically intimate. Eventually, like the Buddhist teacher Thich Nhat Hanh, Field will call it "mindfulness."[8] Like him and like Wordsworth before him, she will reflect on the "miracle" of transformed consciousness that this kind of attention can make available.

Just as it did for Lucy Swithin, genuine engagement with the thing offers Field access to a more broadly conceived space in the material universe and to the mythic dimensions of the temporal one. Engaged by the lump of coal without the blind thinking and narrow-focused perception that demands its future purposiveness to be foregrounded in consciousness, Field begins "to feel its blackness . . . to feel its 'thingness' and the thrust of its shape, to feel after its past in forests of giant vegetation, in upheavings of the land passing to aeons of stillness, and then little men tunneling, the silence and cleanliness of forests going to make up London's noisy filth" (95). In the "physics" of a tin mug, with an awareness of its "stresses" and "strains," "roundness" and "solidity" and its place held up by the table, comes a new significance for "pictures, buildings, statues, which had before been meaningless" (96). The "moments of delight" that these perceptions materialize for her have as their "essential quality . . . a fusing of experience, a flash of significance uniting the meaningless and the separate" (135). They are, in other words, moments of being in which the radical relationship of everything that is can be perceived with utter clarity. And this is wisdom.

In this frame of reference, the question "What makes me happy?" can indeed be seen to be the one that yields a fundamental wisdom—the wisdom of the heart. Blind thinking is bound significantly to the shames, fears, inadequacies, inferiorities, and senses of failure; its hallmarks are the confusion of past and present, the longing to escape from the present moment, and the perpetuation of the distorting effort to make the "might have been" true. Heartfelt thinking waits in the present moment without a fear of the emptiness—of the empty mind—that waits for things rather than "willing" them to be (102).

If the law of the Father, in Lacan's terms, is one of separation and enforced reunion in order that identity can be achieved and affirmed, what Field writes about is her search for the law of the Mother, risky though that search may be in a universe of values informed by the Father's law. The final lesson of this text, to woman and writer, of woman and artist, is that relationship *need not* be merging, that "becoming the thing" *need not* lead to the fearful dissolution of personal identity, but that becoming the thing is indispensable to actualizing some fundamental part of the self, and that, as Heidegger reminds us, becoming the thing is not necessarily becoming exactly like it.[9] Like the town inundated inside and outside by a tidal wave, of which she so frequently dreams, Field recognizes that inside and outside stand always in dialectical relationship to each other, that a rhythmic "thinking backwards," represented so fully in the journal work itself, is genuinely the way to go forward.

So Field, too, is engaged in reinventing Eve, reaffirming as she does so her connection to a tradition of women's power that unraveling her own thinking has allowed her to actualize. "It will be a sore fight letting go and letting the sea in" (101), she had written in an earlier journal entry. Yet in a later chapter, "Fear of the Dragon," she confronts the drawing of a dragon she had made at fifteen and labels it "the original primal fear." While as an adult she writes of it as bathed in a grotesque imagery of blood and death, nevertheless, of Galahad the archetypal dragon slayer she writes: "how I hated him" (149). Far from being the enemy, Field's fearful dragon enables her to confront the fearful potential for dissolution of identity that a genuine engagement both with the world of things and with her own inner impulses, even her sexuality itself, seem to portend. In this personal underworld is Hecate, the goddess, but thinking herself back into it is to risk being "drag-ged," being swallowed up like Jonah in the whale. Nevertheless, out of this primal sea comes inevitably "the day's catch of happiness" (192), and the journey inward is linked inextricably to the outward journey: "for the day's catch," she writes, is seen always "in terms of my relationships with others."

So the issues are separation, loss, (sexual) shame, fear of failure, fear of dissolution. Through all is threaded the longing for relationship and the determined struggle to name all of these. Galahad is to be hated as the dragon slayer, for the dragon is found to be critical to the identification process. Yet he is perhaps to be hated also for the heroic model he offers, an autobiographical narrative no woman can genuinely share.

What Field realizes as well is that the journey inward, symbolic in Western narrative, is both symbol in women's lives and yet more than this: it is actual, a journey into the images that are powerful for them. Galahad's model for seeing the knowledge of good and evil, a search forbidden to Eve, turns out to be of only limited value, in any case. What she recognizes is the folly of believing that dragon—or snake—can ever really be slain. Like the goddesses in the myths preceding the myth of Eve, the new narrative she offers is a myth that embraces the enemy and discovers in its eyes her own face.

Following the Image to Connected Knowing

Joanna Field begins each of her books with a key question: The first is "What makes me happy?" The second, "What interests me?" and the third, "What makes me unable to do what I want to do?" As she explores these questions, both she and her editors propose at various points that these questions take on a different tenor for women. Although some of their reasoning (women have a need to be possessed by people and experiences that men don't) may seem outdated and sexist to contemporary readers, she nevertheless poses problems that articulate themselves in special ways for women and for women in classrooms.

Women often come to college classrooms out of a peer- and teacher-enforced silence.[10] There is ample evidence to indicate that in many college classrooms they are confronted with the same barriers to voicing their experience. In my years of teaching women's journals and personal narrative writing, students young and old will after a time break out of their silence to describe what that silent place was like. "I was always the dumb blond in the family," one woman in class burst out after reading Marie Bashkirtseff's journal. "Now I know that I'm really not crazy— that other women think and feel these things, too." Given the opportunity to write about a family experience evoked for her by a reading in feminist theory, one young woman wrote about hiding on the stairway of her house while the Rabbi gave her brother Hebrew lessons—an opportunity to study her language and cultural tradition that had been forbidden her by her parents. Today, at thirty-five, she is studying the Talmud with a female Rabbi and writing about it as a rhetorical document. Still another young woman used the classroom opportunity to develop a journal that chronicled her feelings about surviving incest, about the complicity of her mother in denying her experience, about the eating disorder that is the legacy of her body's revolt against this violation and the enforced silence whose ban she has begun to defy. Still another young woman attributes her inability to speak in class and her intense difficulty writing to the secret of her parents' alcoholism, and to the blocking factors of the shame, guilt, and fear the experience of co-dependency evokes.

In this chapter I have spoken of writing, as did Joanna Field fifty years ago, as an agent both of separation and connection. What we are able to name finds a place in our experience appropriate to its impor-tance, both separate from and a part of who we are. Writing about an experience, an image, a fantasy, involves giving ourselves up to it. To resist naming these experiences, images, fantasies, as chapter after chapter in Field's second book *(An Experiment in Leisure)* amply demonstrate, is to be stuck in an endless round of their insistent demands upon our attention. We give ourselves up not only in mind, but in body, too. From her reading of the *Tao,* Field is able to adopt the principle of emptiness, here expressed as "I am nothing, I know nothing, I want nothing" (*An Experiment in Leisure,* 40). This is no mere "formula as a cold fact" but "felt in the blood as a giving up of the whole being" (41); it was "giving up myself *to* something" as well, she writes. As such, it is a ritual act. And so, "why not sacrifice to the 'x' . . . instead of trying to build frantic bulwarks against it, why not ritualize my knowledge of my own smallness and make it a bearable thought" (47).

What rapidly becomes apparent in this ritual evocation is that the call to emptiness is paradoxically a call to relationship, too. In the logic of this argument, if writing is about relationship, and if women do indeed have a perspective on relationship that differs from men's, as many kinds of evidence seem to suggest, then Field's intuitions about differences in women's education, and the uses to which they can put the act of writing should themselves be of great interest to writing teachers.

If giving herself up to something is for Field a ritual act, then the kinds of writing that help her to do this are ritual acts, too. If the outcome of ritual activity is the affirmation of community, discoveries that writing allows her to make have all the hallmarks of ritual knowledge leading to this affirmation, as well. In these propositions lies the crux of the paradox in which "inside" and "outside" become indistinguishable. This might be the key to the many paradoxical opportunities that a writing process offers students. For by writing about the material con-crete versus the ideal abstract, by writing about things instead of issues, they are led, in the most profound sense, to write about their *relations* to things. In so doing, they learn something about the opportunities and responsibilities of relationship. And when the time comes to write about issues—about the abstract ideal—they are able to do so from a perspective of embedded engagement that makes the issue—and their connection to it—real. This knowledge, and this practice, is one gift of women's narrative to the West.

In my own teaching practice, encouraging concrete connections to the objects of students' experience is the work of most of our first term together in the writing classroom. I use other media—drawing and film— as well as various kinds of fiction and nonfictional narrative to help us explore our relationship to objects. Students come to class with a drawing pad, a blank writing book, and a book of selected essays, poems, and fiction. Because we are a not yet a community, but must (I believe) become that if our work together is to succeed, we are, in a sense, the first objects for each other's exploration. We introduce ourselves to each other by representing ourselves in a brief series of images (four or five) outlined on a large drawing pad with magic marker. These might be the story of our year before coming to this classroom; they might be images of important life-moments; or they might simply be what occurs to us as a safe way we want to represent ourselves in this particular group. In small groups of three or four, we tell each other what these images represent for us, connecting the pictures to a brief oral narrative. Out of one or more of these, at a later point in the course, some broader narrative will come. Before they begin to write in earnest, I send them out to draw, experimenting with Frederick Franck's technique of never removing the eye from the object as the pencil traces its shape on the page *(The Zen of Seeing)*. In small groups, they talk a bit about why they chose what they drew, and what they may have learned from the activity. At the same time, they see a short film about seeing; I use *The Mood of Zen*,[11] a lovely portrait of the water, fish, and stones in a Zen garden, but there are many films that might serve the same purpose. We also read some of the more accessible psychological literature on adult and childhood memory.[12] At first, little of this seems significant except to the most adventuresome and unrepressed student. The significance of the images and of image making becomes clearer as they start to write narratives that connect their images to people and experiences of their lives. By this time, we have begun to create a larger frame—social, historical, psychological—within which students begin to place their individual lives. Among the elements of this frame are the lives of other students, pieces of which gradually emerge as they write about their experiences and read them to each other in small groups. Other elements include the psychological literature, which demonstrates basic memory processes they share with others, as well as pointing toward ways they can gain access to their own memories and help others to do the same. The literature we read is also of great importance; early on we read many personal narratives, such as, Virginia Woolf's essay on her father, Joan Didion's essay on keeping a journal, Annie Dillard's *Sight into Insight*.[13] Eventually, we will read and experiment with the techniques described by Field in *A Life of One's Own*. As we study these texts, we look particularly at the ways the writers use the objects of their experiences as images that connect them to the persons and experiences they write about, and that help the writers describe themselves. We often read passages aloud, connecting ourselves to the oral tradition I spoke of earlier in this book, and modeling a learning through sound as well as sense. Complementing our reading of the work of professional writers, students frequently sit in small groups, reading their own work aloud to each other. Field's book is a guide to much of this process; in fact, it becomes, with the fiction, the primary text of the course.

All of this work is aimed at getting students in touch with the important objects in their lives that can become the images that help them to write in connected ways. It addresses a basic point about learning that we strive to connect new understandings to previous experience, and that all new experience is viewed through cognitive templates whose power can be great even when we do not realize that this is so. The literature, and other students' writing, are the bridges that connect private and public, self and world. So also is the act of writing itself. Consequently I offer students many opportunities to talk and write about what their previous experiences with reading and writing have been. This often leads to narratives of their experiences in schools—many of which, sadly, have been negative—that can be very helpful in breaking blocks to writing process.

This passage from Gordon Rohman's unpublished research on prewriting is included in my syllabus:

> The late Dorothy Sayers wrote that this process involves what she called a 'conversion' of 'events' from the world into 'experience' in a person. An 'event' she distinguished as something that happens to one—but he does not necessarily experience it. You only learn to experience a thing when you can express it to your own mind. A writer is a man who not only suffers the impact of external events, but experiences them. He puts the experience into words in his own mind, and in so doing recognizes the experience for what it is for him. To the extent that we can do that, we are all writers. A writer is simply a [person] like ourselves with an exceptional

power of revealing his experience by expressing it, first to himself and then to others so that we recognize this experience as our own, too. When an 'event' is so recognized, it is converted from something happening to us into something happening in us. And something to which we happen. The writer gropes for those words which will cause this transformation. ("Pre-Writing: Models for Concept Formation in Writing").

Field puts this connection between inner self and outer experience in yet another way. Like many other of the writers spoken of in this book, she is essentially writing about intimacy. "Out of every plant and beast man's self cries to him," William Blake had written (cited by Field, *An Experiment in Leisure,* 174). "I thought at first" she writes, "that meant a poetic way of stating the fact of evolution, but now it seems to be true in a more intimate way, that these loves are the images which your dim sense of what you are takes to clothe itself, they become the very texture of your sense of being" (174). The ritual submission to what is outside the self, a hallmark of good writing process, is therefore a ritual submission to what is "inside" the self, to the self itself. And the basis of any good writing teaching, then, must be not *productive* but *reproductive* theory.[14]

Writing of her years of fascination with mating birds, Field's epiphanic moment involves the recognition of radical connection:

"[T]he living processes I needed to understand were not exclusively physical, . . . the mind used the idea of the physical facts of sex and maternity themselves as symbols, symbols of the truth that all real living must involve a relationship, recurrent moments of surrender to the 'not self.' Richness from the earth, whether the healing power in herbs, bright colors hidden in the chemistry of leaves and roots, or the dark wealth of mines, all these were equally apt ways of talking about either the powers of generation in the body or the unknown creative depths of the mind. (177)

I believe that students feel the loss of this connection to the earth deeply, and efforts to help them find ways to reconnect with the physical, natural world pervade my teaching. Drawing things outdoors on the campus—outside the world of the classroom and its books—is one way to call attention to this lack. Literature can provide one of the richest ways to enhance students' ecological awareness and their critical thinking about ecological issues; it can also help us form a theory of human ecology. In a way different from scientific knowing, but complementary to it, literature points out the relationships we cannot live without.

That the(se) inner and outer world(s) are bridged by images may be more of an astonishment to the scientist than to the poet. Field herself began with the scientist's facts and was drawn inexorably to the poet's images. One of the greatest services of her journal/commentaries is to teach us how this process works in the nature of narrative, and to demonstrate how critical it is that we help students to seek their own images as a core activity in the ways we teach them to write. Her proposal for the "investigation of images" as the way to proceed with her own self-training as a writer, in fact as key to a writing process, meets the proponents of logic in critical thinking theory with a heads on (or hearts-on) rebuttal. "[M]y mind certainly seemed to prefer [these images] as instruments of reflection, to the more usual and accepted terms of logic and reason . . . they brought meaning and order into the chaos of raw feeling. Whereas conscious reasoning could not touch the chaos, feeling and thought were somehow too much at loggerheads for that" (159–160). Field insists on the embodied nature of the process involved in searching out her images, "a direct touching of something which feels like the raw experience of being alive" (53).

Within the broad narrative investigation of her own writing process, Field writes and records other narratives, the most significant of which are her own fairy tale, and her interpreted recounting of Sean O'Casey's play "Within the Gates." Both are driven by images—largely organic—that continually metamorphose into each other: vegetable becomes animal becomes mineral becomes both human and divine. Their narrators, the hag and the prostitute, can be read as alter egos for dimensions of Field herself, and for all women genuinely in touch with their Otherness in culture. Students are fascinated by it, and it is particularly useful in studying the ways private images join larger archetypes for human experience, something their own writing can aim to achieve. It is worth close explication because in it Field demonstrates so much about the writing process itself.

Field's fairy tale is a fantasy about the phantasms of the unconscious mind and their inevitable (and terrible) surfacing at the behest of those who dare to cast the spell that raises them from the depths. It begins with a little boy who eats a stolen apple, becomes as a result a swollen melon, and is kicked down an embankment. Once burst, the melon's seeds drop into the river, and under the casual eye of an old woman at her window, become little fish, who swim immediately out to sea. There, they discover a gleaming white human skeleton and weave a thick bronze-colored silk spun out of themselves to shroud the bones, pondering all the while how to raise it to the surface. Swimming from the sea upriver in search of advice about how to do this, now grown to be large salmon, they are caught, tinned, and eaten by the little old woman, who mysteriously sets in motion a series of events that lead to the making and striking of a magical gong of seven metals at the North Pole. The earthquake that results heaves the sea's bottom to its surface, forming a small island on which lies the now hardened bronze cocoon. This fulfills the prophecy of one of the little fish that "the bottom of the sea must come to the top" to raise the skeleton. Exposed to the elements, the cocoon gradually breaks down, and from it emerge "like two photographs taken one on top of the other" (*An Experiment in Leisure*, 88) the dark and light warrior gods, Dis and Adonis. Behind him, like the proverbial dragon's teeth, the armies of Dis spring up.

Gradually, exploring each of these images, Field comes to identify their connection with her own otherness. Her greatest terror is the recurring awareness of the "Satanic" presence represented by Dis (elsewhere the snake, the lion, and the dragon), and of his apparent inseparability from the life-giving Adonis. But her greatest insight is recognizing the presence of desire in human processes—including writing processes: "unformulated experience, that is, nature in the raw, nature shut off from awareness, is this the dragon? But isn't nature—that is, human nature, as one feels it in oneself—isn't it desires? Desires without the integrating power of awareness, is this then the destroying dragon? But to become aware of a desire you must somehow let go wanting the thing and simply look" (98). Together with the story of O'Casey's dying prostitute whose song and dance and laughter challenge the upright by making them aware both of their desire and their fear, Field's hag's tale confronts her, and us, with the cost that authentic awareness exacts: a confrontation with the dialectical nature of our experience and of ourselves. What her Christian sensibilities lead her to identify as "Satanic" modulates gradually through the less dualistic perceptions of the Chinese philosophers she is clearly reading.

The terror of the blank page has come not only from "desire without the integrating power of awareness" but also from the intuition of what might indeed (fearfully) emerge if, as she does what she ultimately learns to do: "accept the blankness . . . since it was from this that an image would grow, an image which was communicable because it was a picture of some *thing,* of flames or dust, or a horned beast; but which also somehow contained within itself the inner truth that I had found utterly incommunicable in terms of matter-of-fact statement" (190). The hag strikes her gong, the prostitute sings and dances, and Field writes her narrative within which their stories are contained, calling up her own fear and her own desire in order that she may lay both aside. Writing is an incantatory process, and its confrontation is finally with the "daemonic" in its richest sense:

> It certainly did seem that the lust for security and submission, a primitive instinct which was undoubtedly imperious and strong, could be more safely turned towards something within, whether you called it your fate or your daemon or your God; for to let it find its expression in a blind external slavery would leave you totally at the mercy of chance and circumstance. My conclusion was that there was a psychological necessity to pay deliberate homage to something . . . and also . . . to find your own pantheon of vital images, a mythology of one's own, not the reach-me-down-mass-produced mythology of Hollywood, of the newspapers, or the propaganda of dictators. (233)

The daimonic attaches itself both to Dis and Adonis, both to death and love. It, too, is bittersweet. Silencing language through whose seams intimations of our mortality (and our suffering) may leak, we lose the very life force itself, and with this loss we lose also relationship and ourselves. Writing of the daimonic in *Love and Will*, Rollo May returns us to the discussion of Eros that Anne Carson began in her reflections on song, reminding us of how impoverished contemporary understanding of the daimonic has become in a world of *The Exorcist* and *Omen I, II, III*, etc. May's radical definition returns us to Plato: the daimonic is "any natural function that has the power to take over the whole person"; both creative and destructive, it is "the urge in every being to affirm itself, assert itself, perpetuate and increase itself" (*Love and Will*, 123). Coming through the Latin as *genii*, a spirit presiding over our destiny, as genius, it is associated with our generativity, our creativity, in sum, "the unique pattern of sensibilities and powers which constitutes the individual as a self in relation to his world" (*Love and Will*, 125). Eros, the longing for relationship, is a daimon.

Through an ever-heightened awareness refined and stimulated by the writing process, Field seeks both to arouse and to tame her experience of the daemonic, recognizing that by exploring her images, she will answer the primary question this exploration will arouse: "What makes me happy?" This method, demonstrated both in her fairy tale and the interpretive reflection on O'Casey's play, addresses additionally the necessity of suffering, the untranslatable *souffrance* of which May Sarton wrote so eloquently, copying in her journal the words of Louis Lavelle's *Le Mal et la Souffrance:*

> We sense that there can be no true communion between human beings until they have in fact become beings: for to be able to give oneself one must have taken possession of oneself in that painful solitude outside of which nothing belongs to us and we have nothing to give. . . . Nevertheless this solitude into which we have just come, and which gives us such a strong sense of inner responsibility, and at the same time of the impossibility of being self-sufficient, is experienced as a solitude only because it is at the same time an appeal toward solitudes like our own with whom we feel the need to be in communion. (*Journal of a Solitude*, 103)

It also reaffirms the dialectical nature of the image as a reflection of the dialectical nature of our experience itself: "images, those two-faced gods who bridge the gulf between what is spoken and what is felt, between the seen and the unseen, between spirit and flesh, bridge it because they are an outward and visible sign of an inner and private experience. And the impulse to suffer . . . at first glance . . . just a tendency to self-laceration, but which if accepted and understood could lead to a freeing of the imagination from the dominance of the ego" (*An Experiment in Leisure*, 194). The unconscious heaves up both Dis and Adonis, Eros and Thanatos. We invite students always, as we have ourselves been invited, to taste the bittersweet.

Writing, Literature, and Classroom Praxis

It is not without irony that the question of Field's third book—"What makes me unable to do what I want to do?"—leads to an analysis of theories of education and of schools whose contemporary pertinence has, if anything, intensified in the context of the current critical-thinking movement. *On Not Being Able to Paint* explores and extends the conclusion proposed at the end of *An Experiment in Leisure* that engaging in reasoning processes that have no basis in our experience is in fact no engagement at all, simply learned posturing. Her thesis, then, is that the real work of schools is to provide the environment and the guidance through which students can answer the question "What makes me happy?" and in so doing develop both ethical and aesthetic principles upon which their choices and relationships might be based.

The risks of narcissism, solipsism, and real evil in an educational model rooted in "following our images" are not lost on Field, but neither is the contextual dimension to truth that many discussions of the "true," the "good," and the "just" simply ignore. Ameliorating this last (major) problem—adequate attention to context—is one of the functions of literature study in schools, and a primary argument for the intimate relationship between writing and literature in English curricula.

First, the study of literature in writing classrooms teaches us that our images are both our own and archetypal in that they connect our private experience to the mythologies of the known world, that is, to other people's experiences and truths. When she writes that "we must make myths of our lives," May Sarton means just this, that we must seek and affirm the network of relationships in which we (and our images) live, making them neither solely the materialization of our unexamined attachments and desires, nor the ideas that attach to them ends in themselves to be achieved or fulfilled at any cost.

For example, Sarton's garden is real, its "outwardness," to use Field's language about images, "deeply rooted in simple sensation, in the concreteness of colour and shape and texture and sound and movement." But its mythological dimension lies in its ties to experiences that both intimately bind and radically transcend her own: "[The flowers] live and die in a few days; they keep me closely in touch with process, with growth, and also with dying. I am floated on their moments" (*Journal of a Solitude*, 11). Alice Walker's mother makes an extraordinary garden, "a screen of blooms—sunflowers, petunias, roses, dahlias, forsythia, spirea, delphiniums, verbena" and in so doing, says Walker, she is "Ordering the universe in the image of her personal conception of Beauty" (*In Search of Our Mothers' Gardens*, 241). Hawthorne paints Dr. Rappaccini's garden, on the other hand, as no more than the outward manifestation of his poisoned intellect (i.e. his thought and the thing are one and the same). Its flowers are neither genuinely connected to, nor genuinely transcendent of his own experience. The loss of this double meaning of the image is, in Field's eyes, most worrisome—historically it is the frequent excuse for exploitation and violence on a grand scale.

> Instead of vehicles for the communication of inner private immediate experience, [images] had been taken as real in their own right, because to believe in the innerness of

experience was difficult, but to cling to a concrete statement of apparent external fact was easy. The whole history of popular religions could I thought be looked upon as a materialization of the image; and once it was no longer looked on as a truth of spirit, but instead a truth of external fact, then it became the instrument of all kinds of exploitation—lustful, political, social, the instrument of the crudest infantile desire to be king of the castle and to prove that others are dirty rascals. (*An Experiment in Leisure*, 226).

One need only reflect on the medieval Crusades and the means by which the white man took up his "burden" in the nineteenth century to realize how different the image and experience of the cross must have been for women, Jews, Arabs, and blacks from how it was for the white European man on whose shield, sword, and pastoral staff it was emblazoned.

And so the study of literature can teach us ways that others have followed the images we share, and in so doing it can both encourage us on our own quest and teach us a certain humility, a compassionate restraint conceived in the recognition that the personal is political, that the ways we name our experience and ourselves have broad implications for all those who have come before, and for those who are to come. The image mediates in a special way 'the closeness of the world's body to the text's body' (Said, *The World, the Text, and the Critic*), and the closeness of both to our own bodies. So, teaching students Field's method of following the image is helping them integrate their inner experience of self and world, their thoughts about both, and the world to which both are related. Far from merely remaking the world in our own image through a well-imitated rhetorical posturing, or blindly following the images proffered by the material and ideological salespeople of the world, by naming our images we accept "the horrible experience of being muddled" (*An Experiment in Leisure*, 232) that this inevitably invites—writing, drawing, painting, singing, dancing "even though [we] have no certainty of what will come" (235). The muddled uncertainty in which, at least initially, everything is possible is, writes Rolly May, the *sine qua non* of creative process, and certainly inimical to the logician's prescription for the adequate foundation to critical thinking. Writing is an art, and teaching writers is facilitating the kind of encounter and engagement that May says makes art possible. "Dogmatists of all kinds—scientific, economic, moral, as well as political—are threatened by the creative freedom of the artist. This is necessarily and inevitably so. We cannot escape our anxiety over the fact that the artists together with creative persons of all sorts, are the possible destroyers of our nicely ordered systems. For the creative impulse is the speaking of the voice and the expressing of the forms of the preconscious and unconscious; and this is, by its very nature, a threat to rationality and external control" (May, *The Courage to Create*, 84–85).

It might be argued that the (religious) history of American schools, the philosophic influence of Locke's empiricism, and logical positivist models for knowing, along with some rhetorical models derived from classical and neoclassical traditions, have worked against rather than supported positive outcomes from the teaching of writing in schools. Any willingness to confront the "muddle" of which Field speaks, or to risk the intensity of engaged encounter that May calls central to genuine creative process, has been pretty well ironed out of the body/mind consciousness of most freshman students I have taught, largely overcome by the well-learned sense that classrooms—including writing classrooms—are places to which we go for right answers to preexisting questions. In this model, there is not only no new answer under the sun, there is also no new question. Socratic method is perceived (and often used) as a guessing game in which everyone pretends mystification and the fog lifts for the students *en masse* when the long-hinted-at answer is grudgingly revealed by the teacher-expert. The vast succession of rhetoric and composition books continues to suggest the imposition of writing methods from the top down rather than from the individual experience up (or out). The replication of models for exposition and argument that remain without audience or purpose or—most of all—self, designed *by* academics *for* academics to be written by students, few of whom will seek the academic life, intensifies their sense of a closed system whose rules are learned by those with the energy to try to beat it for the real-world experience it will ultimately buy. Aesthetic questions cannot, of course, be separated from the ethical issues these problems raise.

In response to all of these practitioners, Field cites Aldous Huxley's postulate that "Passions and prejudices notoriously prevent men from thinking clearly and acting justly" (*An Experiment in Leisure*, 224). Still, she writes, "If that was what moralists and philosophers had been trying to do for the last two or three thousand years was it perhaps not time to ask why that had so little succeeded, and whether it might not be that they had been using the wrong method?"[15] *On Not Being Able to Paint* proposes a relationship to objects that rejects the separation and detachment of the reasonable mind, and proposes an ethic and an aesthetic in which we are "mixed up with them" (10) in rich and intimate ways. Objects both seen and experienced in this way are transfigured "comparable in a small way to the transfiguration of falling in love" (21). This transfiguration is actualized in the dissolution of edges (16), in the attention to color as "an experience so intimate and vital" that "it must be kept remote and safe from the cold white light of consciousness" (22), and in a kind of seeing that is indifferent to their utility, but "offering a source of delight simply through the fact of being themselves" (21). "Eros is an issue of boundaries," Anne Carson writes (*Eros the Bittersweet,* 30). "[P]ainting," reflects Field, "is concerned with the feelings conveyed by space." Therefore, "it must also be to do with problems of being a separate body in a world of other bodies . . . deeply concerned with ideas of distance and separation and having and losing" (12).[16]

In a way that we frequently underestimate, writing too is concerned with feelings "conveyed by space." To write to someone we care for, to write of something we have experienced, to write for a cause we believe in is a different, and oftentimes more powerful, act than to *speak* to, of, for, any of these. Words also take up space, and in forming them the hand carves out a boundary that announces one's identity to the world. Just as there is loss when the connection between word and song is broken, so also does the predominant conception of writing as technology rather than art suggest the loss of this relationship between word and identity. Without a sense of this relationship, the writer's struggle to paint, and the rich dialectic between writing and painting, is contained rather than liberated by its metaphoric nature. The somewhat sentimental reawakening of interest in calligraphy and the fascination for fonts facilitated by the explosion of word-processing technology are the strange bedfellows of our defense against this loss of a certain connection to the word.

All of this leads to the argument that what Field proposes to enable herself to paint might equally be proposed to enable students to write. The "spiritual dangers" that face the painter face the writer, as well, and I would argue that it is the intuition of these very dangers that blocks student writing. Like painters, writers have to "create the insides of things," not only physical bodies but also "memories, hopes and ideas" (14), a task Virginia Woolf[17] redefined at the beginning of this century when she challenged the false assumptions about the stability of phenomena made by her Victorian and Edwardian predecessors. Like painters, writers must confront the radical instability of the imaginative act this calls for, since in the Einsteinian universe perspective is all, and in the changing play of light and shadow no line is ever fixed. What is held *in* is as significant as what is held out, but the "*play* of edges" (16) threatens chaos. "So I could only suppose," Field writes, "that, in one part of the mind, there really could be a fear of losing all sense of separating boundaries; particularly the boundaries between the tangible realities of the external world and the imaginative realities of the inner world of feeling and idea; in fact a fear of being mad" (17).

If Nancy Chodorow and other object-relations theorists are right in their assessment of the distinctive permeability of women's ego boundaries,[18] and of women's struggles among the possibilities of fusion, connection, and separation, then, like Virginia Woolf, women who write must in their own way *always* be "writing the body" even when their work seems to them, as it did for Woolf, to proscribe this fact. There are numerous pedagogical significances to this proposal. First, it validates as "knowledge" about things *more than* what we have been taught to "think" about them. This latter definition of knowledge I understand as an essentially separated and separating, male-centered epistemology, which affirms value on the basis of how distant we are from the object rather than how close to it we are; it also makes "distance" from the object the much-valued prerequisite to "objectivity" and consequently privileges both.[19] In classrooms this means that we fear students' writing about things that are "too close" to them because we believe this will preclude their ability to think critically (with distance and objectivity) about issues or problems. It means that narrative is inevitably subordinated to exposition. Too often, it means that thinking critically and thinking objectively—without self-involvement—are considered equivalent acts.

The writing of the women I have studied in this book suggests repeatedly that through the body we have the world. Yet women's inheritance in this culture, and in many others, is a radical distrust, fear, often hatred, of their bodies, and repeated exposure to educational models and experiences that invalidate the body's knowing on many counts. Distrusting the body, they distrust also its experiences and the relationships to the world and other persons that emerge from these relationships. The models for writing that we privilege in schools are implicated in this process of invalidation.

In my own classroom, I try to put students back in touch with the world in multisensory ways. I look for assignments[20] that call upon individual memory, especially childhood memory, in the hope that students can use these assignments to recover something of what Ernest Schachtel calls "the concrete abundance of life" rather than "the cliches which society has come to consider as the main stations of life" ("On Memory and Childhood Amnesia," 193). I look for readings in literature that model other writers seeking this, too. I do this because I believe recovering that "concrete abundance" is the foundation for two important dimensions of education—the ability to think critically, and the ability to find joy in the processes of reading, writing, and thinking. Without both of these, the educational experience, particularly as it manifests itself in writing, is an impoverished one, indeed.

Nevertheless, developing trust for our own experiences and the knowledge we learn from them is no easy task. Field's journals and her later commentaries on her entries reflect recurrent images of being engulfed: to recognize the instability of the boundary between things is to recognize the instability of the boundary between selves.[21] Students need to be deeply supported in making this leap. Interestingly enough, bound up with this process is color: "the forboded dangers of this plunge into colour experience were to do with fears of embracing, becoming one with, something infinitely suffering, fears of plunging into a sea of pain in which both could become drowned" (*On Not Being Able to Paint*, 25). In her essay "Sight into Insight," for example, Annie Dillard writes of the newly sighted for whom seeing is patches of color—"the world unraveled from reason, Eden before Adam gave names"—so extraordinarily, painfully brilliant that one young woman kept her eyes shut for two weeks after successful surgery to restore her cataract-blinded sight. One cannot help but wonder if a fearful intuition of this explains the literal colorlessness of so much student prose.

Finally, there is "what we bring to what we see" (Field, *On Not Being Able to Paint*, 27), something that my emphasis upon recovering childhood memory for writing assignments attempts to address. In this world, "unraveled from reason," as Dillard puts it, the concept of "copy" is virtually useless, for it is precluded by the instability of our visual (or verbal) grasp of the thing that we see, and the nature of our distance and separation from it. Everything, in other words, is possible, and no model will really suffice. For many students the confrontation with this might be the most terrifying of all, for in the act of writing—particularly if we follow the image as our method—we often discover what we have always known but chosen not to see.[22]

Elsewhere I have spoken about the classroom as a community of relationship—a sense that is supported by our experience of it as a ritual space. Those relationships are built and enhanced in a number of relatively simple ways. One way is providing multiple opportunities for reading aloud, both from students' own writing and from literary texts. Another is arranging frequent individual conferences times. During these fifteen- to twenty-minute conferences, students read their work to me, with the option to request that I read it to them. As a matter of fact, I never take their papers away from them, either before or after our conferences, unless there is absolutely no opportunity for a conversation over their final draft. We talk as we go, and our conversation is our collaborative work with their text. Revision is ongoing until students decide they are at closure with a piece. Saying the words of their texts out loud both individually and in class is a way of lessening their fear of the words' power and claiming that power for themselves. For example, students can often hear what they cannot see, errors and awkwardness as well as images and constructions that work well. It also supports certain kinds of learning that silent reading does not allow, and is another way of participating in the oral tradition that underlies the writing process.

Finally, I take as many opportunities as appropriately possible to offer students the narrative of how and from whom *I* have come to certain understandings about the literature we read and my own writing process. Elsewhere I lamented the loss to the educational process of the more direct kinds of mentoring that could come from the plastic arts or apprenticeship opportunities of guilds and unions. As a child, I always wanted to know how people I thought were wise got to know what they know. The narratives of those experiences often taught me more than the moral of the story itself. My own narratives are ways that I test the ideas I think I trust; I recount them with the exploratory tentativeness which often remains underneath my certainty of their lessons for me. Modeling this for students and offering them the opportunity to tell their own stories of coming to wisdom can help fill the gap between school learning and the life experiences that have taught them things they need to be able to trust. It lessens the ways that schools privilege "public" versus "private" kinds of knowing—a version of the old split between the domestic world and the world at large. And it gives them yet another opportunity to be narrators—like those in the literature we read—who have something to give to the classroom community where they will spend almost a year.

What follows is an example of this process at work for one of my students, Kathleen Doody.

Narrative As Mediation for the Problem of the Body

Reflecting upon *A Life of One's Own*, Kathleen wrote on a school experience in this way:

> It was a Wednesday afternoon between the hours of 2:30 and 3:45 p.m. I was sitting in my usual front row seat in Smyth 235. Before me was a woman instructor whose carefully chosen words would open up all kinds of possibilities for me. . . .

I distinctly remember her lectures on the power of "NAMING" our experience. She spoke of the "TEXTURE OF OUR EXPERIENCE" so vividly that I began to have small stirrings of feeling inside of myself: I had been closed off to feeling since I was a child. [The teacher] also pointed out through the books we read in class that "WE ARE AT THE MERCY OF WHAT WE BURY."

It is so clear to me now, three years later, that I have been using these three themes in my own life experience. I have learned that by 'FEELING' the "TEXTURE" of my experience, "NAMING" that feeling so that it is not buried away to leave me at its mercy, then I am open to discover the ebb and flow of who I am.

Feeling, naming, writing, and sharing my experiences have totally transformed me—I am finally able to say in all honesty that I have "A LIFE OF MY OWN" !!!!!!!!!!!!!!!!!!!!!

Later in the month, this same student wrote on "silence and family experience" in response to Susan Griffin's book, *Woman and Nature:*

I have been "locked" in silence all my life. I remember an incident in my childhood that is forever branded in my brain. It defines what my relationship to my mother was as a child and still is. That relationship is based on silence—silence towards the "truths" of our realities.

On this particular day I was home from school faking illness which was not unusual for me. No one ever asked why I was so afraid to leave my mom home alone with the babies (there were always two at any one time in my home). No one ever asked because no one wanted to know. I mean why would a father who was sexually molesting me ask me what's wrong? And why would a mother who was too afraid of hearing the truth ask what's wrong? So I feigned illness on a frequent basis with no questions asked.

As I look back, I see myself staring up into my mother's distraught face as she folded clothes from the dryer and put icing on a cake, and ironed my father's uniforms. Every now and then she would nervously glance at me and our eyes would meet fixed in an intense embrace. It would last only a minute, but that look between us told me that mom knew, but also sadly told me that she could not bear to hear the truth—it was communication without words—KEEP SILENT—I cannot handle what's going on—and that silence still remains between us—and she still cannot handle what's going on.

At the end of the term, she wrote: "I feel my life was the substance of this course. Therefore, I chose myself as my project."

The task that this writer has set for herself—to choose herself as her project—led to an extended series of journal entries and pieces of personal narrative that explored the silence she had recognized in that first confrontation with what she was *not*—a feeling, touching person who experienced her world as textured and was able to name the nature of her experience in it. Intuitively, Kathleen begins to follow her images, and they speak volumes about the task she has undertaken. Each class day she comes to the same seat at the same time, sitting in the front row close to the woman speaking words she perceives as "carefully chosen" because they are in fact carefully heard: she has come to believe that they have been chosen particularly for her. Her back remains always to the rest of the class; she never speaks, never looks back. This is, at first, a monologue for an audience of one. She preserves her anonymity and control by adherence to the unspoken rule by which she has been taught to live: what we cannot see is not there. To begin to hear in this carefully chosen way is the first step; "opening" herself to "discover the ebb and flow of who I am" begins the plunge into memory and imagination that will indeed "transform" her. To begin this process, the gates of silence must be "unlocked," the fire of rage and pain that "brands" memory must be named, and the seeing must be "face to face." She is aware of her mother's struggles to smoothe over and cover up what has occurred: clothes are folded, a cake is iced, but neither steel, heat, nor pressure can iron out the deeply etched patterns of this experience. In this memory, eyes, not bodies, embrace. To be separate is the only way to be safe. But to be together is the only way to be alive.[23]

This young woman uses her writing like Field uses her free-drawing—to create the kind of "reciprocity," to use Field's term, between herself and the phenomenal world that enables her to become the active subject of her own experience. In later journal entries, the free flow of memory is looser and less exact than her measured statements here, and

Kathleen begins, once again using the image, to access "my real, core feelings."

> I didn't even have the words to tell—how could I tell when I didn't know what it was? My horror had no language. I have now chosen to sit in the rawness, bare bones of my real life— my real, core feelings.

> Break down this wall, break down this wall—see me—I have a body—look at me—he touched me—here I am, right behind all these bricks and mortar—this is what happened— this is who I am—I don't want to hide anymore—I don't want to be so horrified and petrified behind these walls anymore—please—come and talk to me—I have to tell you so I can be free—When I turn away from the food thinking, worrying, and go sit in the space that's so terrifying and empty, I know this is my healing space where I must sit and feel and feel and cry and rage—

For this woman, for many women, the concept of eros as "an issue of boundaries" is infinitely complex; for her, and for many women, writing the body means that the flesh must first, and at great risk, be stripped— or more often melted—back to the skeletal frame. Walled into a brick cocoon of her own making, both prison and healing space, the place of Dis and of Adonis, the freedom lies in the telling, and the words become the way of taking flesh once again. The request of language is to touch and be touched, to be separate yet connected, to confront and to affirm both the fear and the desire. The cry for the wall to be broken is addressed to a deliberately ambiguous audience—both herself and the unnamed others to whom she reaches out.

Later in this last entry, she shouts, "Medusa will fight!!!," joining her stock of private imagery to a mythic image from the literature we read that was powerful for her, that is powerful for all women. At the close of the semester, Kathleen read portions of her narratives to other students in the course, facing them to end her self-imposed isolation and silence. Through both of these acts of writing and reading, she joined the larger archetype of other women's journey; she began to mythify her experience, engaging it in the safest way she could so that she can finally both own it and be free of it, entering it in order to leave it behind. And she joined her voice with the stories of other classmates who have themselves read and responded to each other throughout the term.

Despite the dramatic nature of this student's text, I believe it is a superb example of the ways that reading and writing personal narrative offers students a literal and figurative means to join the world. Field insists on the image as being central to this work. At the center of *On Not Being Able to Paint* is a chapter called "The Concentration of the Body." In this book, the question "What makes me happy?" has become a richer one: "What makes me whole?" More particularly, in this chapter, it is the question of how "the capacity to make a whole picture" connects "with the capacity to be a whole person" (111), a question central to Virginia Woolf's autobiographical writing and to her fiction. Through reflection on one of her drawings, an angry parrot defending its egg, Field recognizes how ineffectual typical academic learning is in supporting the kind of wide-focused attention that the total concentration of the body involves. By implication, she argues that this is an education of and for partness, not wholeness, that in its bias for "thinking in the public language of words," it drowns out our thinking "in the private language of [our] own subjective images" (123), and that by separating us from our images it separates us from ourselves and from genuine engagement with others and our experience in the world. When she draws, "this satisfaction in gaining awareness of the object as a whole, through the use of repetition and rhythm of symbol, is like the feeling that exercise gives, particularly dancing or skating. In drawing that tree, the spread of the branches and leaves gives an awareness of my shoulders and arms and fingers and I feel its roots in my feet" (107).

It is not without significance that Virginia Woolf speaks of the "rapture" of making things and experiences "real" and "whole," "by putting them into words" (*Moments of Being*, 72), but that she expresses this realization in terms of an image—the flower in the garden at St. Ives—and her appreciation of its significance in terms of painting. "If I were painting myself," she writes, "I should have to find some—rod, shall I say—something that would stand for the conception [of wholeness]. It proves that one's life is not confined to one's body and what one says and does; one is living all the time in relation to certain background rods or conceptions. Mine is that there is a pattern hid behind the cotton wool" (73).

For Field and for Woolf, the necessity is to discover through image, rhythm, and symbol that sense of pattern in which we participate, and in the process to facilitate (by discovering that it exists already) our own integration, our own wholeness. This is a ritual process. Like my student, these women recognized that the free-writing/drawing of their journaling work named and ordered experiences in such a way that gradually, it was less able to hurt them: "both the gods and the demons" Field wrote, "were brought down to earth, their power more ready to be harnessed to real problems of living" (*On Not Being Able to Paint,* 120). "And by the fact of other people being able to share, vicariously, the moment when one's gods had descended, one then gained a firmer hold on the spiritual reality of one's gods—or one's devils. So one came to know more clearly what one loved and would want to cherish in living and what one hated and would seek to eliminate or destroy; and by this one's life developed a clearer pattern and coherence and shape" (121).

Two primary struggles stimulated Field's writing of the studies she later called *On Not Being Able to Paint.* First, the recognition that imitation[24] is not only impossible but aesthetically damaging led her to explore why we are driven to imitate and why resisting this impulse is so difficult (and important). Second, recognizing how tenaciously the educational model in which she has been trained (as have most of us) privileges rational clarity at the expense of the muddled "con-fusion" that marks the engagement of creative process and prefigures scientific method; denigrates "reverie" and "absentmindedness"; and ignores the fear and anger that accompany both our experience of separation and the longing to fuse. Just as a painting's frame separates its form and content from the reality surrounding it, so also is the page on which we write framed in such a way that its space and the time we spend there are qualitatively different from whatever reality (be it conscious or unconscious) that takes its form as text. Here, the object becomes an image, and that, says Field, has made all the difference.

The paradox lies both in the safety and the danger of this fact. As Field's free-drawing demonstrates to her, the engaged writer is both acutely aware of the separation between self and other and involved in a representational process that must belie that separation if it is to be honestly engaged. The implications for education are profound indeed.

> Observations of problems with paintings had all led up to the idea that awareness of the external world is itself a creative process, an immensely complex creative interchange between what comes from inside and what comes from outside, a complex alternation of fusing and separating. But since the fusion stage is, to the intellectual mind, a stage of illusion, intoxication, transfiguration, it is one that is not easily allowed for in an age and civilization where matter-of-factness, the keeping oneself apart from what one looks at, has become all-important. . . . It surely means that education for a

democracy, if it is to foster that true sanity which is necessary in citizens of a democracy, foster the capacity to see the facts for oneself, rather than seeing only what one is told to see, must also fully understand the stages by which such objectivity is reached. In fact, it must understand subjectivity otherwise the objectivity it aims at will be in danger of fatal distortion. (*On Not Being Able to Paint*, 146–47)[25]

Finally, we cannot speak of "safety" or "danger," of "separation" or "con-fusion," unless we speak also of three themes intimately connected with women's writing: hunger, anger, and reproduction. Kathleen's journal powerfully reveals the paradox of her longing for a separate identity, one that would be realized, nevertheless, through the connection for which she also longs. In both real and figurative terms, this is her hunger: to take what is outside in, to fill up the empty space with food, to fill up the empty page with words. The framed page is by her own definition both a "healing space" and a place of rage and pain. It is the place where she empties herself out, and so the place where she fills herself up. Field subtitles part 3 "The Method of the Free Drawings" with the phrase *"Incarnating the Imagination."* "Write your self," cries Hélène Cixous. "Your body must be heard" ("The Laugh of the Medusa," 250). This French feminist proposal that we "write the body," the concept of *écriture féminine*, addresses the longing of Virginia Woolf, and it reflects also the very real, if unacknowledged, way that she achieves this goal. Her challenge to the conventional novel's prose form, like Field's intersection of drawing, journal writing, and self-analysis, combines with the eccentric prose forms of these French writers to suggest the necessity for more flexible models for academic writing, too.

I have argued earlier that like the lyric, women's writing has its roots in an oral tradition, in song, and that their writing reproduces the relationships articulated in these forms. Her free drawings and her reflection about them taught Field that it was possible to bring "the feeling self and the body self" together with the "knowing self" so that one could "feel what one knew" (*On Not Being Able to Paint*, 125–26). She learns from the poet what conventional "detached" prose—what the stance and language of science—can never do alone: she learns that "dictionary definitions and logical grammatical arrangements" can never teach as fully as language that follows the breath, or words arranged "for their qualities in the ear and on the tongue and between the lips" (126). We need to invite studens to an engagement with language and with theory that also offers an engagement with themselves—to teach them, in other words, to experience the relationship among painter, poet and scientist by allowing them to connect the theories we offer them with the lives they live through the nature of the writing processes we make available to them as options for reflection and response.

> Through the process of giving life to the portrayal of one's subject, of coming to see it as a whole through the discovery of pattern and rhythm and so coming imaginatively to appreciate its nature, one is actually creating something, creating the spiritual reality of one's power to love it—if it is lovable; or laugh at it or hate it—if it is laughable or hateful. Ultimately then it is perhaps ourselves that the artist in us is trying to create; and if ourselves then also the world, because one's view of the one interpenetrates with one's view of the other. (136)

What Field offers here gives a whole new meaning to Aristotle's conception of *ethos*. For her proposal is that making the whole text is making the person whole, an essentially reproductive activity in both cases. It also honors what Madeleine Grumet calls in "The Politics of Personal Knowledge" the "spontaneity, specificity and ambiguity of knowledge" (319) and in so doing offers us a basis for finding an ethical guide to behavior and experience that emerges from our engagement in the very story that we tell. For stories "take place"; that is, "[t]he space and time of our lives are not merely a priori categories but are conditions that we share with other people in neighborhoods were we turn the corner and collide, exchange licence numbers, insurance cards and then go home and tell about it, and dream about it, and tell about it and tell about it" (321). Storytelling, which both reflects and shapes our experience, is always about "a negotiation of power" (320). Ontology and epistemology stand next to ethics and aesthetics, and ethnography holds their hands. As writing teachers, what greater gift can we give to our students than this?

"When I use a word," Humpty Dumpty said, in rather a scornful tone, "it means what I choose it to mean—neither more nor less."

"The question is," said Alice, "whether you can make words mean different things."

"The question is," said Humpty Dumpty, "which is to be master— that's all."

—*Lewis Carroll*, Through the Looking Glass

Perhaps the Freudian discovery of the unconscious was merely the cautious start of an epistemological and existential revolution which destroyed the whole rational system installed by the classical age and marked out before it by ancient philosophy. We know . . . how logic and ontology have inscribed the question of truth within judgement (or sentence structure) and being, dismissing as madness, mysticism or poetry any attempt to articulate that impossible element which henceforth can only be designated by the Lacanian category of the real. After the flowering of mysticism, classical rationality, first by embracing Folly with Erasmus, and then by excluding it with Descartes, attempted to enunciate the real as truth by setting limits on Madness; modernity, on the other hand, opens up this enclosure in a search for other forms capable of transforming or rehabilitating the status of truth.

—*Julia Kristeva, "The True-Real," in* The Kristeva Reader

Where language and naming are power, silence is oppression, is violence.

—*Adrienne Rich*

VI

'Re-membering':
Adrienne Rich and the
Problematic of Experience

Introduction

> The unconscious wants truth, as the body does. The complexity
> and fecundity of dreams come from the complexity and fecundity
> of the unconscious struggling to fulfill that desire. The complexity
> and fecundity of poetry come from the same struggle.
>
> —Adrienne Rich, "Women and Honor: Some Notes on Ly-
> ing," *On Lies, Secrets, and Silence,* 188

At a conference where I read parts of the previous chapter, a male
colleague who had listened with obvious care raised the puzzled question
of biological essentialism. "But aren't you afraid that by emphasizing
women's engagement with and knowledge of reproductivity, you will
reduce them to the same biologically determined status from which they
have sought all their lives to escape? Aren't you doing what men have
done all these years?"

The question ultimately chills and warms. The chill of fearful self-
doubt arises from the reminder of how many times this question has
been raised before, most particularly in response to the (I believe widely
misread) French feminist concepts of *écriture féminine* (i.e., to Cixous)
and of *jouissance* (i.e., to Kristeva). (It has always been fascinating to me
how Wordsworth and the Romantics used notions of joy as the ecstatic
product of the male imagination, with all its sexual connotations, without a battling of the collective critical eye.) The warmth flushes from the
shared belly-laugh of Cixous's Medusa, who, in showing the priests her
"sexts" ("The Laugh of the Medusa," in Marks and de Courtivron 255),
in fact defies the reductiveness of the biological peephole through which
women have been viewed, and who gives her lips voice so that in being
heard they can be truly seen. So to affirm the alarms of the body—its
knowledge, its wisdom, its much-denigrated song and dance—is not to

reduce but to expand both our consciousness and our understanding of our own reproductive possibilities.

Naming writing as a reproductive act, I described exultation in their own reproductivity as a metatheme of many women's narratives. I soothed my puzzled colleague with the reminder that reproductivity was not merely a biological activity, but a broadly based sociocultural activity, a fact that our penchant for novelty and our denigration of ritual relentlessly obscures. His reaction revealed how narrow the accepted cultural (male) definition of reproduction has been. It revealed as well the underlying fear that he and other men would be denied access to reproductive experience if women claimed it as their own. In fact, he looked finally relieved when I reminded him that, when it is appropriately (broadly) defined, men have access to reproductivity, too.

As I write this, the voice of another male colleague, who was glancing at a copy of Adrienne Rich's essays, echoes in memory: "That's the trouble with so many of these books about 'women's things'—there's so much blood in them." As it happens, the blood of which Rich speaks is intimately connected to bread: hers is a book about the connection between revolutionary politics and poetry, a book in which the body politic is deeply implicated but not by any means her sole focus.[1] Still, both men's reactions revealed their similar fear—one rooted in feeling shut out, the other in a rueful and humorous repulsion by what he had to mess with, by what he had to be implicated in.

Adrienne Rich makes three claims about writing that respond to these men. First, she says that writing is about the discovery and expression of the body's truth; second, that poets seek the images that express and access the body's truth for those who seek it; and third, that "fecundity" and "desire"[2] are predicated upon the fierce honesty of this search. Inevitably, the images that write the body and the language that expresses the "complexity and fecundity" of its desires will be critical to understanding writing as a reproductive activity. Writing classrooms must be places where students and teachers are primarily aware of this critical opportunity that writing makes available to us. This chapter is about some ways we can cultivate that awareness.

The first opportunity to explore the meaning of writing as a reproductive act emerges from Adrienne Rich's lessons about writing. In the face of a vast cultural silence in which she says women themselves have been complicit, Rich seeks a language that will enable her to write the body. To do this means challenging the adequacy of the grammar, syntax, and styles of discourse in which language and power have been institutionalized and by which women have been inscribed and colonized. To write the body is to insist upon the significance of context, the radical subjectivity of knowledge, and the epistemologies that describe its process and content. To write the body is to affirm the validity of narrative, to argue that narrative complements, and is indeed *primary* to, exposition and argument in the storyteller's exploration of truth and its contexts. To write the body is to make a place for oneself in the culture's mythmaking tradition. Writing the body, women resist the cultural imperative to validate our brothers', fathers', and sons' stories before our mothers', sisters', and daughters', and further that they resist the demand to repudiate those stories when they do not sound like our own. And doing this means that they have the courage to tell their *own* stories. In both the listening *and* the telling, we become attuned to the silence that marks what is unspoken, and to our own complicity in refusing to hear. Rich's work ultimately suggests that when we read and write the body, we learn resistance to any text—including our own—that tests truth in the abstract and repudiates the embodied truth of plain and ordinary things. These materials form the agenda of this chapter.

Adrienne Rich: Writing As a Reproductive Act

Inevitably, the first problem is silence.

I often ask students to write about a schooling experience as some piece of literature we read might evoke it for them, a technique I learned from my colleague Madeleine Grumet. Reflecting on her experience in traditional college classrooms, Maureen, a student in my feminist theory class, explained her speechlessness this way: "I used to think I had nothing to say because the things they talked about didn't have anything to do with me. Now I know they had a lot more to do with me than I ever wanted to admit." Often, we allow ourselves to be silenced, silence ourselves, because our unconscious intuits our potential to discover what we would prefer not to know. When Rich speaks of women's complicity in their own oppression, this is one part of what she means. The writing process offered Maureen an ephiphanous moment that illustrates an important point about facing the causes of her silence, and facing her own complicity in maintaining it. Later, writing about her family, she described her father as a man behind the newspaper, the man whose chair was to be vacated immediately when he came into the living room to read. This writing exercise offered her yet another opportunity to reflect on the consequences of her silent acquiescence to his authority, and to negotiate the ambiguous territory of respect, love, and subjection to an equally wordless male power. Rich explores much of the same territory. Reading Rich's work as she wrote helped Maureen to feel less alone, and gave her a narrative tradition to which she could join her own voice. In all of this, however, she never writes about her mother—not once.

From this example comes a generalization: recognizing writing as a reproductive activity means that we admit our colony's connection to the parent country, but refuse to privilege the parent. "When language fails us, when we fail each other/there is no exorcism," Rich writes. But "absolute loyalty was never in my line/once having left it in my father's house" ("Rift," *A Wild Patience Has Taken Me This Far*). As the inheritance of our father's house, language must stand as a reminder that our mother was there, too, more often, more intimately, more concretely, than our father may have ever been. She had a language of her own that it is our charge to recover, a mythic story that she waits for us, not to replicate, but to reproduce.

> And did you ever tell me
> how your mother called you in from play
> and from whom? To what? These atoms filmed by
>   ordinary dust . . .
> to which we must return simply to say
> this is where I came from
> this is what I knew.
> ("For Memory," *A Wild Patience Has Taken Me This Far*)

Women need to remember that they are their mothers' daughters, too. What does this mean for women writing? It means that while we have inherited our fathers' forms, it is our mothers' hungers with which we will fill them, and eventually, under the pressure of the content that we pour into them, the forms will no longer serve. In her essay "When We Dead Awaken: Writing as Re-Vision" (1971), Rich reflects upon her experience as a writer through the lens of her remembered experience as her father's daughter, her husband's wife, and as the child of American higher education. To revision these relations is for Rich more than an autobiographical exercise, it is "an act of survival" (*On Lies, Secrets, and Silence*, 35) that she suggests is a necessity for every woman. For, "Until we can understand the asumptions in which we are drenched we cannot know ourselves." (35) Until our students can understand these assumptions, connected writing—authentic writing—cannot occur. We must offer them opportunities to write in ways that allow access to this material in themselves.

The recognition that she wrote always for a male audience (her father, her professors, "the Man"—the idealized literary master) led Rich to a dawning understanding of the formal emotional and psychological consequences of this reality. Anger is buried in the effort not to displease this audience—to achieve the perceived control that, we have learned, formal art requires—most often because it has gone unrecognized for so long. The rhetorical consequences of this denial included for Rich a choice of forms that offered extraordinary kinds of control of rhythm, rhyme, and meter, the rejection of an openly first-person voice, the adoption of a persona (sometimes male) when the first-person voice was engaged, and a tone that flattened out even the deepest feelings. But the conflict between woman and artist showed itself inevitably in her choice of subjects: the Norman invasion seen from Mathilde's court in the famous tapestry made there; many kinds of needlework threaded with unnamed anxiety; starry nights full of fire and ice; conflict-ridden relationships; the demands of children and household; histories of other women's lives called out of anonymity in an epic catalog of literature, science, and history.

In an early poem, Rich had found in Bach an "antique discipline" that "Renews belief in love yet masters feeling/Asking of us a grace in what we bear." Young and afraid, she could argue then that "A too compassionate art is half an art" and, without formal restraint, the heart was "else betrayed" and "too-human" to be acceptable in this classical model of aesthetic decorum ("At a Bach Concert," (1951), *Poems Selected and New*). The terms of mastery appear again in the same book, in the poem "Aunt Jennifer's Tigers," in which a young niece fantasizes her aunt dead, lying in her casket with hands, bearing the "massive weight" of uncle's wedding band, "ringed with ordeals she was mastered by." In this same poem, the rigid order of the needlepoint canvas and its endlessly replicated stitchery is defied by its content: tigers "sleek," "chivalric," and "certain," "prancing, proud and unafraid." In this first book, the catalog was Melville, Mahler, Plato, "expert men/Who do not reckon horoscopes/But painfully extend their ken/in mathematical debate" ("From the Conjunction of Two Planets," (1951), *Poems Selected and New*). Later it becomes daughter-in-law; mother-in-law; Hattie Rice Rich (paternal grandmother); Mary Graveley Jones (maternal grandmother); Emily Dickinson; Ethel Rosenberg; Simone Weil *(A Wild Patience Has Taken Me This Far)*.

By 1955, "To work and suffer is to be at home" ("The Tourist and the Town"), the disillusioned young protagonist of "Living in Sin" wakens to an indifferent lover, banging taps, and daylight shining through grimy window panes on the scattered table-scraps of the night before; soon, "back in love again," she waits nevertheless through another night for "the daylight coming/like a relentless milkman up the stairs." In the midst of the Italian sun, there is autumn, winter, age, change, and death, and only death, at last, gives a wife "an existence of my own" ("The Perennial Answer," (1955), *Poems Selected and New*). Although she maintains a tight regularity of rhyme and meter, the forms, some clearly derivative of Frost's dramatic monologue, become longer and more complex.

In the ensuing eight years, the visual rhetoric of her pages reveals a great deal: the anger that has smoldered in the previous two books bursts through the voices of personae, its only container a thinly veiled irony. The first-person voice announces itself: "Piece by piece I seem to reenter the world." Here the two archaic figures, "a woman and a man," again confront "The old masters," who by now "haven't a clue what we're about" ("In the Evening," (1966), *Poems Selected and New*). No center holds: man and woman, woman and woman, man and man, are at war. Neither inside nor outside is safe, if for different reasons: the hearth is showered by frozen geodes, and star fire burns cold above a volcanic earth, the very walls of the house bleed and every dream becomes a nightmare. Its imagery is volcanic, explosive, the texts begin to fragment and finally to shred, and Rich begins to do what she says every writing woman must: confront the myth of the "exceptional" woman who is enabled by her "specialness" to work in the (male) artist's world, confront the myth of Woman as she emerges in books written by men. In "Snapshots of a Daughter-in-Law," she both wields the camera and is its subject, all framed by the two-sexed epic catalog of the namers—Diderot, Samuel Johnson, Baudelaire—and the named: Boadicia, Dickinson, Wollstonecraft, Corinna, Ovid, mother, daughter, daughter-in-law. If we are to know who we are, can be, we must know the assumptions in which we are drenched: "belle," "harpy, shrew and whore."

The risks of allowing ourselves to be privileged by the term *exceptional* are great. In this poem, such privilege pits woman against woman in "The argument *ad feminam*/all the old knives/that have rusted in my back, I drive in yours/*ma semblable, ma soeur!*" In her later theoretical writing, Rich would argue that academic women must recognize themselves as the "required exceptions used by every system to justify and maintain itself" ("Toward a Woman-Centered University," *On Lies, Secrets, and Silence,* 127). Almost twenty years later, this kind of tokenism is far from dead; once inside such a system, women must work actively to subvert its curriculum, "its subject, lines of inquiry, method" ("Toward a Woman-Centered University," 141). Often, this means reading and writing about persons and experiences who are not on primary or secondary reading lists. It means reading and writing in ways and forms with which these subjects have not been addressed before. It means recovering documents—personal correspondence, diaries—that fall outside the categories of male-defined art and science, as well as public documents—novels, essays, poems—suppressed by the critical and economic collaboration of male writers and their publishers.[3] In these documents, an alternative history, epistemology, ontology, often lie; these will change forever the way we read and write about the malestream, and about ourselves. Above all, it means that no woman's story can be repudiated because it is different from our own, because its knowledge or the behavior it describes are incomplete or inadequate to current theory or practice, because it fails to meet aesthetic criteria developed by and for a class élite, or because the life it reveals is beyond our ken. To be our mothers' daughters is to hear the voices of her mothers, her sisters, our daughters, our nieces—our sisters in the profoundest sense.

One of the most exciting developments in classrooms of the eighties and nineties has been the return of nontraditional students, women who have with us all of these relationships just named, and more; women whose own stories are so rich and diverse that they will change forever the way we read and write about other women's stories and about ourselves. One of the most disheartening developments is how little their wisdom is valued by the younger women in these classrooms, how difficult it is for these young women to hear their anger or to validate its causes, how deep is the denial of ongoing causality in their own young lives, with what insidious effectiveness they have learned the response inculcated by so many years in an academic system that silences by rendering irrelevant that of which it is most afraid. More disheartening still is the ongoing inability of these women most disenfranchised by the system to find their stories in these classrooms: women of color and lesbian women.[4] As teachers, to be our mothers' daughters and be among these various groups of women is to provide opportunities for them to write, read, and talk about each other's work, to help them generate an epic catalog alternative to the traditional canon, and to help them generate criteria to make the painful and realistic judgments about that catalog that will prevent it from becoming romanticized, sentimentalized, or subject to the same nonquestioning nostalgia that inscribes that canon.

For the temptation to sentimentalize or the willingness to settle for the insubstantial in the name of nostalgia, Rich saves her harshest criticism. In "Snapshots of a Daughter-in-Law," she charges that our collaboration with our own invaliding has caused us to settle for "mere talent . . . glitter in fragments and rough drafts." Later, the legacy of nineteenth-century "Heroines"

        exceptional . . . by a collection
            of circumstances
                soon to be known as
                    class privilege

haunts her:

        how can I give you
            all your due
                take courage from your courage
        honor your exact
            legacy as it is
        recognizing
            as well
                that it is not enough?
    ("Heroines," 1980, *A Wild Patience Has Taken Me This Far*)

Of the abolitionist, she writes in "The Spirit of the Place" (1980, *A Wild Patience Has Taken Me This Far*) "it was not enough to name ourselves anew/while the spirit of the masters/calls the freedwoman to forget the slave."

This last statement is a powerful ethical principle upon which our conduct in the writing classroom rests. Engaging our students in a writing process and supporting their journey toward voice is teaching them to read and teaching them an awareness of themselves as readers—of everyone and everything—including themselves and their experience in the world. Indeed, Rich's question of her nineteenth-century "Heroines" is one that informs all of our interaction with students in writing classrooms: how do we put them in touch with the persons and things that mark their "legacy," drenched as these things are in memory and desire—and give them still more—the capacity to read these experiences with a compassion to belie the alien nature of Otherness that every reader must overcome if the act of reading (and so of writing) is to be authentic?

In this task, the kinds of literature read in classrooms and the kinds of writing that support their study are critically related to each other. The current outcry that emphasizing multiculturalism and diversity (categories that have come to include questions of gender, too) will shred the very fabric of the American character (too much *pluribus* and too little *unum*, writes Arthur Schlesinger)[5] can be well answered by curricula that establish a dialectic between texts that have long had a voice in American classrooms and those that are determinedly shouldering their way in. The technique of pairing texts, common now in classes that raise questions of gender, race, and ethnicity, is a provocative aid to offering students multiple points of view about single experiences. For example, reading the autobiographical novels, short stories, and personal narratives of Jamaica Kincaid, an Antiguan-born American writer, enables students to revision the colonial novels of Joseph Conrad or E. M. Forster in radical ways. Students' understanding of the complex interaction between Jim, a runaway slave, and Huckleberry Finn can be widened and deepened when it is read as a complement to the slave narrative of Harriet Jacobs.

Writing in the course can also model shifting points of view and multiple ways of defining the truth of our experience. The relationship between writing and identity making is a powerful one, and students need to see that there is room for the way they look at experience, and room for the way others see their own. They need particularly to see the connection between personal and collective memory. This was brought home in a graphic way when I used a portion of Harriet Jacobs's narrative from Mary Helen Washington's collected edition, *Invented Lives.* In connection with some writing we had been doing about childhood memory, we began a discussion about the significance of knowing our personal and cultural pasts, and about the pain as well as the joy of this knowledge. In response to a question about the difficulties of some kinds of knowing, one young black woman suddenly sobbed: "It means knowing that your grandmother was raped, and having to deal with it all your life . . . " I think that one sentence taught a largely white class as much as any interpretation of the reading could. It brought together the idea of *an* experience and *the* experience, and she made their knowledge real by the telling of it.

In a short essay called "On Seeing England for the First Time," Jamaica Kincaid describes the hazards of pretending that there is only one reality, one truth. The English colonial experience of her native Antigua—an experience that offered England and all that was English as "our source myth"—resulted in what she describes as "my erasure." The utter silence of her schooling about any reality other than an English one is a dramatic way of assuring the oppression and suppression of a colonized people. But there is another, more complex effect that Kincaid describes that bears upon the argument of this book.

> The space between the idea of something and its reality is always wide and deep and dark. The longer they are kept apart—idea of thing, reality of thing—the wider the width,

the deeper the depth, the thicker and darker the darkness. This space starts out empty, there is nothing in it, but it rapidly becomes filled up with obsession or desire or hatred or love—sometimes all of these things, sometimes some of these things. That the idea of something and its reality are often two completely different things is something no one ever remembers; and so when they meet and find that they are not compatible, the weaker of the two, idea or reality, dies. . . .

In me the space between the idea of [England] and its reality had become filled with hatred, and so when at last I saw it I wanted to take it into my hands and tear it into little pieces and then crumble it up as if it were clay, child's clay. (16)

Rather than too much *pluribus* and too little *unum*, the effort to maintain the silence of those things that describe experiences other than the canonical reality might become the guarantor of the very distorted thinking and feeling we seek to avoid by claiming a single truth. Even more powerful is Kincaid's understanding that the "difference" of her reality is predicated upon the body's experience of it. The English books she read in school offered a geography of "gentle mountains and low blue skies and moors over which people took walks for nothing but pleasure" (14). Antigua was a world where "the sun shone with what sometimes seemed to be a desperate cruelty" and a walk was "an act of labor, a burden, something only death or the automobile could relieve" (14). Kincaid's writing traces through things the evolution of desperately formed opinions that are the foundation of prejudice. I believe the ethics of writing classrooms demand that we offer students opportunities to read and write, not merely to reinforce the closed systems of their own words, but so that they can recognize both the relative context and the collective potential of the things they hold most dear.

A recent Charles Schulz cartoon makes this point eminently clear. Reading from the Bible to his sister in the presence of their dog, Snoopy, Charley Brown tells the story of Sodom and Gomorrah, ending with the infamous fate of Lot's wife, turned into a pillar of salt. "But what," Snoopy asks, "happened to their dog?"

Finally, for teachers, developing effective criteria for evaluation is imperative. As Rich argues, it is not enough to settle for the sentimental or the bathetic simply because the writing expresses intense personal experience. The classical rhetorical tradition has articulated very well what some of these criteria are, and is particularly explicit in insisting on what Quintillian called *enargeia*[6] as the *sine qua non* of effective narrative. There is no better way to cultivate this quality in narrative than teaching students the vitality of the image: the expression of their connection to plain and ordinary things that makes a reader feel she has not only heard the story but experienced it, too. Reproducing their own images, they reproduce their experiences for us—and for themselves. Doing this in a context where both formative and summative evaluation is applied can be a valuable learning experience in which judgments of the self's *expression* are separated from judgments of the self—one of the most important lessons any writer/self can learn.

Pedagogy, Curriculum, and Resistance

The second issue, connected to this first problem of silence, is the nature of mythmaking and its relation to culturally received images. Just as the capacity to read and write women's experience involves confronting the inverted myths that have defined them, so also must women confront their image in a mirror held up by men. The importance of this image in women's experience cannot be underestimated. Citing Lacan's understanding of the "mirror stage" of identity formation, Muller and Richardson remind us that between six and eighteen months "an infant first experiences itself as a unity through experiencing some kind of reflection of itself, the paradigm for which would be self-reflection in a mirror." In theory, the infant identifies with this reflection " 'in the full sense that analysis gives to the term: namely, the transformation that takes place in the subject when he assumes an image.' It is this reflected image of itself with which the infant identifies that Lacan understands by the 'I' " (*Lacan and Language,* 29). For our purposes here, there are four attending consequences of the identification that Muller and Richardson point out in Lacan's description.

First, "the essential function of an image is 'in-form-ation,' *i.e.* "giving *form* to something—whether this be the intuitive form of an object as in knowledge, or the plastic form of an imprint as in memory, or the form that guides the development of an organism. . . . [T]he image is a form that in-forms the subject and makes possible the process of identification with it" (28). We become, in large part, what we think we see. Second, images are constelled with each other in complexes through which "images are established in the psychic organization that influence the broadest unities of behavior: images with which the subject identifies completely in order to play out, as the sole actor, the drama of conflicts between them" (28). Unlike Freud, Lacan sees complexes as largely social rather than biological and thus instinctual. Our becoming occurs in a contextual network that is greater than just mother or father, but clearly begins there. Third, the mirror that reflects the infant's form need not be a literal physical one, but is often a person and generally *the* person who functions as its mother. Last, the reflection the child sees imaged in the mirror is an inversion of him or herself, and stands among images of other subjects with which the infant also identifies. We are, in fact, captivated—held captive—by the images of ourselves that we see, misidentifying ourselves with them. Identity begins here—in misidentity. As exemplary of this, Lacan points to early language stages in which infants speak in the third person before the first, and "The child who strikes another says that he has been struck, the child who sees another fall, cries" (32). From this distorted "social dialectic" comes our understanding of the self as "fictional." So also, I would propose, does the narrative by which we seek to mediate the gap between ourselves and the inverted images we see in the mirrors where we find ourselves.

In curriculum there is little respite, offering as it does an ongoing narrative marked by women's silence or by gendered subjects reinforcing woman's role as victim, outcast, eccentric, spinster, prostitute, or some combination of all the above. Without feminist paradigms to reread these texts, the average high school student finds the story of adolescence remains largely a male adventure told through the eyes of J. D. Salinger and James Joyce and Ernest Hemingway. Emily Dickinson becomes a writer of short little poems about trains and snakes (never mind that there were fifteen hundred of them) whose unrequited love caused her lifelong, well-protected spinsterhood; in this model for the artist-adventurer, her writing can't hold a candle to the expansive sexuality of Walt Whitman. Tess D'Urberville is hung, Jane Eyre marries in the end; Miss Havisham is permanently deranged when her affianced leaves her at the altar, and Agnes becomes David Copperfield's "Angel of the House."

Pedagogy reinforces the problem. The first mirror is mother, but she speedily disappears from children's educational experience. The data on self-esteem and academic confidence in women graduating from high school is dismal in its record of how precipitously both decline during their high school years.[7]

Inverted and fictional already, the images of themselves women see pose a double problem, for them, well-articulated by Christine de Pisan in her *Book of the City of Ladies*. How could it happen, she wonders:

that so many different men—and learned among them—have been and are so inclined to express both in speaking and in their treatises and writing so many wicked insults about women and their behavior. (3–4)

. . . . .

I finally decided that God formed a vile creature when He made woman, and I wondered how such a worthy artisan could have deigned to make such an abominable work which, from what they say, is the vessel as well as the refuge and abode of every evil and vice. . . . I detested myself and the entire female sex, as though we were monstrosities in nature. (4–5)

Christine's experiential knowledge includes many interactions with "princesses, great ladies, women of the middle and lower classes, who had graciously told me of their most private and intimate thoughts" (4). She says repeatedly that she has observed nothing in their nature or character that remotely resembles the claims of male canonical scholarship. Yet her reading evokes such emotional abjection, she prays at first that she might have been born into the world as a man.

How does one begin to seek to untangle the real self and forge a new identity from an inversion of an inversion? Turning from the canonical mirror in which she has been schooled to see herself and other women, Christine looks into an alternative mirror held up by her own Reason, allegorized in *The Book of the City of Ladies* as a woman accompanied by two other women, Rectitude and Justice. The text itself is an alternative canon of queens, princesses, scholars, goddesses, weavers, tapestry makers, good (if ordinary) women, offered to Christine by this mythical fairy godmother, in fact a commonsensical reminder from herself *to* herself about her own experience as a woman and a scholar. In short, Christine becomes her own fairy godmother, teaching herself—and us—in the allegory of this book how to read again, and how to respond in writing to the arguments that would keep women silent. How then can this mirror, a pervasive and restricting image in women's lives and in the literature about them, be reread?

The power of the mirror as an image in literature about women suggests the extent to which the larger (male) culture has presumed women's narcissistic self-examination. Indeed, the sometimes-realized potential for sentimental self-absorption presented in and by the journal form has often been a criticism for its categorization as an (inferior) social document and therefore as something other than art (and thus its general exclusion from canonical literature). In "Orion" (1965), *Poems Selected and New,* Rich writes:

A man reaches behind my eyes
and finds them empty
a woman's head turns away
from my head in the mirror
children are dying my death
and eating the crumbs of my life.

In this mirror there is no familiar face, but a stranger's, and the horror of this realization can be first paralyzing, eventually exhilarating. In Lacan's theory, both men and women move through, and pass beyond, the mirror stage. But stringent cultural efforts to maintain a woman's infantilization include maintaining her captivity by an image in the mirror that she does not hold. Yet in a real way this is *not,* as we are told, narcissism. At this pivotal point in Rich's development as woman and poet, she realizes, standing before the domestic mirror, that the head she sees there has never been her own, that few women indeed could reenact Narcissus's deadly plunge because the image they see is rarely theirs. For even when they hold it in their own hand, despite the fact that it was first maternal, all too soon the mirror from which they read becomes the surrogate of the male eye in which the text of self must be read and the text of identity negotiated and written. Thus

When to her lute Corinna sings
neither words nor music are her own;
only the long hair dipping
over her cheek, only the song
of silk against her knees
and these
adjusted in the reflections of an eye.
"Snapshots of a Daughter-in-Law,"
(1958–60, *Poems Selected and New,* italics mine)

Like the gardens in which they have also been placed by men's texts, so too have women gazed at themselves for centuries in the mirror of men's reflecting eyes. But women, too, suffer these "adjusted" reflections, in Rich's pun both their *vision* itself and their *thoughts* about what they see. The problem for narrative arises when we understand that it is these very "adjusted" reflections that become the markers of the story women will tell about themselves.

Milton's narrative of Eve's self-introduction to Adam is a fitting paradigm for women's double bind. Seeing her own image, a pleasing

"Shape within the watery gleam" of an Edenic lake, Eve is warned away
from her "vain desire" by a (theoretically angelic) voice that calls her to
Adam and to her biological destiny: "hee/Whose image thou art, him
thou shalt enjoy/Inseparablie thine, to him shalt bear multitudes like thy
self" (*Paradise Lost,* IV, 461, 471–74). Eve is at first repelled, but when
Adam calls out to her and takes her hand, the "smooth watry image"
that had so attracted her fades: "I yeilded, and from that time see/How
beauty is excelld by manly grace/And wisdom, which alone is truly fair"
(IV, 489–91). Eve finds a new mirror—in Adam's eyes.

But in the nineteenth century, Lewis Carroll invents a girl so fascinated by her own image that she leaps into the mirror that shows it to
her—leaps into a dimension of herself that most of us fear—and learns a
method of operating in its inverted world in order to defy the very
inversion to which she is subject there. The dream begins, in fact, with
her defiance: "Oh, what fun it'll be, when they see me through the glass
in here, and can't get at me!" (*Through the Looking Glass,* 9). Associated
by the White Queen with the image of a volcano, Alice takes immediate
possession of the ink pot and the pencil, exerting her superior physical
strength to control the king's memorandum. The house represents for
her the world where she must submit to all kinds of authority, not the
least of which is to stay back from the warm hearth. Returning there, and
consequently ending her adventure into adult autonomy, Alice overtly
resists at all costs. She has an individual educational plan of her own
making that no classroom or governess is going to impede. In this inverted world, the house (and all the demands for conformity it represents) intervenes multiple times, magically, frustratingly, blocking the
way in her effort to get to the garden. But Alice remains resolute. Once
she arrives there, she is astounded to discover that the flowers talk "when
there's anybody worth talking to" (15), and, indeed, they talk to her.

Yet despite her commitment to this adventure and to defiance of
the first world that the looking glass reflects, she repeats with facility its
well-learned creed about the connection between language and power.
Asked by the Gnat if insects in her world answer to their names, Alice's
reply is a telling one:

"I never knew them to."
"What's the use of their having names," the Gnat said, "if
they won't answer to them?"
"No use to *them*" said Alice; "but it's useful to the people
that name them, I suppose. If not, why do things have names
at all?" (30)

. . . . .

"I suppose you don't want to lose your name?"

"No, indeed," Alice said a little anxiously.

" . . . only think how convenient it would be if you could manage to go home without it! For instance, if the governess wanted to call you to your lessons . . . she would have to leave off, because there wouldn't be any name for her to call, and of course you wouldn't have to go, you know."

"That would never do, I'm sure," said Alice: "the governess would never think of excusing me lessons for that. If she wouldn't remember my name she'd call me 'Miss' as the servants do" (32).

Alice's dreamy leap through the looking glass takes her into a world where there is at least the opportunity to see and know in a different way, a world where a Pawn can become a Queen. It is a tantalizing image among the catalog of mirrors in which women find themselves reflected. But the rules of Carroll's chess game are very much those that Alice learned as a child of that first world from which she comes; while she nevertheless dreams herself physically inside the looking glass, she remains still the little girl gazing into it from the other side, extraordinarily ethnocentric down to the proper intercourse of mistress, teacher, and servants, and finally unable to determine whether the Red King was in *her* dream—whether the dream was *hers*—or whether *she* was in *his* dream, and thus the dream was *his*. Humpty Dumpty sums it up in a single sentence about who owns language: "The question is, which is to be master—that's all" (66).

Traditional criticism sees Carroll's book as extending to his character Alice a "last fling at childhood" (*Through the Looking Glass,* xii). The paradox is that she perceives the invitation as an offer of adult adventure—an opportunity to become an adult by escaping adult power. As such, *Through the Looking Glass* can be read as a kind of paradigm for a pedagogy of the repressed. Alice rejects the stifling demands of domesticity and schooling that keep her infantilized and warn her from the place too close to the fire that adults must inevitably risk. The role of Pawn is as tiresome as the role of child, and Alice wants, after all, to be Queen— that is, to share, and then usurp, the power of the king. The series of steps she takes are themselves paradigmatic of Western notions about child development; they are predicated on separation from the domestic sphere (i.e., from mother), a separation assisted by schooling at the hands of surrogate mothers (and fathers) in the looking-glass world, and, finally, engagement with the wide world "out there" as far away from both school and domesticity as possible.

Echoing Humpty Dumpty, whose language is it, anyway? That question of whose dream—whose image it is—haunts Adrienne Rich's poetry and her poetics. Like Alice, she repeatedly leaps through the looking glass to examine the inverted realities that are reflected from there back to her, to examine herself and the identity that has been cultivated for her there. Confronting the assumptions we are drenched in means plunging whole-heartedly into self-exploration. But it also involves rejecting the charge of narcissism, a charge that holds women captive by enforcing cultural pro-scriptions making self-affirmation a matter of disinterest if not dismay. For Rich's keystone is that the personal is political: we examine ourselves in the cultural images that begin to emerge from the mirrors of early life, in our mothers' eyes, in her songs, and in our fathers' language—in the language that those songs become. In so doing, we become in fact least narcissistic of all, because this examination—like the question "What makes me happy?"—must lead inevitably to a critique of the culture in which those images reside and of which they are the expression. The assertion of the continuity of self and world is a primary defense of narrative and explains its survival as a chief means of imparting knowledge and wisdom in cultures outside of the West. It also explains the extent to which narrative operates as cultural critique and consequently must be denigrated when mass culture's demand for conformity makes the power of narrative—especially personal narrative—too great to be tolerated.[8]

The Classroom through the Looking Glass

Going to school gets heavy billing in America as a child's first step toward adulthood. Despite the prevalence of day care as the (now) most literal first separator of mother and child, the symbolic value of this first day remains paramount, and the battle for primacy between what "mommy says" and what "teacher says" is engaged the moment a child lets go of mommy's hand at the classroom door. Here, the child quickly learns that experiential knowledge and the narratives that so often express it—the ways of the domestic life—will be gradually undervalued and, in time, repudiated as inadequate to the educational enterprise. Repudiating this way of knowing and telling, children will inevitably repudiate the images and rhythms that mark their identity as *connected* persons in the world.

Just as the knowing is denigrated, so also will its telling be. Schools are places where reading and writing (and arithmetic) are the chief lessons to be learned, so they are also places where school*work*—the work of becoming literate—is privileged and orality inevitably denigrated. This fact and its implications cannot be stressed enough. In their study of silence as it relates to knowledge and voice, Belenky and her coauthors warn that

> Language—even literacy—alone does not lead automatically to reflective, abstract thought (Scribner & Cole 1981; Sigel & Cocking 1977). In order for reflection to occur, the oral and written forms of language must pass back and forth between persons who both speak and listen or read and write— sharing, expanding, and reflecting on each other's experience. Such interchanges lead to ways of knowing that enable individuals to enter into the social and intellectual life of their community . . . without tools for representing their experiences, people also remain isolated from the self. (*Women's Ways of Knowing*, 25–26)

Lev Vygotsky and his colleagues speak of "exterior dialogues" as necessary to "inner speech and an awareness of one's own thought process," arguing that "play itself is a precursor to symbolization and meaning making." Crucial to the argument of this book is the injunction that "Growing up without opportunities for play and for dialogue poses the gravest danger for the growing child."[9] Play provides children with their first experiences in creating metaphors, where an object and the children's actions combine to suggest other objects and events" (*Women's Ways of Knowing*, 32–33). It is a book about the significance of "plain and ordinary things" as the raw materials of the images in dialectical relation to which self and identity are formed. The numbers of women found to be truly "silent" in their ability to access and express the voice of self was small in the study by Belenky and her coauthors, yet gradations of their self-described "deafness and dumbness" are present in every poor writer I have taught.

The denigration of experiential knowing and the narrative that represents it is coupled in contemporary schools with reference to "symbols and metaphors . . . dissociated from the concrete referents, actions and experiences that the symbols stem from and express (Greenfield 1972; Greenfield and Lave 1982; Scribner and Cole 1973, 1981)" (*Women's Ways of Knowing*, 34). Schools remain places where the authority of the teacher's voice (first or finally) silences all others—where genuine dialogue is at least artificial, if not difficult or impossible. And eventually they become places where the story of the dominant culture, told by the privileged few, drowns out even the most resilient students' belief in the validity of their own narratives.

> While the lack of dialogue and the dissociation of language from experience is problematic for all children, concentrating on the written forms of the language before children have developed proficiency in wielding oral forms is likely to be tragic. The silent women had limited experience and confidence in their ability to find meaning in metaphors [and] were lost in the sea of words and numbers that flooded their schools. For them school was an unlikely place to "gain a voice." For them the experience of school only confirmed their fears of being "deaf and dumb." (*Women's Ways of Knowing*, 34).

Earlier in this book I argued through the stories of preliterate people the significance of recovering the concept of song—particularly our mothers' songs and the wisdom those songs express. As Lacan's model for development suggests, the loss of this primary oral tradition parallels the demand—in the name of separation—that our connection to the first image of ourselves in our mother's eye be severed as well. Drawing children from orality to literacy, schools actively support both of these demands. The research on women's ways to knowing asks us to confront the cost of the theory and pedagogy that informs our choices about schooling and curricula.

So what can we learn by reading about Alice? Rushing through the looking glass in search of experiential knowledge, she nevertheless learns little, turning a deaf ear to the realities that offer themselves with this kind of knowledge: separation, love, death. Her dream of the looking-glass world is an extended dialogue with all kinds of creatures who seek to draw her into an adult's engagement with language. The gentle Gnat's message is finally that death is a permanent reality of life, but that we are far more able to construct reality through language and the choices we make as we play with it than we might perhaps believe. Thus his insistent effort to teach Alice how to make jokes. His earlier dialogue is silenced with the same resistance to this world's ways of knowing that is the hallmark of Alice's response to what he and the others offer her.

> "Well if she said 'Miss' and didn't say anything more," the Gnat remarked, "of course you'd miss your lessons. That's a joke. I wish *you* had made it."

"It's a very bad joke."

But the Gnat only sighed deeply, while two large tears came rolling down its cheeks.

"You shouldn't make jokes," Alice said, "if it makes you so unhappy." (*Through the Looking Glass*, 32)

This is a world, much like life, where apparent nonsense can make the greatest sense, a world "riddled" with metaphor and paradox where one must run very fast simply in order to stand still, go one way in order to go the other, where many riddles have no answers. That she insists on the primacy of her governess and her lessons—of received knowledge as opposed to the experiential knowledge of which she has "dreamed"—says a great deal about the comfort and safety of the "real" world before the glass.

How safe should schools be? On the one hand, in the nature of the process they offer and the means by which they allow students to access their own knowledge through telling and finally writing narratives of experience, I would argue that schools should be places of great safety. On the other hand, in recognizing and honoring the risk that such a process involves, because of the pain and madness this invitation to narrative can often invite, I would argue that schools should be places of great risk, and so by definition radically unsafe—if safety means, as I believe it often does, supporting and rewarding conformity. In this critique, then, I would argue that writing classrooms should be at once the "most—and least—safe places of all.

I must reiterate that I do not believe this to be a narcissistic enterprise. Writing of the relationship between the individual, her writing, and politics, Rich offers this summary reflection: "Trying to construct ideas and images afresh, by staying close to concrete experience, for the purpose of alleviating a common reality that is felt to be intolerable—this seems to me fair work for the imagination" (*Blood, Bread, and Poetry*, xi). From the narrative tradition, we can learn that there are many kinds of politics, and by teaching them to participate in this tradition, we can teach students their connection to the body politic in which the individual body belongs. When the Buddha enunciated a first principle that "all life is suffering," for example, he enunciated a political reality that came from a highly personal process—years of practicing *zazen* (following the breath), still and alone, under the bodhi tree. The tradition that represents this principle and a number of other realities that attend to it, like the experiences of change and loss, is told largely through *koans*,[10] apparently paradoxical formulations, riddles of a sort, often beginning with a dialogue between a teacher and a student, which are very concrete in the solutions they suggest to this common reality of suffering that we share. Narrative power resides in the images of concrete experience, and following our images, like the Buddha following the breath, is a powerful act. Schools need to enable students to do this; writing classrooms are superb places for this work—this play—to occur. Above all, the kinds of reading that happen there—reading of students' texts, readings of short stories and diaries and personal essays, memoirs, autobiographical narratives—can invite students to affirm and engage themselves with the wisdom of their culture and that of others. They learn how it is accrued, how it is transmitted, how to develop a community of elders and peers, how to take from it and contribute to it. They learn that they are not alone. And all of this is ritual.

Before returning to Rich, I would like to offer one last example of this point.

Meinrad Craighead is an artist and mystic whose book *The Mother's Songs: Images of God the Mother* is an exquisite collection of her paintings accompanied by personal narrative material. As a child separated from her grandmother by the distance from Chicago to Little Rock, Craighead began to draw in response to one of those political realities we all face: "to assuage my loss of her." She introduces her book this way:

God the Mother came to me when I was a child and, as children do, I kept her a secret.

Instinctively I knew that this private vision needed protecting; my identity, my very life depended upon its integrity. But as she guided me as an artist, illuminating my imagination, her presence in my life could not really be veiled. She erupted in my imagery. And it is as an artist that I am compelled to reveal this secret life we have shared for nearly fifty years.

My grandmother was a storyteller. I remember the telling. Lying in her arms, I heard her voice gather in the rhythm of the front porch swing, the night chorus of cicadas, the flashes of the fireflies in the boxwood hedge. I remember her voice but not many of the stories she told me. My imagery originates here, not in the memory of verbal content but in the pulse beat I learned from her body and the breath of her dark imagination which I still feel in the wonder of the natural world.

I draw and paint from my own myth of personal origin. Each painting I make begins from some deep source where my mother and grandmother, and all my fore-mothers, still live; it is as if the line moving from pen or brush coils back to the original Matrix. Sometimes I feel like a cauldron of ripening images where memories turn into faces and emerge from my vessel. So my creative life, making out of myself, is itself an image of God the Mother and her unbroken story of emergence in our lives.

Craighead's narrative summarizes and exemplifies all that has come before in this chapter. It is a powerful example of the process of following the image, and what can be achieved when we allow ourselves to do it, and support students to do the same. It expresses the reproductive quality of this activity and affirms Lacan's insight that identity comes through the ways images of ourselves are reflected back to us through constellated complexes that are part of early childhood experience. And it suggests a way out of the puzzle by which women must seek a voice for their own experience—an experience drenched in the interaction of mothers and daughters—that will be actualized in their fathers' language. For the images that form her "myth of personal origin," as Craighead's narrative makes explicit, lie in the place of memory that is "before" or "behind" the language with which her grandmother told her stories: "not in the memory of verbal content, but in the pulsebeat I learned from her body and the breath of her dark imagination which I still feel in the wonder of the natural world."

Finally, in her language is also the answer to the charge of narcissism, an answer that lies, paradoxically, in the concept of *écriture féminine*—the text as body and the body as text. The personal becomes mythic and consequently *more than personal* through the agency of the image; when the imagery is organic, as is often the case in women's texts, it becomes the agency of connection among the personal, the natural, and finally the supernatural. This is the experience of those engaged in ritual behavior. In Craighead's grandmother's voice, pulse and breath are also the rhythm of the cicadas' chorus and the firefly's flash, and, in the midst of the world's apparent chaos, the myth of origins—the "unbroken story" that every culture seeks of the god "ever emergent" in our midst—in this case, of the mother god long-silenced by the father's omnipresent voice.

Alternative *Herstories* and the Writing Classroom

In the context of a lecture on feminist history, Rich asks the question: "What, then, is the meaning of history if one is a woman?" ("Resisting Amnesia," *Blood, Bread, and Poetry,* 145). Her response to her own question becomes in effect a prescription for what it means to *write* feminist history:

Our theory, scholarship, and teaching must continue to refer back to flesh, blood, violence, sexuality, anger, the bread put on the table by the single mother and how it gets there, the body of the woman aging, the pregnant body, the body running, the body limping, the hands of the lesbian touching another lesbian's face, the hands of the typist, of the midwife, of the sewing-machine operator, the eyes of the woman astronomer, of the woman going blind on the transistor assembly line, of the mother catching the briefest expression on the child's face: the particularity and commonality of this vast turbulence of female becoming, which is continually being erased or generalized. (154–55)

I believe that before students can learn the history of culture, they must learn personal history and engage themselves in writing processes that encourage and allow them to do this. Jonathan Edwards articulated the Puritan belief, long ingrained in the American character, that understood history as the individual writ large.[11] This has become the impetus for the autobiographical impulse recording lives of the great men—heroes—of the American experience: Benjamin Franklin, Thomas Jefferson, Paul Revere, George Washington, Abraham Lincoln—the list goes on. And it has fueled the image of the archetypal American hero, a radical individualist, a white-skinned loner, accompanied (if at all) by a dark-skinned, loyal (if inferior) sidekick painted in silhouette against the backdrop of an apparently boundless frontier and an ideology of manifest destiny. To this tradition and to this way of writing history, Rich's response is direct and clear: "it is not enough" ("Heroines," *A Wild Patience Has Taken Me This Far*).

Of her own struggle to record the alternative herstory of "heroines" she will say as well, "it is not enough." Why this is so suggests yet another dimension of the problem of otherness that Rich explores in this poem—and elsewhere: when the privileged class writes the narrative of those who cannot speak for themselves, or when those of that class write their own narrative, they write always from the position of privilege, and inevitably from the position of an Other. There is, in other words, a dual problem of locus and of language. Rich's irony is double-edged when the word *privilege* appears in "Heroines":

> You are spared
> illiteracy
>   death by pneumonia
>   teeth which leave the gums

the seamstress' clouded eyes
          the mill-girl's shortening breath
by a collection
          of circumstances
                    soon to be known as
class privilege . . .

"[Y]ou begin speaking out/," she says of/to her "heroines,"

and a great gust of freedom
          rushes in with your words
yet still you speak
          in the shattered language
                    of a partial vision . . .

Rich's work as a poet is very much focused upon addressing this dual problem: how to bridge the gap between self and other, how to find a language that will appropriately represent this effort. We need to offer our students this same awareness, as well as the opportunity to experiment with ways that will help them deal with these same issues. We need to help our students "relocate" themselves. In academic institutions, I believe students experience a profound sense of their own otherness. Too often, schools feel for students like places where teachers work, places where teachers belong but students are invited only to visit for awhile. Indeed, the ways schools canonize knowledge and control its dispensation reinforce students' sense of being privileged, if sometimes bored, voyeurs.

The writing classroom is no different in this regard. Little, for example, is taught of a now-rich cross-disciplinary theory about the writing process itself. Enormously significant work has been done, providing teachers with insight regarding their students' and their own writing processes, but little is ever shared with students in freshman writing classrooms except in the partially digested form served up in the repetitive plethora of rhetoric and composition textbooks. In order to trust the knowledge that is applied from it, students need some understanding of the theory from which the knowledge has come, and they need to test both in the context of their own experience. Trust is the forerunner of connection, and in trusting our connections, we learn to trust ourselves.

With support, students are capable of reading theory and using it to reflect on their own processes, learning in the process to become apt theoreticians in their own right. In short, I believe students should be encouraged, especially early on, but also throughout, to write (and talk) about what writing has been, is, and is becoming for them.

Rich's comments in this regard are fascinating, turning as they do upon the question of trust. In an essay on her experience of teaching language in an open-admissions situation at City College of New York, she comments astutely: "The whole question of *trust* as a basis for the act of reading or writing has only opened up since we began trying to educate those who have every reason to distrust literary culture. For young adults trying to write seriously for the first time in their lives, the question 'Whom can I trust?' must be an underlying boundary to be crossed before real writing can occur" (*On Lies, Secrets, and Silence*, 64). Her comments reinforce the thesis that much can be learned by novice writers from reading the work of many groups, especially the work of those "on the margin" who have nevertheless been educated in the mainstream. Women are the primary reference group for this book, although there are obviously numerous others. These are groups who have learned a certain articulateness about their distrustfulness, and hearing their ambivalence articulated can help students begin to understand some of their unease with the educational system and with the writing they do in that system. The work of Jamaica Kincaid about her own education in the British system, cited in the previous chapter, is an excellent example of the kind of reading I am describing.

Young people—not only (but especially) young women—have much to mistrust in the ways that literacy has functioned in relationship to language: indeed, their naiveté and cynicism about the politics of language are of a piece, and these conjoin with a preference for the image that is equally naive and cynical. Together, they are powerful explanations for why so many eschew a command of written or spoken language, but most especially confrontation with the ethical responsibilities such a command, such a gift, entails. The most obvious answer to the question "Whom can I trust?" is "myself." Yet a precious few can answer with the determination of Ann Bradstreet: "I am obnoxious to every carping tongue/Who says my hand a needle better fits."[12]

Over and over again as a writing teacher I have found myself in situations where unwittingly, through the assignments I made or the responses I gave, I have talked students out of rather than into trusting themselves. While I believe it is unethical practice to lead students into a blind and uncritical trust of their own language and ideas, it is equally unethical to use the model of received knowledge to cow them into submission to a syllabus or class agenda, to render them so mistrustful of their own experience that they can never say "myself." Like Rich, I believe the solution lies less in prescription of books or even methods than it does in the capacity to create a community of collective wisdom where each student's experience can be turned over—tongued, if you will—to find a fit as part of the whole. Communities of wisdom are very much a part of oral traditions, and the search for them is not incoherent with the impulse to write personal narrative, itself always an extended exploration of the question of trust.

In their simplest form, such communities might resemble those from which the songs of oral poets came. Speaking of their songs, Alfred Lord notes: "in a very real sense every performance is a separate song; for every performance is unique, and every performance bears the signature of its poet singer. He[13] may have learned his song and the technique of its construction from others, but . . . the song produced in performance is his own. . . . The singer of tales is at once the tradition and an individual creator" (*The Singer of Tales*, 4). Gathering in private homes, coffee houses, taverns, marketplaces, at weddings and festivals, singers take the occasion for song as a chance for reward—approbation, money, food, or drink. This occasion offers the community an opportunity to affirm its tradition and learn the theme and variation of its own tradition and that of others. Their strong sense of audience leads singers to assess carefully what songs will please and consequently garner the desired reward.

Their apprenticeship is marked by three phases. First, they sit aside while others sing in order to learn character, place, event, and theme as well as the rhythm both of singing and thought. In the literate context, this is the phase of the naive reader-listener, the early weeks when a class is first coming together over their own and others' texts. The tasks of this period involve primarily the establishment of trust, along with a common method and language for listening and responding to each other. In the second phase, would-be singers open their mouths to sing. The primary enterprise of this phase involves "fitting thought to rhythmic pattern" (22). In the literate context, it might involve learning the rhythms of basic sentences and their variations, not necessarily content-based but expression-based formulas. The imitative quality of this stage is initially marked in the literate tradition by the desperate sameness of many freshman papers, but in later stages, as students become more free to experiment with basic phrases and rhythms, it marks the beginning of their discovery of their own voices. The third phase in an oral poet's apprenticeship is marked by "an increase in repertory and growth in competence," beginning from the "point at which he sings his first song completely through for a critical audience" (25). The songs they can sing multiply, and the songs they know are refined, not as acts of memory but of composition and recomposition. In the literate tradition, this is the process of revision in the hands of a skilled writer.

I have returned again and again to the issue of orality in this text because its importance is repeatedly reiterated in the tradition of the wisdom community out of which this book comes. Becoming literate, we have both gained and lost. What we have lost becomes clearer when the "technologization of the word," to repeat Walter Ong's phrase, becomes so pervasive and (paradoxically) specialized that we are less and less able to talk to each other, less and less able to speak about our own experiences or to count on an ongoing viable connection to those of others. A culture obsessed with specificity in what is *said* can, ironically, cease to recognize, or care about, what is *meant*. Narrative in such a culture becomes largely irrelevant. Furthermore, such a utilitarian view of language, one that I believe many schools support, can, equally ironically, block rather than encourage revision: if we have said what is necessary to communicate the message, the incentive to enhance or enrich meaning, or to evoke context, is surely limited. This may indeed explain why, so frequently, students say "You know what I mean."

And so in the shift from oral to written "texts," we understand the intent of what is written to be unlike the intent of the oral performance, "not . . . the recording of a moment of the tradition, but as *the* song" (*The Singer of Tales*, 125). In the name of specificity, context and all that goes with it is irrelevant, and this is a great loss. Under these circumstances, the formation of genuine community—let alone the cultivation of its collective wisdom—is impossible.

Speaking of her own translation and recording of Quechua songs, those of an Andean tribe with whom she lived, Regina Harrison puts it another way: "Their songs, beautiful in their own right for their melodies alone, also articulate indigenous cultural values and allow us to enter their world" (*Signs, Songs, and Memory in the Andes*, 4).

> In these pages, the selection of historical texts, linguistic analyses, stories, and songs should not overshadow the personal enthusiasm of the "telling of the tale" in a manner that does not alienate the "other," that very human person who may wear a poncho or a necklace of jaguar teeth. In the process of understanding the Quechua-speakers' system of values we may come to embrace the mystery of our own selves, which we often neglect in the pursuit of our own revered objectivity. "Sing, sing your own song," my Quechua-speaking friend coaxed me after she explained her visit with her song mentor,

the *ukumbi* snake-woman. Her careful teaching, combined with my hours in libraries away from the tropical forest, enables me now to sing those words with some measure of their profound significance. (4)

"Trust yourself," the message of her friend, the Quechua singer, emerges in Harrison's negotiation of oral and written traditions. I believe that classrooms should also be places where this relationship is negotiated. In short, I believe that classrooms, particularly writing classrooms, should be places where written texts are addressed as oral performances over and over again, where students read their own work and the work of others, where how it sounds counts as much as how "correct" it is, where voice is a living thing and not merely a literary—or literate—concept. The mutual interdependence of reading and writing suggested here is critically important. Students need to hear and overhear themselves, each other, and other singer-writers, before "voice" has any real meaning in their experience as writers—and persons. Indeed, the relationship among hearing, speaking, reading, and (by implication) writing to human knowing and being in the world is so important, that when oral-auditory language areas are destroyed, normal reading becomes impossible (Gardner, *Frames of Mind,* 87).

The negotiation of the personal and the political, central to feminist work, is finally what both this discussion and the activity it describes are about. Indeed, the same separation between the private and public worlds that has maintained women's oppression has functioned to support false dichotomies for appropriate kinds of academic writing. This separation has allowed schools to valorize and privilege that which irons out the subjective experience from the truth a subject seeks to tell. When the private voice seeks access to the text, it challenges the system, it threatens change. The assumption, sadly, is always that change will mean loss. The reaction is resentment, anger, resistance. Women who have a story to tell have faced this reaction over and over again. Adrienne Rich puts it this way:

> The fear of change thus intersects with a fear that lucidity and love cannot coexist, that political awareness and personal intensity are contradictions, that consciousness must dissolve tenderness, intimacy, and loyalty. Lucidity, political awareness, and consciousness are equated with intellectual nihilism, with depersonalization, with the spirit of objectification. This is itself a measure of the way in which Western culture in its

intense patriarchalism has polarized thought and feeling. In a society so dismembered, anonymous, and alienating, tenderness and intimacy are precious and rare and—apart from all other forces which oppose feminism—it is no wonder that people fear the loss of what emotional intensity they still have. ("Husband Right and Father Right," *On Lies, Secrets, and Silence*, 216)

Elsewhere, Rich has written, "All silence has a meaning" ("Disloyal to Civilization," *On Lies, Secrets, and Silence*, 308). As I write this, I am reminded of the long silence that followed my own years as a graduate student, of my certainty that my scholarship could reside only in my teaching—that I was not nor ever would be a "scholar," in the circumscribed way I had learned to think of that term, that so much of what I had written in those graduate years was a skillful fraud, a sleight (and slight) of tongue. I had heard there no voices remotely like what I imagined my own might be, experienced no literate context in which I could imagine making significant contributions. It was a problem of locus and of language—largely, though not wholly, without malicious intent. And it silenced me for many, many years.

What we do not recognize as part of our own experience we inevitably impose upon others as a silently agreed-upon norm. I believe that for a period of time at least, through my own unawareness, I silenced my students as I was silenced before them.

A good teacher can inspire awe at her knowledge and skill. I have come to believe that this is no compliment, for in this culture awe functions most frequently as an invitation not to access or participation, but to distance and to silence. Awe is a value of a particular brand of patriarchal culture, and it has no place in schools. I do not want my students to believe that they can be like me any more than I want them to believe they can never attain the kinds of knowledge that I have, or can attain only this kind of knowledge. I want them to believe, always, that they can be and know *more* and *differently* than I do, and my greatest joy is their triumph in doing this.

Thinking Back through Our Mothers

I look at my face in the glass and see
a halfborn woman.
    (Rich, "Upper Broadway," (1975, *The Fact of A Doorframe*)

Almost a quarter century separates this poem and Rich's first efforts to impose the order of men's forms on her own feelings. Ten years separate her from the mirror that reflected a head her poetic persona could no longer identify as her own. In the interim, she muses upon "The humble tenacity of things/Waiting for people, waiting for months, for years" (1974, "From an Old House in America" *The Fact of a Doorframe*). The ritual quality of her poetry is distinguished in two ways: by her persistent commitment to recovering and renaming the persons and relations—private and public—that inform women's history and experience, and by her repeated invocation of "plain and ordinary things" ("From an Old House in America"). Both of these distinguish themselves by the ways they express Rich's overweening interest in looking for the silences and exposing their meaning.

"We think back through our mothers, if we are women," Virginia Woolf had written a half century before (*A Room of One's Own*, 79). Lacan suggests that the first mirror is mother, yet prevailing theories of child development, predicated upon the importance of separation and the child's attraction for the father's (public) world, fall silent about an ongoing role for this first object of a child's fascinated attention. In her discussion of curriculum, Madeleine Grumet expresses it this way:

> Lacan's account of the relational triangle collapses into a dyad. In his account . . . the symbolic overwhelms the imaginary, and even though the child continues to look for the mother in the forms of the father's culture, the gratification of that look is forever deferred. For the father, or "phallus" in Lacan's account, is merely the marker for that power we attribute to someone else, always imputed to another—the father, the word, the law, the state, the science, the deity—but never realized. This account makes the third term an unrepentant murderer, destroying the illusion of completion given in the dyadic romance of mother and child and never providing the compensation it promises. Lacan accomplished both matricide and patricide, and because Lacan has effaced touch and sound, his domain of the "real," even though it contains the imaginary and the symbolic, loses the world and reduces culture to nostalgia. (*Bitter Milk*, 108)

Yet of even greater importance to a secure sense of self is the child's relation to her or his mother before the father enters the mother-child dyad. Nancy Chodorow's work offers us a cautionary tale related to earlier stages of the child's development, counterbalancing traditional theory's emphasis upon the stage where father intervenes. As infants grow less "absolutely dependent," "The mother is no longer interchangeable with any other provider of care. . . . The developing self of the infant comes to cathect its particular mother, with all the intensity and absoluteness of primary love and infantile dependence. . . . Separation from her during this period, then, brings anxiety that she will not return, and with it a fundamental threat to the infant's precarious sense of self. Felt dependence increases as real dependence declines" (*The Reproduction of Mothering*, 68). In summary, "Father and other people are important as major constituting elements of the 'reality principle,' and as people enabling differentiation of self and differentiation among objects. Yet it is the relation to the mother, if she is primary caretaker, which provides the continuity and core of self, and it is primarily the relation to her which must be worked out and transformed during the child's earlier years" (71).

Too often, schools collaborate in the loss or distortion of this mother-child relation. As Grumet points out, when the maternal (domestic) gives way to the symbolic (public), the material goes with it. This "development" is reflected in the distinction that arose in the relations between master and apprentice, teacher and pupil.

> Apprentice and master were engaged in a similarly purposeful yet barely rationalized relation where the work literally *at hand* defined the dimensions of their task. In contrast, the relation of the contemporary teacher to student has evolved into one which, though less clearly instrumental, has become more self-consciously intentional as the press of material necessity seeps out of schooling. Teachers and students manipulate signs and symbols. The medium through which we communicate is knowledge, the codes and methods of the academic disciplines, by now highly abstracted from the material necessity and politics that originally shaped them.
>
> . . . . .
>
> The purposes that pulse through a family's labor—the blanket that is spread, the dish that is washed—or through the work of the apprentice and master—the glass that is blown, the bricks that are laid—mark their shared attachment to the world. The material, sensual presence of the world draws the one who teaches and the one who learns to each other as they approach it. (*Bitter Milk*, 107–8).

I believe that in this century we are reaping the cost of this dematernalization/dematerialization of education. I believe that this loss is most evident in writing classrooms—that it explains our students' broken texts, their struggle with critical thinking that requires substantial and substantive connection-making, and the bleached, sparse quality of their narrative efforts. I believe as well that it explains the resistance to validating experiential knowledge and the forms of writing that express it as fit objects of study or practice in higher education. And with Grumet, I believe that these are problems of intimacy: "if touch and sound are the sensual passages between parent and child and world, those modes of contact are associated with an intimacy that we limit to erotic or familial relations or to some strenuous forms of labor. In contrast, the look dominates the classroom. As centralized and efficient urban schools draw large numbers of students together, intimacy diminishes. Touch is avoided, and sound is muted in the corridors of the nation's schools" (*Bitter Milk*, 111). Sadder still is our collaboration in this process; in the name of "classroom management," "the look of pedagogy as it has evolved in schools repudiates touch. The teacher is untouchable, invulnerable. . . . By arranging students in rows, all eyes facing front, directly confronting the back of a fellow's head, meeting the gaze only of the teacher, the discipline of the contemporary classroom deploys the look as a strategy of domination" (111).

As I read Grumet's remarks, I cannot help but remember my own discomfiture with a day as the "sub" in a third-grade classroom where the little girls had already been socialized to be quietly—or rather, disquietingly—still, and the little boys squirmed in captive desperation. Intuitively, I was unsure which group—boys or girls—was more imprisoned, my despair less a function of my inability to exert control than it was a function of my desire to make them free. I feel that same discomfiture in the college classroom with the distance that separates my position in "front" of the class, a physical but, more profoundly, psychological reality that no circling of chairs ever seems to mediate. I reach out naturally to touch every person that I meet, the laying on of hands a way to affirm that the greeting is more than *empty* ritual, *is* ritual indeed. In the classroom I chafe at the lost opportunity that was the particular grace of "master" and apprentice, an opportunity to touch that only the writing conference offers enough potential intimacy to actualize at times, and in these times only with a guarded care. I want my students to be touched by what they learn. I want more for them than metaphor. I want them to know the thing itself.

The project of this book has been to learn about writing by reading women—by reading their texts and exploring the ways they use those texts to read themselves. The women I have spoken of argue that if we are to recover the material, we must recover the maternal. This is the meaning of Virginia Woolf's statement, and it informs the ways she works with language and with the image in her fiction. The question "What makes me happy?" leads Joanna Field to a method for "following the image" and to a theory of education radically embedded in the material reality of her own experience. The difficulties and self-doubt they express along the way are a function of how powerful the enforcement of silence about the nature of women's experience has been. Adrienne Rich's gloss on this problem is bitterly direct:

If I remind you of my father's favorite daughter,
look again. The woman
I needed to call my mother
was silenced before I was born
("Reforming the Crystal," 1974, *Poems Selected and New*)

In her poetics and in her poetry, hearing the silence that follows the period when mother is mirror, Rich attempts to formulate a theory of identity constructed on connection, not separation from her. The fact that much of this work is done in the context of examining lesbian existence offers her readers another opportunity to address the problem of otherness as they learn more about the process of those who write "from the margins" of what this culture has defined as the "tradition" of human experience. In her essay "Compulsory Heterosexuality and Lesbian Existence" (1980) Rich argues that the "eroticization of women's subordination" is less an expression of men's " 'fear of women' and of women's sexual insatiability" than it is a fear of denied access. "It seems more probable," she writes, "that men really fear not that they will have women's sexual appetites forced on them or that women want to smother and devour them, but that women could be indifferent to them altogether, that men could be allowed sexual and emotional—therefore economic—access to women *only* on women's terms, otherwise being left on the periphery of the matrix" (*Blood, Bread and Poetry,* 43). The kinds of fearful connections between men and women formulated as the salve to this fear have distorted for all of us what the possibilities might be for a rich and fulfilled connection to the material/maternal. We have learned too well a leap to metaphor, to mastery, when the thing itself frightens us by its resisting, embodied being-in-the-world. The organization of schools and the pedagogies that inform our work there reflect this longing for control. Rich's poetry argues over and over again that our connection to things is what will set us free. No ideas without things: the classroom as a ritual space: this is the real work of schools.[14]

Orality, Memory, and Classroom Praxis

No one who survives to speak
New language, has avoided this:
the cutting away of an old force that held her
rooted to an old ground
the pitch of utter loneliness
where she herself and all creation
seem equally dispersed, weightless, her being a cry
to which no echo comes or can ever come.

At the psychological center of this pellucid poem, "Transcendental Etude" (1977, *The Fact of A Doorframe*), Adrienne Rich places one line: "a whole new poetry, beginning here." In the poems that precede it, she shows us how to come to this place, this work, modeling for teachers and students the importance of visions and the ways to trace them, find them, sing them. To find the texture of our experience again, to draw and keep it "at hand" to "re-member" (Rich's word) it, and ourselves, we must seek the things that make it what it is because they made us who we are. Rich's poems begin always with the texture of her experience with things. We must show students how to do the same. In "From an Old House in America," "the carcasses/of old bugs crumbled/into the rut of the window" give way to "rusted screws, this empty vial/useless, this box of watercolor paints/dried to insolubility . . . this pack of cards with no card missing/still playable/and three good fuses/and this toy: a little truck/scarred red, yet all its wheels still turn." (*The Fact of A Doorframe*)

In the catalog of the useful and the useless, we find the materials for a narrative that will enable us to connect the material (semiotic) and the symbolic, making the leap to metaphor a substantial one, and in this leap a model for the kind of critical thinking that roots us in our own experience, yet multiplies available perspectives and connections. The connection to things in Rich's work is expressed with a kind of tenderness, her catalogs in poem after poem no mere list but a lesson in the laying on of hands. When the leap to metaphor comes—as it does in this and each of her poems—it is vested in the compassion that the connection to things has taught. Connecting them to her, refusing alienation as a condition of affirming their difference, their otherness, paradoxically

enables the connection to persons that negates false categories of time
and space:

> All my energy reaches out tonight
> to comprehend a miracle beyond
>
> raising the dead: the undead to watch
> back on the road of birth
> ("From an Old House in America")

Rich refuses the kind of separateness that necessarily renders us alien
from whatever is "other," and her refusal is a compassionate one. Perhaps our students are such poor critical thinkers because we spend so
much time on *problems* of difference that we neglect to examine the
presumptive *definition* of difference as alien as a problem of itself. We
neglect, in other words, to help students cultivate the kind of compassion
that real connection, which honors difference, is about.

It is a perpetual problem of context, a perpetual dialectic between
things and theories about them. Echoing Bachelard, Rich recognizes in
things yet another paradoxical version of "intimate immensity":

> The enormity of the simplest things:
>
> . . . . .
>
> These things by women saved
> are all we have of them
>
> or of those dear to them
> these ribboned letters, snapshots
>
> faithfully glued for years
> onto the scrapbook page
>
> these scraps, turned into patchwork,
> doll-gowns, clean white rags
>
> for staunching blood
> the bride's tea-yellow handkerchief
>
> the child's height penciled on the cellar door
> In this cold barn we dream

> a universe of humble things—
> and without these no memory
>
> no faithfulness, no purpose for the future
> no honor to the past
> ("Natural Resources" (1977), *The Fact of A Doorframe*)

I have argued throughout this text the importance of memory and desire being palpably present in writing classrooms. Rich argues, and I join her in the argument, that if they are to be real, these must be embodied: "a universe of humble things—/and without these no memory" ("Natural Resources"). New writers need to know that others have sung before them. This remains a particular problem of women's experience in classrooms. The disparity between the reality of women's lives and what the texts of the Western canon have said about them is a specter each new writer must face. It did not go away when Christine de Pisan constructed her "city of ladies." And it is intimately bound to the agenda of separation from mother, an agenda pervasive to most developmental theory. Rich writes about it in this way:

> At most we're allowed a few months
> of simply listening to the simple line
> of a woman's voice singing a child
> against her heart. Everything else is too soon,
> too sudden, the wrenching-apart, that woman's heartbeat
> heard ever after from a distance
> the loss of that ground-note echoing
> whenever we are happy, or in despair.
> ("Transcendental Etude")

Her response is to propose multiple ways of constructing texts of relationships, texts that address the problems of memory and of desire as they emerge from the mirrors of our mothers' eyes, and from those held up by men who have told us what we should see there. Things are the key to memory, the overt manifestation of our desire for connection and our recognition of the salvation that lies in affirming it. Things give us, through the network of memory, access to the mirror of our mothers' eyes where we first found ourselves. In this context, grammar, syntax, and styles of discourse that have described—and inscribed—us can be deconstructed, and a space for a recontextualized experience can be realized. To "write the body" is to write this experience.

Everything else seems beyond us,
we aren't ready for it, nothing that was said
is true for us, caught naked in the argument
the counterpoint, trying to sightread
what our fingers can't keep up with, learn by heart
what we can't even read. And yet
it *is* this we were born to. We aren't virtuosi
or child prodigies, there are no prodigies
in this realm, only half-blind, stubborn
cleaving to the timbre, the tones of what we are
—even when all the texts describe it differently.
("Transcendental Etude")

In her essay "Women's Time" *(The Kristeva Reader)*, Julia Kristeva responds to why contemporary women's artistic aspirations have turned so strongly to literature. Her response takes the form of three questions illuminating the "revolution in poetic language" she first wrote about in 1974 in her doctoral thesis. Her questions propose that literature counterposes the socially normative with "a certain knowledge and sometimes the truth itself about an otherwise repressed, secret and unconscious universe," in short, that its imaginative space "of fantasy and pleasure" is a wonderful place to play, counterposed as it is to the "abstract and frustrating order of social signs, the words of everyday communication." That women identify themselves with these possibilities in poetic language suggests for Kristeva a good deal more than their desire to possess the phallus by possessing the pen. More appropriately, she argues, it "also bears witness to women's desire to lift the weight of what is sacrificial in the social contract from their shoulders, to nourish our societies with a more flexible and free discourse, one able to name what has thus far never been an object of circulation in the community: the enigmas of the body, the dreams, secret joys, shames, hatreds of the second sex" ("Women's Time," *The Kristeva Reader*, 207).

The operative concept in Kristeva's text is "nourishment," and it is the operative word for this book's proposal, too. Kristeva does not romanticize the maternal in a way that suggests that invoking this original mirror might offer a magic cure to broken lives or broken writing. Nor do I. Like Rich, Kristeva appeals for a "more flexible and freer discourse"—an appeal for what she calls "*a signifying space,* a both corporeal and desiring mental space" in which the core violence (what I have called the "brokenness") of the human experience can genuinely be recognized and addressed.

What I mean is, first of all, the demassification of the problematic of *difference,* which would imply, in a first phase, an apparent de-dramatization of the 'fight to the death' between rival groups and thus between the sexes. And this . . . [is] in order that the struggle, the implacable difference, the violence be conceived in the very place where it operates with the maximum intransigence, in other words, in personal and sexual identity itself, so as to make it disintegrate in its very nucleus. ("Women's Time," *The Kristeva Reader,* 209)

In 1972, Rich had written: "The tragedy of sex/lies around us, a woodlot/the axes are sharpened for" ("Waking in the Dark," *The Fact of A Doorframe*). Poet-theorist and theorist both call us to the recognition that the ways we are living, the categories of our description that perpetuate this life, are no longer real, have *never* been real. This book proposes that classrooms—any classrooms where writing and conversation take place—can be ritual spaces in which the original relations of connection can be, in Rich's words, "re-membered." And where we can be re-membered, too. This, I believe, should be the ultimate goal of the writing classroom's project.

Conclusion

> We cannot sing without changing our condition. The song
> will maintain the air as a territory. . . . What are the songs that
> have taken up residence in your head?[1]

Part of my own discovery in writing this book has been how many of my
own images also pervade other women's stories. Song, mirror, garden,
mother. Writing the images and writing *about* them is a way to ask
Berneice Johnson Reagon's question: "What are the songs that have
taken up residence in our heads?"[2] If there is one thing most important
for us to discover in writing classes, I believe it is this: the writing and the
asking are one and the same. When we have the experience of the writing
and the asking as one and the same, we experience the writing as song.
We claim the territory of the page. It becomes for us not only space, but
place.

The classroom, so often a space as stark and blank as the empty
page, can become a place, too. But whose place? Teachers have owned
classrooms for a long time. Students come to us there, asking one question: "What songs have taken up residence in your head?" We sing to
them, most often, all the other people's songs-in-residence that we know.
But how often do we truly sing our own? More seriously still, how often
are we unable to tell the difference? Most seriously of all, how often do
we invite their own singing? How often do we teach them how to sing
songs other than those we have sung to them? Whose song is it, anyway?

Reading Virginia Woolf, Carolyn Heilbrun reflects on the costs to
Woolf (and to herself) of the choice to write about women's experience.
"The first," she writes,

> was the ridicule, misery, and anxiety the patriarchy holds in
> store for those who express their anger about the enforced
> destiny of women. . . . Even today, after two decades of
> feminism, young women shy away from an emphatic statement
> of anger at the patriarchy. Perhaps only women who have
> played the patriarchal game and won a self despite it can find
> the courage to consider facing the pain that the outright

expression of feminism inevitably entails. (*Writing a Woman's Life*, 125)

Explicitly this is a book about reading writing women and about students' experiences in writing classrooms; implicitly and at times quite specifically it is a book about women in writing classrooms, women who are both reading and writing there, about other people (about other women, if they are lucky) and about themselves. Obviously, I am one of those women.

When I first began to do feminist work, I taught a course called "The Artist and the Problem of Anger." Now I propose a phenomenology of intimacy as the theoretical basis for reading and writing women. I ask my students to write about families and schooling because these two crucibles are among the most gendered places in their lives; they are also places where a kind of knowing is *engendered* whose effects, examined or not, will last a lifetime. Unexamined, the potential for damage done by prejudice and opinion passing for knowledge can be very great indeed.

Both—the anger and the intimacy—have been the subject of some significant ridicule among my peers. Both, because they belong to the body, are considered anathema to the acquisition of knowledge and are consequently forbidden in most schools. Both, in the context of the violence and the denial that marks our current cultural experience, have been the subject of some puzzlement and resistance among my students. Their schooling has provided them with precious little to account for the presence of these in the classrooms where they have been sitting for the twelve or so years before they come to college.

This evolution in my own feminism—the shift from anger to intimacy—has paralleled a growing understanding of the elements of invention in women's writing, and of the contextual specificity in which invention processes must be understood. We need to understand the objects, persons, landscapes—and our relations to them—that inform the stories we tell and the selves who tell them. Writing anything costs something. Writing from the outside increases the cost. Students recognize both of these things: they recognize the risk to the writer, and they recognize their own inevitable position "outside" in schools. They also recognize that some of us are more "outside" than others. Whose song is it, anyway? In the face of these costs, is it any wonder that we are all reluctant to say "mine?"

Richard, my colleague-reader, is himself a writer. Throughout his reading of my text, he has asked me to say what to *do* to make happen in classrooms the kinds of things I have proposed as significant and important. I have as much resistance responding to his question as I do to ordering a writing textbook each term. I tell him to stop listening to other people's songs (including mine) and start listening to his own. Then he'll know what he wants to make happen—in his writing and in his classroom—and he'll know how. So the first question is *not* how we can do it with *students,* but how we can do it with ourselves, or, better, how we can do it together.

Making classrooms ritual spaces means that we have to make group decisions about how to take possession of them. The power of the historical tradition remains strong: classrooms feel like worship spaces where people gather to hear "the word" pronounced by the teacher whose function remains priestlike, mediating between Truth and those who seek access to it. In this context, questions like "How many pages?" and "What do you want me to do?" and "Is this right?" are more than appropriate, because there is an unspoken agreement that we are all here to have these questions answered in a public, efficient manner before a group of witnesses.

Writing classrooms should be places where the collaboration of reading, writing, and speaking models ways of forging connections among objects, persons (including oneself), and the knowledge that they mediate. If we believe this, then the notion of a gathering to witness to a Truth is a disastrous one. It is particularly disastrous when Truth is defined as something someone else has said at some other time in some other situation (apparently) unrelated to our own. It is disastrous for all students because it creates indifference. Why connect to anything that can be looked up later—in a book or in class notes? In an age of information overload this seems unnecessary and, to any sensible person, highly inefficient. Furthermore, the disconnection from objects, persons, and the knowledge they mediate makes ethics and aesthetics finally no more than mouthed platitudes, regardless of how learned those platitudes might be. Without an interpenetrating ethics and aesthetics that is accessible to us, however limited that might be at first, the capacity to evaluate our own work or that of others, including the reading of the course, is simply unavailable because the criteria for evaluation remain outside—disconnected from—the lifeworld of our experience. Finally, this disconnection is most disastrous for women students who find themselves mirrored in worlds that offer them inverted images and inverted narratives of their connections themselves. For these students, writing is a powerful act of reclamation; its questions are gendered in complex ways. And because its hallmark is resistance to the received tradition at every turn, it requires the ongoing support of reading other women writing.

As I write this, I remember that teachers are students, too.

What are some of the ways that we can repossess this classroom space, re-member it, in Adrienne Rich's words? First, by celebrating its potent theatricality and the possibilities for experiment that it offers to us, teacher and student alike. There is a rich literature on this subject[3] and it is not my intent to replicate it here. To put it simply, in our houses we rearrange the furniture when we want to change our experience in and of a room. Sometimes this involves accommodating new furniture or new people. Inevitably it involves accommodating new feelings. In classrooms there is no reason why we cannot do the same.

Often I part my classroom down the middle and turn the chairs facing center. I am a peripatetic teacher. I am on walkabout all the time. I find the space of a huge circle alienating. This arrangement helps students to see a lot more of each other, and of me, at the same time. Walking that center aisle helps me feel closer—within a row or two, of the thirty-some bodies in my classroom.

But there are other options—and other questions worth asking— about the values of shifting conventional classroom arrangements. What would a classroom be like with no desks or chairs that are the familiar armature of our separation from each other? Where does the center of power shift in the absence of a blackboard and an identified "front" of the room? Which way do students face when the familiar, well-internalized command to face front is absent? How does our sense of groundedness change when we are close to the floor, pushing at the very perimeters of the space to which we have committed ourselves on particular days at particular times for particular numbers of weeks? What is the nature of the intimacy that can be cultivated through the arrangement of our bodies in space, through the way we read and speak to each other, sometimes one-to-one, sometimes to the group?

In ritual places, there is a good deal of reading and speaking aloud arranged in a rhythm with other kinds of silent activity—sitting, praying, dancing, writing. In each case, the rhythm of speech and silence, stillness and movement, is appropriate to what the ritual seeks to achieve. Classroom space and time can be orchestrated in this way, too; attention to rhythm should complement attention to content, an insight that I would wager every writer knows, an insight that every writer I have read here has spoken of in one way or another.

What are some ways that writing teachers can re-member their own experiences as writers and readers of literature in the face of the politics of an academy disinterested in this continuous dimension of their teacherly lives? One means is cultivating the kind of reading and writing—for ourselves and for our students—that accesses memory, reminding us that all of our knowledge is an appeal to already-existing contexts that it will complement or contradict. This is an appeal for a recovery of narrative as the cradle song, melody, threnody, of exposition, argument, and theory. It is a request that we question all the kinds of writing that the academy demands we teach. It is a suggestion that the disciplines take responsibility for teaching the formal constraints of their various discourses when (and if) it is necessary for students to learn them, and that writing teachers cease perceiving ourselves as servants to these multidisciplinary demands. It is a proposal that we read, write, and talk about the major contexts out of which our lives emerge, in which new knowledge, as well as our own subjectivity, is grounded: the family, schooling, object relations, nature, the images we have of all of these. One of my poorest writers wrote best about a Tonka truck he played with endlessly as a small child; one of my brightest yet most withdrawn students occasionally interrupted her correct but desperately controlled and stilted sentences with descriptions of natural settings she remembered that rivaled the best nature writers I know.

Writing the narrative that introduces the first chapter of this book, I learned a good deal about myself as a teacher, and as a learner. It is threaded with my life values and images. It expresses a good deal about the way I read literature, and so about the way I teach it. Making those values explicit to myself is eminently valuable to me as a teacher. Sharing them explicitly with my students—offering them my own text for interpretation—models what I ask them to do with their own work.

Reading writing theory and asking students to write about how they respond from their own experience as writers hearing theoretical propositions about the work they are engaged in can operate the same way. For one of my students, an early article about what makes "good writing" by Linda Flower and John Hayes,[4] two writing theorists originally from Carnegie Mellon University, evoked tremendous shame that had always been part of his sense of himself as a writer. It also provided him with some language to analyze why much of what he did in writing didn't work. Writing about both the emotional and the cognitive content of his response to the article helped him move through some significant blocks in his own writing process—helped him become not only a better writer but a better student overall.

I need at this point to pause and say that in privileging a connection between the reader/writer and the life world, I am not privileging the autobiographical essay as an entity unto itself, nor am I arguing that students' relationship to knowledge should be expressed as an endless series of feature stories. I am, however, arguing that the self-conscious exploration of our relationship to knowledge is efficacious. I am also arguing that comparison and contrast between the ways *we* get to questions and conclusions about ourselves and our relationships to knowledge and the ways *other* people get to the same or different questions and conclusions is valuable. I think that these questions and explorations should be the primary content of reading, writing, and conversation in the freshman composition classroom, and frankly that they should be a significant portion of the reading, writing, and conversation in every other classroom, too.

Finally, I challenge the adequacy and accuracy of the claim that "objectivity" as a goal and a value informing the pursuit of knowledge is either real or desirable. "All men are mortal beings/Socrates is a man/ Socrates is a mortal being" we intone in our logic classes: a basic model for the inevitability of the truth that a thing cannot be and not be at the same time, a "universal" model for beginning the discussion of the difference between truth and validity. But what would happen, asked one of my students, if the second premise had read "Antigone is a *woman*." Respond to that first premise from another center, one that rejects "man" as a universal term, and the changed context renders the original conclusion rather inconclusive indeed. Add the dimension that mortality in human beings involves the question of soul, and that the classical world questioned whether women actually had one, or at least one equally as good as men's,[5] and a vast philosophic tradition of ontology, epistemology, and metaphysics splits head and heart, mind and body, knowledge and experience, men and women, in the name of an objective truth. In the life world *some* things *are* and *are not* at the same time. Argument is best reasoned when we claim to leave ourselves, the texture of our lives, the very ground of knowledge, out of the equation? In the face of this prescription, whose truth is it, anyway?

Public language that continues to address writing solely as a "skill" rather than as a process reflecting multifaceted relational dimensions of the human experience marks the limitations and sometimes outright wrongheadedness of theories on writing failure. More seriously, it has helped reinforce an already-existing dissonance in traditional English classrooms about the place of literature in the teaching of writing—in short, about the relationship between reading and writing themselves.

Over the past twenty-five years, writing teachers have witnessed the old house of their professional theory and practice undergo a spectacular renovation. This "new rhetoric" offered a politic answer to the rhetoric of writing failure. It also became a powerful heuristic for examining the relationships with self, and with the world of objects, personal and natural, that this book argues are the real predictors of writing success. However, as Walter Ong's work suggests, the agonistic roots of rhetorical practice often cause these relationships to be perceived in adversarial and therefore dualistic ways. Consequently, the answer of this "new rhetoric" to the problem of writing failure—a problem of connection—is not a complete one.

Virginia Woolf, Joanna Field, and Adrienne Rich search for a revised (or revisioned) form and language to express their connection to "plain and ordinary things." They use personal narrative to explore, refine, and remake their connection to objects (i.e., to persons, to nature, and to self or selves) and to create fictions that assert connections to experience. Telling their own stories, they show us ways to heal the brokenness inherent in modern object relations. Journal writing, whose impulse is inherently narrative and conversational, shares the intent of oral narrative, a bardic, troubadourian tradition damaged or lost by the conditions of modern urban living. As private work, it has a very public, revisionist intent: it suggests ways that writers can read themselves back to recover their oral roots. As story, it can be used *not*, as those fearful of these revisionist demands would have it, to encode brokenness, but *in fact* to forge and enhance connection.

Women's personal narrative work and the movement of this work into their fiction can have a significant impact on contemporary pedagogy. It suggests first how damaging the false dichotomy between ontology (who we are—the narrative) and epistemology (what we know—the expository) has been. Secondly, its storytelling impulse offers to contemporary teachers fruitful possibilities for analyzing the nature of students' writing problems and working in a way that addresses the split between students' private worlds and the public demands of the academy and the larger worlds of discourse. Above all, it validates the critical need for students to discover their own voices so that they can make authentic choices among the selves in life's numerous rhetorical situations that will demand their story be told. In so doing, it shows us all ways, both real and imaginary, that our own stories can be used to help constitute communities, answering the charges of narcissism and solipsism that every inherently Romantic project like this one must face.

Whose song is it, anyway? Ours.

NOTES

Preface

1. *New Standard Dictionary of the English Language,* New York: Funk and Wagnell, 1959.

2. As the expression is used throughout this book, "personal narrative" is writing whose subjects or topics are rooted in the personal experience of the writer—e.g., journals, first-person essays, letters, writers' notebooks, autobiographical fragments. While there are obviously distinctions between this kind of writing and fiction, in much women's writing the relationship between personal narrative and fiction is very fluid indeed.

3. *Circles on the Water: Selected Poems.*

4. *The Holy Bible: Revised Standard Edition* (New York: World Publishing, 1962).

5. I understand *productive values* to be linear, future- and outcome-directed, and indifferent to process except as its efficiency guarantees the desired end. Contemporary production models seem particularly intent on repudiating past efforts in light of the "bigger" or "better" product or experience that can come after, and frequently the product itself is disposable, a "throw-away," valuable only so long as it serves its often-temporary purpose. I understand *reproductive values* to be circular, i.e., valuing a continual return to the past and recognizing the ongoing presence of the past in the present. The quality of "now" is significant in this model, as is the quality of the process that yields the product, be it culture, education, kinds of emotional or psychological bonds between persons, or persons themselves. And that product is valued for its uniqueness, its nondisposability, and its significance as an enduring presence in our lives.

6. In theories of knowledge, subject/object relations stand for the relationship of the knower (subject) to the known (object). In object-

relations theory, the same term represents the relationship between infant (subject/knower) and caretaker (object/known). A child's first object is almost always mother. In the mother/child relationship, the father comes as the third term, calling the child away from the mother and thus toward differentiation, that is, toward his or her place with the father in the public world.

7. In "La chair linguistique" (*Nouvelles littéraires,* May 26, 1976, reprinted in translation in *New French Feminisms*), Chantal Chawaf writes: "Isn't the final goal of writing to articulate the body? For me the sensual juxtaposition of words has one function: to liberate a living paste, to liberate matter." (*New French Feminisms,* 177)

8. Judith Gardiner, "On Female Identity and Writing by Women," in *Writing and Sexual Difference,* edited by Judith Abel.

9. Cf. especially Anne Fausto-Sterling's *Myths of Gender: Biological Theories about Women and Men* (New York: Basic Books, 1985).

10. I am grateful to Sandra Jamieson both for her fine summary of the misunderstanding I might face without being more clear about my position on this issue and for proposing, in her review of my book for SUNY Press, language that I could use to talk about it here.

11. Jessica Benjamin, *Bonds of Love: Psychoanalysis, Feminism and the Problem of Domination* (New York: Pantheon Books, 1988).
Nel Noddings, *Caring: A Feminine Approach to Ethics and Moral Education* (Berkeley: University of California Press, 1984).
Sara Ruddick, *Maternal Thinking: Toward a Politics of Peace* (New York: Ballantine Books, 1990).

12. Nancy DeJoy, *Rhetoric of Critique/Critique of Rhetoric: Towards Criticial Discursive Practice in the Academy,* Unpublished Dissertation, December, 1992. Available on microfiche through University Microfilms International, Ann Arbor, Michigan.

13. Citing both Aquinas's *Summa Theologica* and Heidegger's *Being and Time,* William Luijpen understands the concept "ground of being" in this way: "The participating being, which does not have the ground of its 'to be' in itself and yet *is,* must find this ground in something other than itself, it must *be*-under-the-influence-of-something-else, it must be-

caused.... What is sought by the metaphysician is the cause which draws back from nothing and prevents it from falling back into nothing, for of itself being is nothing and, while being, it can also not-be" (*Existential Phenomenology*, 62, 63).

14. "Many bright colours; many distinct sounds; some human beings, caricatures; comic; several violent moments of being, always including a circle of the scene which they cut out: and all surrounded by a vast space—that is a rough visual description of childhood" (Woolf, *Moments of Being*, 79).

15. These drawings of women dancing, their menstrual streams conjoined in a circle around their paired bodies, are located on a site sacred to the aboriginal people. This precludes my reproducing them here for my readers. However, a selected set of them can be found reproduced in the article by anthropologist Chris Knight cited in my bibliography.

16. For some interesting examples of writers talking about their own process, see, among numerous others, Zinsser, *Inventing the Truth;* Heilbrun, *Writing a Woman's Life;* Sternburg, *The Writer on Her Work;* and Wandor, *On Gender and Writing.*

17. "[Vorticism] is traceable to [Ezra] Pound's figure ... of words as electrified cones, charged with 'the power of tradition, of centuries of race-consciousness, of agreement, of association,' an image simplified by Lewis in *Blast's* emblem (a cone and a wire) for all that the artist does not invent but must know" (Kenner, *The Pound Era*). *Blast* was a quarterly publication started by Lewis in 1914 that became at Pound's behest "the organ of the great English Vortex" (Kenner, *The Pound Era*, 238).

18. Primary references for this book are the essays by Heidegger in *Poetry, Language, Thought* and in *The Basic Problems of Phenomenology,* both translated and edited by Albert Hofstadter.

19. I want to say a brief, if digressive, word at this point about method, particularly as it relates to my use of Heidegerrian theory in reading Woolf. As Sandra Jamieson has suggested I point out, there are a number of issues, as well as ways of articulating them, that Heidegger shares with Woolf, Sarton, and Field. She astutely suggests in her review of this book for SUNY Press that these include, among others: "the fear

of the loss of identity and the embrace of the 'other' as it relates to the Heidegerrian notion of *Dasein* as the 'being towards death'; the relationship between creativity and identity-making; the role of conflict in intimacy as it plays itself out in the work of art, and the artist's mediating function in this regard; the Heidegerrian concept of boundaries, which is strikingly similar to how Field attempts to explain the artist's (her) experience of form; Heidegger's *Mitsein,* the understanding that 'Being with others belongs to the being of Dasein that is an issue for Dasein in its very being' (SZ 123/160)."

Where it is interesting and appropriate, I have cited Heidegger's text as it reflects some of what I am reading in the literature. In this regard I wish to note and thank Professor Jamieson, who pointed me toward a number of the references from "The Origin of the Work of Art" and in Fynsk's *Heidegger: Thought and Historicity.* Her remarks and references were extremely helpful to me in constructing my revisions of chapter 4, where I have used some of Heidegger's work extensively in the reading of *Between the Acts.* However, I have elected for several reasons not to further elaborate these relationships in the text itself. First, this is not a comparative study of Heidegger and Woolf or any other of these writers, although it seems to me that an interesting book could be written on the subject. Secondly, I do not wish to privilege any theoretical position—including Heidegger's—to validate the reading of a literary text, nor do I wish to appear to subordinate the literary text to a theoretical one, something I consider a standard patriarchal critical practice. It is the tension between the style of Woolf and the style of Heidegger when they address similar phenomena that I want to highlight, while not privileging one against the other. It has always been a matter of fascination to me that *Being and Time* and *To the Lighthouse* were published in the same year. I believe their two authors confronted the same issues, although they clearly represented their confrontations with these issues in very different ways. Consequently, Woolf can be read in relation to Heidegger, and Heidegger can also be read in relation to Woolf. I am not using any theory to make the voices of any of the women I read in this book more authoritative, or to legitimize their stories. Finally, I do not believe that expanding the discussion of Heidegger in a way that threads it throughout the text will enhance the reader's understanding of my thesis, and indeed it might destabilize an already tenuous balance between my own voice and (more importantly) those of the other women writers whose voices I intend to be the primary voices of this text.

20. The use of a "dialectical notebook" as an aid to reading and to the composing process has become popular in current writing pedagogy.

Students split a notebook page down the middle, writing their lecture notes on one side and their summary/thoughts on the other side; sometimes a third column is left for peer comments. For a description of this and some other uses of the journal form in the writing classroom, cf. Linda Stanley and David Shimkin, "The Triadic Journal: The Purposes and Processes of Journal Writing across the College Curriculum," *Writing across the Curriculum* 5, no. 1 (December 1987).

21. "[T]he thesis of Western secular *ethnocentrism* [is that] the *West* became the *we* to the *ethnos* of all other peoples, who became THE OTHER."

In economic (and racial) terms, "The *cheap labor far away* was to become the concrete OTHER of the West, the ultimate polarity in a series of hierarchical polarities."

In religious and cultural terms, "it was the essentially *economic* impact of the New World upon the Old, that would essentially transform that Old World from one civilization amongst others—the Christian, to THE ONE, the West, to which all other civilizations were OTHER" (Wynter, "Ethno or Socio Poetics," 79, 80, 81).

In this book I argue that in a patriarchal culture women also function in the economy and in other cultural institutions like religion and the family, as Other, and in psychoanalytic terms, this also implicates a woman's role as (m)other.

22. Cf., for example, Griffin, *Woman and Nature;* Starhawk, *Dreaming the Dark,* appendix A; Martha Vicinus, ed., *Suffer and Be Still: Women in the Victorian Age* (Bloomington: Indiana University Press, 1973); Carolyn Merchant, *The Death of Nature: Women, Ecology, and the Scientific Revolution* (San Francisco: Harper & Row, 1980).

23. Chicago, in *The Dinner Party,* 159ff, cites the figure of nine million women burned as witches.

Chapter I

1. In one sense, of course, the Romantic experiment succeeded: its proponents *did* offer us an alternative, "wholistic" vision counter to the "broken" one that I propose as marking the modern and postmodern periods. Nevertheless, the very fact that virtually every successive generation of poets from Tennyson and Arnold to Eliot and Stevens and beyond finds itself struggling to come to terms with that vision of 150 years ago

suggests to me that it has indeed *not* been integrated into the collective psyche, and in that sense I stand by my argument that it has failed.

2. In his essay "The Metaphysical Poets" (1921), T. S. Eliot cited the beginnings of this changed "sensibility" as belonging to the seventeenth century, although the reasons he cites are literary rather than sociological or psychological. He uses the occasion of this reflection to valorize the rational at the expense of the affective, a typical Eliotic dodge of his own discomfort with feeling: "[S]omething . . . had happened to the mind of English between the time of Donne or Lord Herbert of Cherbury and the time of Tennyson and Browning; it is the difference between the intellectual poet and the reflective poet. Tennyson and Browning are poets, and they think; but they do not feel their thought as immediately as the odour of a rose. . . . In the seventeenth century a dissociation of sensibility set in, from which we have never recovered" (*Selected Essays*, 287, 288). His solution to the problem of expressing emotion, a remarkably "dissociated" one in itself, was offered in an earlier essay, "Hamlet" (1919): "The only way of expressing emotion in the form of art is by finding an 'objective correlative'; in other words, a set of objects, a situation, a chain of events which shall be the formula of that *particular* emotion; such that when the external facts, which must terminate in sensory experience are given, the emotion is immediately evoked" (*Selected Essays*, 145).

3. In *Dreamtime: Concerning the Boundary between Wilderness and Civilization,* Peter Duerr expresses the concept of wildness or wilderness in this way:

> Archaic humans . . . still possessed the insight that one had to leave the world, that one could become 'tame' only if before one had been 'wild,' that one could only live in the true sense of the word if one had proved one's willingness to die.
>
> In order to be able to live within the order, in other words, to be consciously tame or domesticated, one had to have lived in the wilderness. One could know what inside meant only if one had once been outside. (42–43)

Duerr goes on to say:

> In small, non-Western societies today a more "archaic" attitude is often still encountered towards that part of the self that is

sited on the other side of the fence of civilization, in the wilderness. For the Bakweri of Mount Cameroon, the world of the "outside" is the world of the mermaids *(liengu)*. This world includes the sea and the primeval forest. . . . All women are outside, but the mermaids are "more outside" than all the others. (45)

4. I believe the current revival of '60s folk/rock music with its narrative lyrics and the media fascination with "talk shows" on which people often reveal the most intimate life experiences is a manifestation in popular culture of this longing for story.

5. Advertisement to the *Lyrical Ballads,* in *Prose Works,* 116.

6. "[W]hereas the Semitic genius placed its highest spiritual life in the religious sentiment, and made that the basis of its poetry,—the Indo-European genius placed its highest spiritual life in the imaginative reason, and makes that the basis of its poetry" (Arnold, "On the Study of Celtic Literature," *Complete Prose Works,* 3:369).

"The present has to make its own poetry, and not even Sophocles and his compeers, any more than Dante and Shakespeare, are enough for it. That I will not dispute; nor will I set up the Greek poets, from Pindar to Sophocles, as objects of blind worship. But no other poets so well show to the poetry of the present the way it must take; no other poets have lived so much by imaginative reason; no other poets have made their work so well balanced; no other poets, who have so well satisfied their thinking power, have so well satisfied the religious sense" (Arnold, "Pagan and Medieval Religious Sentiment," *Complete Prose Works,* 3:231).

For the definition of objective correlative, cf. note 2 above.

7. Several books address this issue: Gallagher and Laquer's *The Making of the Modern Body;* Suleiman's *The Female Body in Western Culture;* and Showalter's *The Female Malady.*

8. Lane, Ann J., editor, "The Yellow Wallpaper," in *The Charlotte Perkins Gilman Reader* (New York: Pantheon, 1980) 3–20.

9. Wynter, "Ethno or Socio Poetics," 84. Introducing this point in her article, Wynter notes that Gines de Sepulveda, a sixteenth-century Spanish theologian, argued the Spanish right to enslave the Indians on

the grounds of their illiteracy, literacy being synonymous in his argument with culture. " 'Now compare those gifts of prudence, sharpness of wit, magnanimity, temperance, humanity and religion (of the Spaniards) with those of those little men (homuncili) in whom you will hardly find a trace of humanity. They have no culture, no system of writing (nor do they) preserve monuments of their history; they have the vaguest obscure memory of facts recorded in certain pictures, they lack written laws and have barbarous institutions and customs' " (Gines de Sepulveda, cited by Wynter in "Ethno or Socio Poetics," 84).

10. For a discussion of this, see Walter Ong's *Orality and Literacy*.

11. Despite the predominance of men among the group of troubadours, Judy Chicago's research team found that "Of the one hundred known minstrels between 1150 and 1250, twenty were female" (*The Dinner Party*, 141).

12. *Poems Selected and New* and *The Fact of a Doorframe*.

13. "When a man reflects upon his existence, it is undoubtedly true that he finds himself 'already' involved in a definite body and in a definite world. He is never sheer indetermination. He finds himself as an American, a Hebrew, as intelligent, a cripple, a laborer, rich, fat, etc. All this constitutes what he 'already' is, or to say it differently, his past. Sometimes the term 'determination' is used to describe this condition, for there is question here of that which is meant by all kinds of 'determinations.' The most current terms, however, are *situation* and *facticity*. . . . "

" . . . every determination that is 'already' present in a human existence implies also something that is "not yet" there; every past implies a future. Existence is oppositional unity, unity in opposition of what *de facto* is and what can be. As such, man's existence is called *project* or plan" (Luijpen, *Existential Phenomenology*, 40). Luijpen's primary reference here is Heidegger's *Being and Time*.

14. In her essay on French feminist theory, Domna Stanton paraphrases Julia Kristeva, whose work is perhaps the most helpful in addressing this question of voice. "All subjects articulate themselves through the interaction of the semiotic and symbolic modalities, Kristeva insists, but the first of these has been consistently repressed by the Logos because it is experienced as a threat. Only the eruption of the semiotic into the symbolic can give reign to heterogeneous meaning, to difference, and thus

subvert the existing systems of signification. . . . In much of women's writing, she discovers that 'the notion of the signifier as a network of distinctive marks is insufficient, because each of these marks is charged over and beyond its discriminatory value as a carrier of signification, by an instinctual or affective force which, strictly speaking, cannot be signified but remains latent in the phonic invocation or the inscribing gesture. . . . Poetic language has always shared analogous traits' " ("Language and Revolution: The Franco-American Dis-Connection," p. 75 in *The Future of Difference,* ed. Eisenstein and Jardine, pp. 73–87).

15. Langbaum goes on to say: "For Wordsworth the self is memory and process—the memory of all its phases and the process of interchange with the external world. The movement of thought into sensation and back again corresponds to the circular movement of self into nature and back again and to the circular movement from the subjectively individual to the archetypally objective phases of identity and back again. Each circular movement, which could be conceived as starting from outside as well as inside, is a new creation, a new confirmation, of self—and is impelled by joy" (*The Mysteries of Identity,* 46).

16. Albert Lord, cited in Neisser, *Memory Observed,* 243.

17. All citations of *The Waves* are from *Jacob's Room and the Waves: Two Complete Novels.*

18. Cited in Makward, "To Be or Not to Be . . . A Feminist Speaker," 96.

19. Cf. Schachtel, cited in Neisser, *Memory Observed,* 192, 193.

20. "Kristeva has posited two types of signifying processes to be analyzed within any production of meaning: a 'semiotic' one or a 'symbolic' one. The semiotic process relates to the *chora,* a term meaning 'receptacle' which she borrowed from Plato *[Timaeus],* who describes it as 'an invisible and formless being which receives all things and in some mysterious way partakes of the intelligible, and is most incomprehensible.' It is also anterior to any space, an economy of primary processes articulated by Freud's instinctual drives *(Triebe)* through condensation and displacement, and where social and family structures make their imprint through the mediation of the maternal body. While the *chora's* articulation is uncertain, undetermined, . . . it is the aim of Kristeva's practice to remove what Plato

saw as 'mysterious' and 'incomprehensible' in what he called 'mother and receptacle' of all things. . . . The symbolic process refers to the establishment of sign and syntax, paternal function, grammatical and social constraints, symbolic law. In short, the signifying process, as increasingly manifest in 'poetic language,' results from a particular articulation between symbolic and semiotic dispositions" (Leon Roudiez, Introduction to Kristeva's *Desire in Language* 6–7).

21. Schachtel, cited in Neisser, *Memory Observed*, 195.

22. Ibid., 194. In *Feeding the Hungry Heart* (New York: Signet, 1982), Geneen Roth records the literal self-starvation of thousands of contemporary women. This collection of Roth's own and other women's journal entries regarding their struggles with eating disorders is a powerful statement of the body-mind-spirit connection at the heart of the Romantic argument, and of the consequences when our sense of that connection is lost. While the need for nourishing food is a real and desperate one, Roth, herself a therapist, views the symptoms of eating-disordered women as a manifestation of the longing for satisfying (loving) relationships— with themselves and with other persons.

23. Cf. chapter 5, note 6.

24. This notion of prayer need not be understood in a Judeo-Christian or formally religious sense at all; it might be understood as an "attention to," to use Weil's word, or a "mindfulness of," to use the Buddhist term, that which is intimately a part of and yet powerfully transcends the self—a moment when epistemology and ontology come together. And so Wordsworth's poems to daffodils and clouds, and numerous moments in the sonnets when his apostrophe turns to God; Shelley's skylark, the vision of Coleridge's Mariner, etc.

25. In "The Origin of the Work of Art," Heidegger defines the same experience as a moment of Truth, "the primal conflict in which . . . the Open is won within which everything stands and from which everything withholds itself that shows itself and withdraws itself as a being." He goes on to say: "In referring to this self-establishing of openness in the Open, thinking touches on a sphere that cannot yet be explicated here. Only this much should be noted, that if the nature of the unconcealedness of beings belongs in any way to Being itself . . . then Being, by way of its own nature, lets the place of openness (the lightning-

clearing of the There) happen, and introduces it as a place of the sort in which each being emerges or arises in its own way" (*Poetry, Language, Thought*, 60–61, 61). In the addendum to this essay, he qualifies his language about the process of experiencing these moments: "the " 'fixing in place' of truth, rightly understood, can never run counter to the 'letting happen.' For one thing, this 'letting' is nothing passive but doing in the highest degree . . . in the sense of *thesis, a 'working' and 'willing'* which in the present essay . . . is characterized as the 'existing human being's entrance into and compliance with the unconcealedness of Being.' For another thing, the 'happen' in the letting happen of truth is the movement that prevails in the clearing *and* concealing or more precisely in their union, that is to say, the movement of the lighting of self-concealment as such, from which again all self-lighting stems. What is more, this 'movement' even requires a fixing in place in the sense of a bringing forth, where . . . the creative bringing forth 'is rather a receiving and an incorporating of a relation to unconcealedness' " (83–84).

26. In Levertov, *Candles in Babylon*.

Chapter II

1.

According to the Aranda, the great cosmological force, The Dreaming, first moved when the earth's surface was barren and featureless. Beneath this surface lay many totemic ancestors, essentially human, but closely associated with natural species. These beings one day rose up and their actions and their wanderings brought into being all the physical features of the Central Australian landscape. . . .

An important aspect of the ancestral transformation is the creation of totemic landscape—'the country.' This creation has two facets: the emergence of actual landscape forms through 'imprinting' (Munn 1970: 142), and the emergence of sacred objects *(tjurunga)*. Both facets are intimately associated with the creation of totemic animals and human beings.

Imprinting conflates a number of notions to do with marking, naming and singing (cf. Munn 1970: 142). A mark

is a design on the landscape, a natural feature, such as a
mountain or swamp, which an ancestor makes. The paradigm
case of a mark is a track or footstep—a sign through which
one may read the past (Strehlow 1964[b]: 47). But a mark is
also stylesed *[sic]*, and in art forms it is found not as a
naturalistic representation, but as an ancestral 'signature' placed
at a site. (Morton, "The Effectiveness of Totemism," 455)

2. "A totemic 'signature' is a name sung out by an ancestor. Songs
are conceived in terms of names, each composing a stanza or *'tjurunga
retnja'—'tjurunga name'* (Strehlow 1971: 119). Verse composition is
described as 'throwing out' or 'calling out names,' 'calling out one's own
names,' or 'calling oneself by names' *(makalama)*. The last word comes
from *tnakama* ('to name'), which also has the sense of 'to trust' or
'believe in.' In The Dreaming, ancestors first called out their own names,
then those of their place of origin, and finally those of all the places and
living things encountered during their journeys. Each song was thus
inscribed on the country as an expression of ancestral will and left behind
for the benefit of living human beings" (Strehlow 1971: 126);" (Morton,
"The Effectiveness of Totemism," 455–56).

3. "For the expansion of the Western self, the auto-creation in the
sixteenth century was only made possible by the damning up of the
potentiality of non-Western man, by the negation of his Being. Once the
idea of the Christian medieval ethnos of the West had broken down, it
was replaced by another universal, the secular ideology of the bourgeoisie,
the concept of HUMANISM. This was the new conceptualization of the
new ethnos of Western Man, as compared to his former Christian *ethnicity*.
It would be part of the ideology of humanism that whilst it saw itself as a
universal, it was universal only in the context of a WESTERN-
DOMINATED WORLD. To quote Orwell, and to paraphrase: ALL
MEN WERE EQUAL BUT WESTERN MAN WAS MORE EQUAL
THAN OTHERS" (Wynter, "Ethno or Socio Poetics," 83).

4. Hélène Cixous, cited in Gilbert and Gubar, "Ceremonies of the
Alphabet." I understand the term *phallocentrism* to refer to Jacques Lacan's
use of the term *phallus*, which, as suggested by his text *Feminine Sexuality*,
does not refer to an actual father but to the power of the symbolic,
paternal/patriarchal order as it stands between mother and child in the
post-Oedipal relationship and between nature and culture in the social
order. As Juliet Mitchell and Jacqueline Rose point out in their

introduction to *Feminine Sexuality*, a phallocentric takes "man as the norm and woman as what is different therefrom" (8). In the linguistic sense, the phallus is a "signifier"; it is this relation to the subject that most interests Lacan.

5. The aboriginal term for "increase ritual" means "to throw out seed" (Morton, "The Effectiveness of Totemism," 458).

6. Citing Roland Barthes in *Writing Degree Zero* (p. 11), Kristeva argues that "style as a 'frame of reference is biological or biographical, not historical [. . .] indifferent to society and transparent to it, a closed personal process [. . .] a *sublanguage* elaborated where flesh and external reality come together; its secret is *recollection* locked within the *body of a writer*' (p. 12)" (cited in *Desire in Language*, 111–12).

7. For an interesting contemporary recovery of women's ancient song tradition, see Starhawk's *Dreaming the Dark*, chap. 2, "Thought-Forms: Magic As Language."

8. Lacan, *Feminine Sexuality.*

9. Chodorow, *The Reproduction of Mothering.*

10. Another configuration of this relationship is the pairing of women with space and men with time, noted in Alice Jardine's *Gynesis* (24–25).

11. Alfred, Lord Tennyson, "Merlin and Vivien," in *Idylls of the King* (New York: New American Library, 1960), 116–38.

12. Sutherland, trans., *The Bacchae of Euripides.*

13. Lacan, *Feminine Sexuality.*

14. Woolf writes in *Moments of Being* that the novel came "in a great, apparently involuntary rush. One thing burst into another. Blowing bubbles out of a pipe gives the feeling of the rapid crowd of ideas and scenes which blew out of my mind, so that my lips seemed syllabling of their own accord as I walked. What blew the bubbles? Why then? I have no notion. But I wrote the book very quickly and when it was written, I ceased to be obsessed by my mother. I no longer hear her

voice; I do not see her" (81). The novel was published on the anniversary of her mother's death.

15. "Since all naming and symbolic identification is a function of the Law of the Father (the law of language), [the] earliest moment in which the 'first words' are spoken involves an eventual barring of the subject, an acknowledgement of a lack in both mother and infant, and a kind of anticipated castration" (Muller and Richardson, *Lacan and Language*, 402).

16. "Devoid of baby talk, insulated from the earliest life of childhood where language has its deepest psychological roots, a first language to none of its users, pronounced across Europe in often mutually unintelligible ways but always written the same way, Learned Latin was a striking exemplification of the power of writing for isolating discourse and of the unparalled productivity of such isolation" (Ong, *Orality and Literacy*, 113).

17. Virginia Woolf wrote to Vita Sackville-West: "Style is a very simple matter, it is all rhythm. Once you get that, you can't use the wrong words. But on the other hand here am I sitting after half the morning, crammed with ideas, and visions, and so on, and can't dislodge them, for lack of the right rhythm. Now this is very profound, what rhythm is, and goes far deeper than words. A sight, an emotion creates this wave in the mind, long before it makes words to fit it; and in writing [such is my present belief] one has to recapture this, and set this working [which has nothing apparently to do with words] and then, as it breaks and tumbles in the mind, it makes words to fit it" (*Letters*, 3:247, cited by Dick in her edition of the holograph draft, 14–15).

18. "Oral noetic processes are formulaic in design because we know only what we can recall. If I think of something once and never again, I do not say that I know it. To 'know geometry' is to be able to bring it into consciousness. Knowing requires memory. But an oral culture cannot remember by formulating something first and then memorizing it afterward. Once the words are said, unless they are said in a way that is itself memorable, they are gone for good: there is nothing there to return to for memorizing. *Verba volant:* Homer's 'winged words.' That is to say, an oral culture does not put its knowledge into mnemonic patterns: it *thinks* its thoughts in mnemonic patterns. There is no other way for it to proceed effectively. An oral culture does not merely have a quaint liking for proverbs or 'sayings' of all sorts: it is absolutely dependent on

them. Cliches constitute its thought. Constant repetition of the known is the major noetic exercise. Narrative, poetic or prose, tells the old stories and tells them in formulaic style. The closer orators are to the purely oral tradition, the more their style, too, will be like the poets' and the prose narrators' styles, filled with commonplaces or formulas" (Ong, *The Presence of the Word*, 57–58, cited in Ong, *Fighting for Life*, 123–24).

19. For a definition and overview of the research about whole language, see Robert Blake, ed., *Whole Language* (Schenectady, N.Y.: New York State English Council Monographs, 1990).

20. In *Writing a Woman's Life,* Carolyn Heilbrun cites an extensive literature distinguishing women's biographical and autobiographical efforts from men's. Her book is a rich resource for study and reflection about the difficulties of this particular use of voice for women.

21. Gates, *The Signifying Monkey.*

22. Washington, *Invented Lives.*

23. Buber, *I and Thou.*

Chapter III

1. I have not found any research, including Diane Bell's, that contradicts this reading of Aranda initiation rites. Anthropologist Chris Knight's reading of the Rainbow Serpent myth and of male ritual activity concurs with mine in the larger context of the ways male ritual expresses the desire to appropriate female power.

In her discussion of *yilpinji,* love rituals among the aboriginal tribes she studies, Bell refers to these as necessarily located "within the context of the land" and to the myths told in these rituals as requiring interpretation "in terms of power symbols." She goes on to say, "Love and sex are only aspects of *yilpinji,* which encompasses the sweep of tensions and emotions engendered by male-female relationships. These, however, must be seen in their cultural context where country is a major symbol of personal and social identity" (163). When Kaytej dreaming sites were cut off by a road built through the center of their territory, women lost ready access to their sacred sites. The consequence was a weakening of women's position, and this is characteristic of what has occurred with the coming of Western men and their ideas to aboriginal Australia. "One ritual object associated with this area was so powerful that it was believed that if a man came within close range, he would meet a violent death. This terminal sanction is no longer available to women. *Men have, however, retained violent sanctions which they apply during initiation time*" (164, italics mine).

2. Knight draws on "four independent recordings of the key myth" ("Lévy-Strauss and the Dragon," 22). Her sources are: W. L. Warner, *A Black Civilization,* revised edition (New York: Harper, 1957), 250–259; C. H. and R. M. Berndt, *Sexual Behavior in Western Arnhem Land* (New York: Wenner-Gren, 1951) 19–26; R. Robinson, *Aboriginal Myths and Legends* (Melbourne, Australia: Sun Books, 1966) 37–43; W. S. Chaseling, *Yulengor, Nomads of Arnhem Land* (London: Epworth Press, 1957) 139–46.

3. Knight details the sociobiological recognition of menstrual synchrony and male efforts to usurp this synchrony (32–36). See note 3 in Knight's article for examples of the rock drawings of women dancing, often in pairs, encircled by their flowing menstrual streams.

4. Regrettably, because these figures of dancing, menstruating women are found at sacred sites and are central to ritual activity, they cannot be replicated here. Some examples of various types of Aboriginal drawings can be found in *Australian Aboriginal Paintings in Western and Central Arnhem Land,* text and editorial work by E. J. Brandl (Canberra: Aboriginal Studies Press, 1988).

In this book, Aboriginal informants are cited as saying that present-day rituals involving the Rainbow Snake are: "men's business which should not be looked at by women" (181). Later, Brandl notes that "In the Aborigines' conception, the Rainbow is not always a snake or a snake-like creature. It can be manifested and painted as a composite figure incorporating human features and/or those of several animals, or be almost completely human in shape. Further, the Rainbow is not a single being but several that are linked in genealogical order; it may not only be either male or female but can also be bisexual. The bisexual Rainbow is said to have come from, and now dwells, under the world. It is credited with creating the country, the 'Dreaming places,' and with the institution of the social order. The male and female Rainbow, in contrast, live above ground residing in the rocks and waterholes at particular sites. They are also creators but appear less powerful than the bisexual Rainbow" (181).

5. Xavière Gauthier, "Pourquoi Sorcières?" [Why Witches?], in *New French Feminisms,* edited by Marks and de Courtivron, 199.

6. G. Roheim, *The Eternal Ones of the Dream* (New York: International University Press, 1945); cited in Knight, "Levy-Strauss and the Dragon," 37, emphasis added.

7. Cf. Chodorow, *The Reproduction of Mothering;* Chodorow, "Mother-Daughter Relationships," in *The Future of Difference,* ed. Eisenstein and Jardine; and Dinnerstein, *The Mermaid and the Minotaur.*

8. Hélène Cixous, "The Laugh of the Medusa," in *New French Feminisms,* edited by Marks and de Courtivron, 255.

9. Chernin, *Reinventing Eve.*

10. "The poetic is the basic capacity for human dwelling" (Heidegger, "Poetically Man Dwells," in *Poetry, Language, Thought,* 228).

11. Nathaniel Hawthorne, "Rappaccini's Daughter," in *The Complete Novels and Selected Tales,* 1046.

12. "For world and things do not subsist alongside one another. They penetrate each other. Thus the two traverse a middle. In it, they are at one. Thus at one they are intimate. The middle of the two is intimacy—in Latin *inter.* . . . The intimacy of world and thing is not a fusion. Intimacy obtains only where the intimate—world and thing—divides itself cleanly and remains separated. In the midst of the two, in the between of world and thing, in their *inter,* division prevails: a *dif-ference*" (Heidegger, "Language," in *Poetry, Language, Thought,* 202).

13. Having argued earlier in "The Origin of the Work of Art" that "Createdness of the work means: truth's being fixed in place in the figure" (*Poetry, Language, Thought,* 64), Heidegger explicates this "fixedness" in an addendum that can further illuminate the sense of "intensity" of the vision/consciousness about which Woolf, Sarton, and Field write:

> [I]n the context of our essay on the work of art, we keep in mind the Greek sense of *thesis*—to let lie forth in its radiance and presence—then the 'fix' in 'fix in place' can never have the sense of rigid, motionless, and secure.

'Fixed' means outlined, admitted into the boundary *(peras)*, brought into the outline. . . . The boundary in the Greek sense does not block off; rather, being itself brought forth, it first brings to its radiance what is present. . . . The boundary that fixes and consolidates is in this repose, repose in the fullness of motion—all this holds of the work in the Greek sense of *ergon;* this work's 'being' is *energeia,* which gathers infinitely more movement within itself than do the modern 'energies.' (83)

14.

In the creation of a work, the conflict [of world and earth], as rift, must be set back into the earth, and the earth itself must be set forth and used as the self-closing factor. This use, however, does not use up or misuse the earth as matter, but rather sets it free to be nothing but itself. This use of the earth is a working with it that, to be sure, looks like the employment of matter in handicraft. Hence the appearance that artistic creation is also an activity of handicraft. It never is. . . . The production of equipment is finished when a material has been so formed as to be ready for use. For equipment to be ready means that it is dismissed beyond itself, to be used up in serviceability.

Not so when a work is created. (Heidegger, "The Origin of the Work of Art," in *Poetry, Language, Thought,* 64)

15. "It was agreed," Coleridge wrote, "that my endeavors should be directed to persons and characters supernatural, or at least romantic; yet so as to transfer from our inward nature a human interest and a semblance of truth sufficient to procure for these shadows of imagination that willing suspension of disbelief for the moment, which constitutes poetic faith" (*Biographia Literaria,* chap. 14).

16. "These then were two very genuine experiences of my own. These were two of the adventures of my professional life. The first—killing the Angel in the House—I think I solved. She died. But the second, telling the truth about my own experiences as a body, I do not think I solved. I doubt that any woman has solved it yet. The obstacles against her are still immensely powerful" (Woolf, "Professions for Women," 62).

17. In his essay "What Are Poets For?" Heidegger echoes Hölderlin ("Long is the destitute time of the world's night"), finding with him in Dionysus both a reminder of the abyss of a world without ground and a hope for its "turning" from it. Of the poet he writes: "He among mortals who must, sooner than other mortals and otherwise than they, reach into the abyss, comes to know the marks that the abyss remarks. For the poet, these are the traces of the fugitive gods. In Hölderlin's experience, Dionysus the wine-god brings this trace down to the god-less amidst the darkness of their world's night. For in the vine and in its fruit, the god of wine guards the being toward one another or earth and sky as the site of the wedding feast of men and gods. Only within reach of this site, if anywhere, can traces of the fugitive gods still remain for god-less men. . . . To be a poet in a destitute time means: to attend, singing, to the tracer of the fugitive gods. This is why the poet in the time of the world's night utters the holy" (*Poetry, Language, Thought*, 93–94).

18. In Woolf's case this was a both literal and critical experience. As her own memoirs suggest, she was apparently sexually molested as child by her half brother, Gerald Duckworth, and her father was a tyrannical ruler over their house and her consciousness. An equal or greater threat lay at the hands of male critics whose judgment of her work Woolf awaited with profound terror.

19. Cf. Schlissel, *Women's Diaries of the Westward Journey;* Jeffrey, *Frontier Women;* Schlissel, Ruiz, and Monk, *Western Women;* and Stewart, *Letters of a Woman Homesteader.*

20. "For men and women often held different visions of community. Men sought a community marked by outward order, but it was to be a place where individuals had freedom to pursue their fortunes and their pleasures. The vision could allow compromises with strict morality as the frontier habit of doing business on the Sabbath and condoning prostitution testified. Indeed, nineteenth-century norms, in a sense, legitimated such compromises, for men were not really responsible for the moral order; women were. Many women, probably middle class in background, saw the ideal community in a different light; it was to be a place of real, rather than apparent, order, a place without disruptive threats to family unity and purity" (Jeffrey, *Frontier Women*, 180).

21. Henri Bergson, *An Introduction to Metaphysics: The Creative Mind* (Totowa, N.J.: Littlefield & Adams, 1965).

Chapter IV

1. The care and specificity with which words must be used in the effort to characterize intimate relationship is demonstrated in Heidegger's gloss on the word *dif-ference* as it follows the discussion of intimacy cited earlier (chap. 3, note 12). "The intimacy of world and thing is present in the separation of the between; it is present in the dif-ference. The word difference is now removed from its usual and customary usage. . . . It exists only as this single difference. It is unique. Of itself, it holds apart the middle in and through which world and things are at one with each other. The intimacy of the difference is the unifying element of the *diaphora,* the carrying out that carries through. The dif-ference carries out world in its worlding, carries out things in their thinging. Thus carrying them out, it carries them toward one another. The dif-ference does not mediate after the fact by connecting world and things through a middle added on to them. Being the middle, it first determines world and things in their presence, i.e., in their being toward one another, whose unity it carries out" ("Language," 202).

In his earlier essay "What Are Poets For?" Heidegger shares a sense remarkably similar to Woolf's of the extraordinary power of language and the "daring" of those who speak: "The nature of language does not exhaust itself in signifying, nor is it merely something that has the character of a sign or cipher. It is because language is the house of Being, that we reach what is by constantly going through this house. When we go to the well, when we go through the woods, we are always already going through the word 'well,' through the word 'woods,' even if we do not speak the words and do not think of anything relating to language. Thinking our way from the temple of Being, we have an intimation of what they dare who are sometimes more daring than the Being of beings. They dare the precinct of Being. They dare language. All beings . . . are *qua* beings in the precinct of language. This is why the return from the realm of objects and their representation into the innermost region of the heart's space can be accomplished, if anywhere, only in this precinct" (*Poetry, Language, Thought,* 132).

2. "To know means to have seen, in the widest sense of seeing, which means to apprehend what is present, as such. For Greek thought the nature of knowing consists in *aletheia,* that is, in the uncovering of things" ("The Origin of the Work of Art," 59).

3. Woolf, *Letters,* 3:247, cited by Susan Dick in *To the Lighthouse: The Original Holograph Draft,* 14–15.

4. Woolf, *Moments of Being*, 81, cited in Dick, *To the Lighthouse*, 25, emphasis added.

5. The concept of writing as a process of discovery, as well as Janet Emig's speculations on composing strategies and the writing process, address this dimension of ritual behavior. Cf. especially "Hand, Eye and Brain: Some 'Basics' in the Writing Process' in Janet Emig, *The Web of Meaning*, 110–21, and "Writing As a Mode of Learning" (123–31 in the same text). The importance of communication to ritual does not negate its significance for the journal writer. Roy Rappaport, a prominent spokesperson among those who study ritual, speaks of the autocommunicative dimensions of solitary ritual as putting various parts of the psyche in touch with each other (LaChapelle, *Sacred Land*, 163).

6. Roy Rappaport, *Ecology, Meaning, and Religion* (Richmond, California: North Atlantic Books, 1979), cited by LaChapelle in *Sacred Lands*, 163.

7. The term *deep ecology* was coined by the Norwegian philosopher Arne Naess. Neither a philosophy nor a political movement, *deep ecology* is defined by Naess in contrast to "shallow ecology"—"the fight against pollution and resource development," an essentially anthropocentric approach. "Deep ecology" is "rejection of man-in-environment image in favor of the relational, total-field image." A primary objective is recognizing and acting on the principle that "Every form of life has the equal right to live and blossom; diversity and symbiosis; and local autonomy and decentralization" (LaChapelle, *Sacred Land*, 11, 12). In her introduction to *Sacred Land*, LaChapelle discusses the origins and history of the "deep ecology" movement in the United States and elaborates the statements of its tenets (10–15).

8. For Heidegger and for Woolf, the artist aids a process of disclosure and in the work mediates the conflict of clearing and concealing: "to create is to cause something to emerge as a thing that has been brought forth. The work's becoming a work is a way in which truth becomes and happens. . . . Truth is un-truth, insofar as there belongs to it the reservoir of the not-yet-uncovered, the un-uncovered, in the sense of concealment. In unconcealedness, as truth, there occurs also the other "un-" of a double restraint or refusal. Truth occurs as such in the opposition of clearing and double concealing. Truth is the primal conflict in which, always in some particular way, the Open is won within which everything

stands and from which everything withholds itself that shows itself and withdraws itself as a being. Whenever and however this conflict breaks out and happens, the opponents, lighting or clearing and concealing, move apart because of it. The openness of this Open, that is, truth, can be what it is, namely this openness, only if and as long as it establishes itself within its Open. Hence there must always be some being in this Open, something that is, in which the openness takes its stand and attains its constancy. In taking possession thus of the Open, the openness holds open the Open and sustains it" (Heidegger, "The Origin of the Work of Art," 60–61).

9. In his introduction to Heidegger's *Poetry, Language, Thought,* Albert Hofstadter notes that the absence of commas between the three is deliberate, reinforcing the "essential continuity of being, building, dwelling, and thinking. Language makes the connection for us: *bauen,* to build, connects with *buan,* to dwell, and with *bin, bist,* the words for be. Language tells us: to be a human being is to be on the earth as a mortal, to dwell, doing the 'building' that belongs to dwelling: cultivating growing things, constructing things that are built, and doing all this in the context of mortals who, living on earth and cherishing it, look to the sky and to the gods to find the measure of their dwelling. If man's being is dwelling, and if man must look to the way the world fits together to find the measure by which he can determine his dwelling life, than man must dwell poetically" (xiii–xiv).

10. For the fictional elaboration of the philosophic *Being and Nothingness,* cf. Sartre's *Nausea.* William Luijpen says of this book: "In *Nausea* Sartre describes the subject as pure disgust with beings. This disgust or nausea-over-beings is a mode of nihilation, a rejection and a refusal of beings on the level of affectivity. Through this rejection and refusal the whole attitude of Sartre with respect to being is determined" (*Existential Phenomenology,* 111).

11. "I was looking at the flower bed by the front door; 'That is the whole,' I said. I was looking at a plant with a spread of leaves; and it seemed suddenly plain that the flower itself was a part of the earth; that a ring enclosed what was the flower; and that was the real flower; part earth; part flower. It was a thought I put away as being likely to be very useful to me later" (Woolf, *Moments of Being,* 71).

12. "[Heidegger] uses etymology as much to uncover human misadventures in thinking as to bring to light what has been obscured in history. An example is his account of the words for "thing"—*das Ding, res, causa, cosa, chose,* where from the fundamental original sense of 'gathering' there is a movement toward 'that which bears on or concerns men,' 'that which is present, as standing forth here,' eventually leading to 'anything that is in any way,' anything present in any way whatever, even if only in mental representations. . . . The ancient thought of gathering falls into oblivion as the later thought of abstract being and presence takes over and occupies the foreground of thinking. Yet the ancient thought—an original discovery of the poets and thinkers who spoke the Indo-European languages into being—is the one that is truest to the nature of the thing as it is knowable in and from living experience" (Hofstadter, Introduction to *Poetry, Language, Thought,* xvi–xvii).

13. "[B]oth a cosmic and human time are essentially cyclic and must return to the beginning to initiate a new creation" (Chuang Tzu, cited by LaChapelle, *Sacred Land,* 157).

14. Cf. Grumet, "In Search of Theatre" and "Curriculum as Theatre."

15. Elaine Showalter, "Feminist Criticism," in *Writing and Sexual Difference,* edited by Elizabeth Abel, 34.

16. "So male educators invited women into the schools expecting to reclaim their mothers, and the women accepted the invitation and came so that they might identify with their fathers. Accordingly, female teachers complied with the rationalization and bureaucratization that pervaded the common schools as the industrial culture saturated the urban areas. Rather than emulate the continuous and extended relation of a mother and her maturing child, they acquiesced to the graded schools—to working with one age group for one year at a time. Rather than demand the extended relation that would bind them over time to individual children, they agreed to large group instruction where the power of the peer collective was at least as powerful as the mother/child bond. Deprived of the classical education that most of the males who organized the schools enjoyed, normalites accepted the curriculum as bestowed, and deviations from it remained in the privacy of the classroom and were not presented to principals or committees of visitors" (Grumet, *Bitter Milk,* 55).

17. "Cut off from their mothers by the harsh masculine authority of church and fathers, theorists like [Horace] Mann sought the reclamation of mother love by promoting women as teachers of the young. Overwhelmed by the presence of their mothers, women entered teaching in order to gain access to the power and prerogatives of their fathers" (Grumet, *Bitter Milk*, 54).

18. "[I]t seems to me that each of us, in a considerable part of his life or of his being, is still unawakened, that is to say that he moves on the margin of reality like a sleepwalker . . . It is, however, precisely against such a condition that what I consider the essential characteristic of the person is opposed, the characteristic, that is to say, of availability *(disponibilité)*.

"This, of course, does not mean emptiness . . . it means much rather an aptitude to give oneself to anything which offers, and to bind oneself by the gift . . . to transform circumstances into opportunities, we might even say favours, thus participating in the shaping of our own destiny and marking it with our seal" (Gabriel Marcel, *Homo Viator*, 23). Later, Marcel will say on the same subject: "The being who is ready for anything is the opposite of him who is occupied or cluttered up with himself. . . . We go wrong when we confuse creating with producing. That which is essential in the creator is the act by which he places himself at the disposal of something which, no doubt in one sense depends upon him for its existence, but which at the same time appears to him to be beyond what he is. . . . [W]hat the person has to create is not some work in a way outside himself and capable of assuming an independent existence, it is his own self in very truth" (25).

19. Cf. note 14 this chapter.

20. See Schechner, "Towards a Poetics of Performance," 44ff.

21. For an explication of historical background to these evolved spatial relations, see chapter 2, "Pedagogy for Patriarchy," in Madeleine Grumet's *Bitter Milk*. Of nineteenth-century American schools Grumet writes, "The intimacy, spirituality, and innocence that teachers and students were to inherit from the mother/child bond—the prototype of their relationship—collapsed into strategies for control. The ideal teacher was one who would control the children and be controlled by her superiors. In 1867 visitors to Boston's Emerson School noted its exemplary order: 'Every pupil appears to be in anxious waiting for the word of the teacher, and when issued it is promptly obeyed by the class. The movements and

utterances of the class are as nearly simultaneous and similar as they can be' " (43).

22. LaChapelle cites Victor Turner's distinction between "univocal" (having one meaning) and "multivocal" (having many meanings) symbols, clustering around two poles:

> In the story recounted in the myth or in the actions of ritual, an interchange occurs between these 'poles of meaning.' Norms, values and ideas cluster at the 'ideological pole'; while the physiological aspects of the body, including emotion, cluster at the other pole. . . . [R]itualization occurs when both these poles are present in a culture's major symbols and 'deritualization takes place when the bond between the poles is broken, for whatever historical reasons.' When this happens all the many aspects of the symbol 'are released from their connectedness and centrifugally diverge to start upon separate futures as concepts, rules and beliefs.' In other words, when a many faceted symbol such as the gourd is lost and replaced by a univocal symbol such as money, 'many of the concepts of the 'ideological' pole become the univocal notions of philosophical and scientific thinking. Of course, the myriad other important meanings of life are lost from this univocal symbol.
>
> What multivocal symbols accomplish is that the culture's values and ideas located at the 'ideological' pole become saturated with emotion, while the 'gross and basic emotions,' associated with the physiological pole, become 'ennobled or sublimed' through contact with social bonding notions and values of the 'ideological' pole. The irksomeness of moral constraint is thereby transformed into the 'love of virtue.' (*Sacred Land*, 159)

23. To those who would raise questions of the place of values in a world where every person is invited to the mythmaking feast, Susanne Langer speaks of sacred stories as "a form of play that has as its purpose, not wishful distortion of the world, but serious envisagement of its fundamental truth" (*Philosophy in a New Key*, 153)—a description that is not eccentric to the goals of the writing classroom's narratives.

24. In her essay "How Does One Speak to Literature?" Julia Kristeva writes of Barthes in context: "The *reading* of a text is doubtlessly the first

stage of theoretical elaboration. A reading, whose conceptual supports are muted, is the terrain of the reading subject's desire, his drives, sexuality, and attentiveness toward the phonematic network, the rhythm of the sentences, the particular semanteme bringing him back to a feeling, pleasure, laughter, an event or reading of the most 'empirical' kind, abounding, enveloping, multiple. The identity of the reading *I* loses itself there, atomizes itself; it is a time of jouissance, where one discovers one text under another, its other. This rare capacity is a condition of Barthes's writings on the frontiers of 'science' and 'criticism' " (*Desire In Language*, 119).

25. Nancy K. Miller, "Women's Autobiography in France: For a Dialectics of Identification," in *Women and Language in Literature and Society*, edited by Sally McConnell Ginet, Ruth Borker and Nelly Furman (New York: Praeger Press, 1980).

26. Gilligan, Carol, *In A Different Voice*.

Chapter V

1. "[T]he Jews—like most early peoples—were matriarchal and worshipped a goddess. It required six centuries for Yahweh to replace Ashtoreth as the primary deity of the Jews; for a long time their temples were side by side. After the Jewish patriarchs succeeded in destroying goddess worship, women came to be treated like chattel. The same story is repeated in culture after culture" (Chicago, *The Dinner Party*, 64B–67).

2. See Rollo May's *Love and Will* and *The Courage to Create* for superb explications of the relationships among myth, the ecstatic, and the demonic dimensions of both creative and religious practices.

3. In *Being and Time*, Heidegger poses the question "What is Being?" Formally, *Dasein* is the subject, the questioner. Heidegger claims that Dasein is the only being for whom Being is a question. He challenges the metaphysical tradition when he argues that Dasein is by definition the Being-in-the-world: "Being-in is thus the formal existential expression for the Being of Dasein, which has Being-in-the-world as its essential state" (*Being and Time*, 80). I am grateful to my editorial assistant, Laura Kroetsch, for her help in developing this footnote.

4. Describing male and female responses to a narrative that poses an apparent conflict between responsibilities to self and other, Gilligan generalizes in this way: "Proceeding from a premise of separation but

recognizing that 'you have to live with other people,' he seeks to limit interference and thus to minimize hurt. Responsibility in his construction pertains to a limitation of action, a restraint of aggression, guided by the recognition that his actions can have effects on others, just as theirs can interfere with him. Thus rules, by limiting interference, make life in community safe, protecting autonomy through reciprocity, extending the same consideration to others and self. . . . Proceeding from a premise of connection, that 'if you have a responsibility *with* somebody else, you should keep it," she then considers the extent to which she has a responsibility to herself. . . . the primacy of separation or connection leads to different images of self and of relationships" (*In a Different Voice*, 37–38).

5. "Examine for a moment an ordinary mind on an ordinary day. The mind receives a myriad *[sic]* impressions—trivial, fantastic, evanescent, or engraved with the sharpness of steel. From all sides they come, an incessant shower of innumerable atoms; . . . Life is not a series of gig lamps symmetrically arranged; life is a luminous halo, a semi-transparent envelope surrounding us from the beginning of consciousness to the end" (Woolf, "Modern Fiction," in *Collected Essays*, 2:106).

6. Making semantic networks, "the mind . . . can creatively summon up words, images or memories by proceeding along one or several interlacing networks of association" (Morton Hunt, "How the Mind Works," *New York Times Magazine*, 24 January 1982, 30ff). These networks are strategies for organizing sensory and other kinds of input as well as for generating ideas in preparation for writing.

7. Perry argues that from freshman to senior years in college, there is a basic progression in the ways of thinking of traditional-age students. Analyzing student protocols, Perry concludes that their stages of moral development begin in basic duality—black/white, right/wrong thinking about issues and experiences, extend through various stages of relativism, and end in a willed commitment to "a way of life" *(Forms of Intellectual and Ethical Development in the College Years)*. For Lawrence Kohlberg, the final (and therefore valorized) stage of moral development assumes "guidance by universal ethical principles that all humanity should follow" (Kohlberg, *The Philosophy of Moral Development*, 412).

8. In *The Miracle of Mindfulness*, Thich Nhat Hanh uses the term *mindfulness* to refer to "keeping one's consciousness alive to the present reality. . . . I think the real miracle is not to walk either on water or in

thin air, but to walk on earth. Every day we are engaged in a miracle which we don't even recognize: a blue sky, white clouds, green leaves, the black, curious eyes of a child—our own two eyes. All is a miracle" (11, 12).

9. "The ontological relation between *Daseins* implies a separation. This ontological relation is in turn the foundation of the existential relations in which *Dasein* can exist in a liberating or dominating mode. The second possibility—the mode of rivalry in which *Dasein* loses its being—is founded in distantiality, itself forgotten or dissimulated by the they. (In this way, Heidegger affirms that the harmony of the everyday world dissimulates a constant and more primordial conflict.) The menace, evoked at both levels, is a loss of identity, a dissolution of *Dasein's* being in the being of the other. . . . Heidegger's decision in relation to it, and with the autonomy of *Dasein* at stake, is to turn to what we have referred to as "the scene of death"—the agon where Dasein, confronting death, comes into its individual being" (Fynsk, *Heidegger, Thought and Historicity,* 36). Confronting our thrownness, in the anxiety of recognizing our being toward death is the confrontation with sheer existence and the possibility that ultimate freedom offers us: "anxiety first discloses *Dasein's* essence as thrown possibility and first discloses the possibility of freely assuming this essence by being toward death. Being-toward-death, then is a repetition that brings Dasein into the very possibility of repetition . . . : *Dasein's coming into the fascination of thrownness is its emergence from it*" (40). Heidegger's reflection in *Being and Time* as Fynsk interpolates it here is an interesting gloss on Field's ambivalent terror and attraction as manifest in the dream of Dis and Adonis.

10. Hall, "The Classroom Climate."

11. Available on VHS from the Hartley Film Foundation/Cat Rock Road/Cos Cob, CONN/068078.

12. E.g., Elizabeth Loftus, *Memory* (Reading, Mass.: Addison-Wesley, 1980); Neisser, *Memory Observed;* and David Rubin, "The Subtle Deceiver: Recalling Our Pasts," *Psychology Today,* September 1985, 39–46.

13. All three of these essays are available in *The Norton Reader,* 7th edition, ed. Arthur Eastman (New York: W. W. Norton, 1988). They are frequently anthologized. The *Norton* is an excellent resource for this kind of writing.

14. "[A]s a world opens itself the earth comes to rise up. It stands forth as that which bears all, as that which is sheltered in its own law and always wrapped up in itself. World demands its decisiveness and its measure and lets beings attain to the Open of their paths. Earth, bearing and jutting, strives to keep itself closed and to entrust everything to its law. The conflict is not a rift *(Riss)* as a mere cleft is ripped open; rather, it is the intimacy with which opponents belong to each other. This rift caries the opponents into the source of their unity by virtue of their common ground. It is a basic design, an outline sketch, that draws the basic features of the rise of the lighting of beings. This rift does not let the opponents break apart; it brings the opposition of measure and boundary into their common outline" (Heidegger, "The Origin of the Work of Art," *Poetry, Language, Thought,* 63).

15.

. . . Three dangers threaten thinking.

The good and thus wholesome
    danger is the nighness of the singing
    poet.

The evil and thus keenest danger is
    thinking itself. It must think
    against itself, which it can only
    seldom do.

The bad and thus muddled danger
    is philosophizing. (Heidegger, "The Thinker as Poet," *Poetry, Language, Thought,* 8).

16. "The earth appears openly cleared as itself only when it is perceived and preserved as that which is by nature undisclosable, that which shrinks from every disclosure and constantly keeps itself closed up. All things of earth, and the earth itself as a whole, flow together into a reciprocal accord. But this confluence is not a blurring of their outlines. Here there flows the stream, restful within itself, of the setting of bounds, which delimits everything present within its presence. Thus in each of the self-secluding things there is the same not-knowing-of-one-another. The earth is essentially self-secluding. To set forth the earth means to bring it into the Open as the self-secluding" (Heidegger, "The Origin of the Work of Art," 47).

17. Woolf, "Modern Fiction," *Collected Essays*, 2:103–10.

18. Essentially, Chodorow argues that because mother and daughter are the same sex, the ability to differentiate from her mother as part of a process of individuation is more difficult for girls than for boys. A mother experiences a sense of "oneness and continuity" with infants of both sexes, but "this sense is stronger and lasts longer, vis-a-vis daughters." She goes on to argue: "Early psychoanalytic findings about the special importance of the preoedipal mother-daughter relationship describe the first stage of a general process in which separation and individuation remain particularly female developmental issues. The cases I describe suggest that there is a tendency in women toward boundary confusion and a lack of sense of separateness from the world. Most women do develop ego boundaries and a sense of separate self. However, women's ego and object-relational issues are concerned with this tendency on one level (of potential conflict, of experience of object-relations), even as on another level (in formation of ego boundaries and the development of a separate identity) the issues are resolved. . . . As long as women mother, we can expect that a girl's preoedipal period will be longer than that of a boy and that women, more than men, will be more open to and preoccupied with those very relational issues that go into mothering—feelings of primary identification, lack of separateness or differentiation, ego and body-ego boundary issues and primary love not under the sway of the reality principle" (*The Reproduction of Mothering*, 109, 110).

19. "Truth means the nature of the true. We think this nature in recollecting the Greek word *aletheia*, the unconcealedness of beings. . . . the hidden truth of Greek philosophy consists from its beginning in this, that it does not remain in conformity with the nature of truth that flashes out in the word *aletheia*, and has to misdirect its knowing and its speaking about the nature of truth more and more into the discussion of a derivative nature of truth. The nature of truth as *aletheia* was not thought out in the thinking of the Greeks nor since then, and least of all in the philosophy that followed after" (Heidegger, "The Origin of the Work of Art," 51).

20. These can be as varied as the student audience facing a teacher. Frequently, I ask students to write about persons and things that have been part of their past in their families and in school; as often as possible I ask students to begin by looking at or visualizing the thing itself, perhaps through a photograph. Students learn interviewing techniques

with each other to help them do a mental inventory of the things and people in their lives and to explore how we get to know and name others and our relationships to them. One goal is to enforce the idea that memory is highly associational but not random, and that it can be investigated in a somewhat systematic way. Informal writing in class offers opportunities to write about their experience of reading different pieces of literature and to facilitate discussion. These are often shared in small groups before the class begins discussion. Brainstorming lists, drawings, doodles, and semantic networks about ideas leading to writing are always a prerequisite to beginning an assignment and are brought to conferences or shared with small groups along with their first drafts. Students keep reader-response notebooks in conjunction with the reading we do in class. Some assignments attempt to tie student writing to their studies in other disciplines, especially when they write about schooling experiences. These are offered in the hope of helping students identify strengths in their own ways of knowing and learning, and to explore the blocks that may be preventing successful learning in other disciplines. Eventually, they will learn simple skills like summary of what they read in order to help distinguish between this and higher-order thinking skills like interpretation and evaluation, and we will look at some critical thinking models (sometimes I use portions of Bloom's taxonomy of educational objectives) to explore some of the ways we think through problems or issues. Assignments generally take a case-study form, with some suggestions for audience, self, and purpose; many leave students free to develop subject matter in a creative way within these suggested parameters. All specify some learning goal related to the literature and theoretical reading we are doing when the assignment is made, and all make clear how individual assignments fit into a larger whole of course reading and writing.

21. "The nature of the earth, in its free and unhurried bearing and self-closure, reveals itself, however, only in the earth's jutting into a world, in the opposition of the two. This conflict is fixed in place in the figure of the work and becomes manifest by it. . . . how can the rift-design be drawn out if it is not brought into the Open by the creative sketch as a rift, which is to say, brought out beforehand as a conflict of measure and unmeasure? True, there lies hidden in nature a rift-design, a measure and a boundary and, tied to it, a capacity for bringing forth—that is, art. But it is equally certain that this art hidden in nature becomes manifest only through the work, because it lies originally in the work" (Heidegger, "The Origin of the Work of Art," 69–70).

22. "Earth juts through the world and world grounds itself on the earth only so far as truth happens as the primal conflict between clearing and concealing. But how does truth happen? We answer: it happens in a few essential ways. One of these ways in which truth happens is the work-being of the work. Setting up a world and setting forth the earth, the work is the fighting of the battle in which the unconcealedness of beings as a whole, or truth, is won" (Heidegger, "The Origin of the Work of Art," 55).

23. In his book *Heidegger: Thought and Historicity*, Christopher Fynsk cites a passage from *Being and Time* as Heidegger's effort to come to terms with "how Dasein is to encounter the other as *other*—that is, how Dasein is to discover the other's relation to itself as an instance of alterity" (33). Heidegger, he says, explores the various possibilities that mark the encounter with the other, starting with the premise that "Being with others belongs to the being of Dasein. (*SZ* 123/160)," (cited by Fynsk, 31). Being-with the other [Mitsein] in its genuine sense is not simply projection of oneself, not merely a relation of identity. The fear is always the loss of identity, "a dissolution of Dasein's being in the being of the other" (Fynsk, 36). This conflict is inevitably present in any relation, and most certainly must mark the intimate relation of which I have tried to speak throughout this text. Yet our power lies in recognizing the very fact of our "thrown being," in the anxiety of giving ourselves up to a world that is without significance and, so "uncanny," a world in which we are "not-being-at-home." But being faced with the inevitability of our annihilation, our death, is what enables the experience of being-possible, and in it lies our ability to hear the call of conscience that in its turn enables us to understand our thrownness as *possibility*. *Dasein* calls, and *Dasein* must hear. Our history, Heidegger says, is always co-history, and we learn this in the act of listening, for "when *Dasein* is listening, it is never alone" (Fynsk, 42). Fynsk cites *Being and Time*: "Listening to . . . is the existential being-open of *Dasein* as being-with for the other. Indeed, hearing constitutes the primary and authentic openness of *Dasein* for its most proper potentiality of being—as in hearing the voice of the friend that every *Dasein* carries with it. *Dasein* hears because it understands. As a being-in-the-world that understands, with the others, it is 'in-thrall' to *Mitdasein* and to itself; and in this thraldom it 'belongs' to these. Listening to one another, in which being-with develops, can be done in several possible ways." (*SZ*, 163/206, cited by Fynsk, 42). Opening to the possibility of death, *Dasein* is able to hear the voice of this friend who is always with us, hears, paradoxically, silence; in this silence is the

conversation about death, a mutual conversation, and consequently, again paradoxically, we live our death with one another. Fynsk writes: "Bearing witness of its own death, the friend *gives* to the other, speaks of, its possible death. And *Dasein*, become silent and reserved, will speak of death in its turn. Listening will become a speaking-giving, provoking and made possible by a speaking-giving that becomes a listening, and so on in an endless return" (43). Thus, he continues, the acts of giving and receiving are "implied, one in the other, in a kind of infinite interlacing" (43)—and finally, even in death, we are not alone. Still, this is a project of transcending self in order to find self—and certainly Heidegger recognizes that the self, like its projects, is a multiple one. The dialectic in the authentic relation he describes of itself would preclude fusion or dissolution—the friend remains other and is *valuable* as such—because, despite the mutuality of the actions the friend describes, there is always giver-receiver, a speaker-listener, and always a third term, world, as well. In fact, part of the richness of Heidegger's definition of hearing is that it is a kind of *sharing* of a kind of seeing, one that "let[s] someone see with us what we have pointed out by way of giving it a definite character. That which is 'shared' is our *being toward* that sees in common what has been pointed out (*SZ* 155/197" cited by Fynsk).

24. *Imitation,* as Field understands it, is the slavish effort to reproduce exactly the object or scene that she sees, or some learned idea of "beauty" as opposed to "what my eye liked" (4). In the first chapter, she writes, "There was no doubt that drawings which were a fairly accurate copy of an object could produce an almost despairing boredom; so I was forced to the conclusion that copies of appearances were not what my eye liked, even though what it did like was not at all clear" (4). Her remarks about the failure of her early, tenacious efforts to reproduce the object or scene before her and her explorations of free-drawing as method are similar to Heidegger's rejection of a certain kind of "human willing." "To put something before ourselves, propose it, in such a way that what has been proposed, having first been represented, determines all the modes of production in every respect, is a basic characteristic of the attitude which we know as willing. The willing of which we are speaking here is production in every respect, placing-here, and this in the sense of objectification purposely putting itself through, asserting itself" (Heidegger, "What Are Poets For?" 110). His complement to Field's abandonment of willed representation for the method of free-drawing is a proposal for "the daring that is more venturesome," about which he writes: "The daring that is more venturesome, willing more strongly than

any self-assertion, because it is willing, 'creates,' a secureness for us in the Open. To create means to fetch from the source. And to fetch from the source means to take up what springs forth and to bring what has so been received. The more venturesome daring of the willing exercise of the will manufactures nothing. It receives, and gives what it has received. It brings, by unfolding in its fullness what it has received. The more venturesome daring accomplishes, but it does not produce. Only a daring that becomes more daring by being willing can accomplish in receiving" ("What Are Poets For?" 120). Rather than the "detachment and separation" of the observing eye, Field reflects in a similar vein to Heidegger, "It seemed one might want some kind of relation to objects in which one was much more mixed up with them than that" (*On Not Being Able to Paint*, 10).

25. Speaking of her eventual ability to paint, Field describes the reason for having become able: "I had discovered in painting a bit of experience that made all other usual occupations unimportant by comparison. It was the discovery that when painting something from nature there occurred, at least sometimes, a fusion into a never-before-known wholeness; not only were the object and oneself no longer felt to be separate, but neither were thought and sensation and feeling and action. All one's visual perceptions of colour, shape, texture, weight, as well as thought and memory, ideas about the object and action towards it, the movement of one's hand together with the feeling of delight in the 'thusness' of the thing, they all seemed fused into a wholeness of being which was different from anything else that had ever happened to me. It was different because thought was not drowned in feeling, they were somehow all there together" (*On Not Being Able to Paint*, 142).

Chapter VI

1. In this book, *Blood, Bread, and Poetry*, Rich links radical feminism and women's liberation to the kinds of political action called for when gender, race, and class are implicated collectively in multiple kinds of political oppression. She says that the title reflects her efforts to link poetry with the social and historical conditions in which it is made, asking the question: *"What happens to the heart of the artist, here in North America?"* (xiv).

2. Julia Kristeva's use of this term can be helpful as a gloss on what Rich intends: " 'art' reveals a specific *practice* crystallized in a mode of

production with highly diversified and multiple manifestations. It weaves into language (or other 'signifying materials') the complex relations of a subject caught between 'nature' and 'culture,' between the immemorial ideological and scientific *tradition,* henceforth available, and the present, between *desire* and the *law,* the body, language and 'metalanguage' " (*Desire in Language,* 97).

"The desire of a subject that ties him to the signifier obtains through this signifier an objective, extraindividual value, void-in-itself, other, without, for all that, ceasing (as it does in science) to be the desire of a subject. This happens only in literature. Writing is precisely this 'spontaneous motion' that changes the formulation of desire for a signifier into objective law, since the subject of writing, specific like no other, is 'in-itself-and-for-itself,' the very place, not of division but, overcoming it, of motion. Consequently, it is the place where the subjective/objective distinction proves invalid, where it is erased, where it appears to be dependent on ideology.... [Barthes's] undertaking makes it clear that literature's specificity resides in the pasage betwen this *desire* to signify the asymbolized and the asymbolizable, where the subject coalesces, and historically sanctioned *objectivity*" (*Desire in Language,* 117–18).

3. On the changing status of women writing in the Victorian period, see Tuchman and Fortin, *Edging Women Out.* Tuchman begins this way: "Before 1840 the British cultural élite accorded little prestige to the writing of novels, and most English novelists were women. By the turn of the twentieth century 'men of letters' acclaimed novels as a form of great literature, and most critically acclaimed successful novelists were men. These two transitions—in the prestige of novel writing and the gender distribution of lauded novelists—were related processes, constituting complementary elements in a classic confrontation between men and women in the same white-collar occupation" (1).

4. For the silence on lesbian women, see Adrienne Rich's "It Is the Lesbian in Us" (1976) and "The Meaning of Our Love for Women Is What We Have Constantly to Expand" (1977) in *On Lies, Secrets, and Silences.* In the former essay Rich writes poignantly: "Two women, one white, one black, were the first persons I loved and who I knew loved me. Both of them sang me my first songs, told me my first stories, became my first knowledge of tenderness, passion, and finally, rejection. Each of them, over time, surrendered me to the judgment and disposition of my father and my father's culture: white and male. My love for the white woman and the black woman became blurred with anger, contempt,

and guilt. I did not know which of them had injured me; they became merged together in my inarticulate fury. I did not know that neither of them had had a choice. Nor did I know that what had happened between—among—the three of us was important. It was *unspeakable*" (199–200).

For the silence on black women, see Spelman, *Inessential Woman*.

5. Arthur Schlesinger's remarks respond to the proposal of the New York State Board of Regents for an integrated multicultural curriculum in elementary and secondary schools in the state. They were widely reprinted, but here I cite "Toward a Divisive Diversity" from the *Wall Street Journal,* 25 June 1991.

6. "[I]t makes us seem not so much to narrate as to exhibit the actual scene, while our emotions will be no less actively stirred than if we were present at the actual occurrence' " (Quintilian, *Institutio Oratoria,* VI, ii, 32, cited in Edward P. J. Corbett, *Classical Rhetoric for the Modern Student* [New York: Oxford University Press, 1971] 27).

7. See, for example, *Women in Higher Education,* ed. W. Todd Furniss and Patricia Albjerg Graham (Washington, D.C.: American Council on Education, 1974); *Meeting Women's New Educational Needs* (Washington, D.C.: Josey-Bass, 1975); *Reconstructing the Academy: Women's Education and Women's Studies,* ed. Elizabeth Minnich, Jean O'Barr, and Rachel Rosenfeld (Chicago: U. of Chicago Press, 1988); "The Inferiority Curriculum" by Jessie Bernard, *Psychology of Women Quarterly* 12, no. 3:261–68.

8.

The question is unavoidable: if we are not on the side of those whom society wastes in order to reproduce itself, where are we?

Murder, death, and unchanging society represent precisely the inability to hear and understand the signifier as such—as ciphering, as rhythm, as a presence that precedes the signification of object or emotion. The poet is put to death because he wants to turn rhythm into a dominant element; because he wants to make language perceive what it doesn't want to say, provide it with its matter independently of the sign, and free it from denotation. For it is this *eminently parodic* gesture that changes the system. (Kristeva, *Desire in Language*, 31)

9. Belenky and her colleagues are citing research from two of L. S. Vygotsky's books: *Thought and Language* (Cambridge, Mass.: MIT Press, 1962) and *Mind in Society* (Cambridge, Mass.: Harvard University Press, 1978).

10. "In Zen, a koan is a formulation, in baffling language, pointing to ultimate truth. Koans cannot be solved by recourse to logical reasoning, but only by awakening a deeper level of the mind beyond the discursive intellect. Koans are constructed from questions of disciples of old together with the responses of their masters, from portions of the masters' sermons or discourses, from lines of the sutras, and from other teachings" (Roshi Philip Kapleau, *The Three Pillars of Zen* [Garden City, N.Y.: Anchor Press/Doubleday, 1980], 369).

11. "The world, the kingdom, and the divine plan! Separately and together, the terms bespeak the comprehensive self-concept that united the colonists (in another of their familiar phrases) 'as One Man with one soul in one body.' To be sure, the terms equally imply the contradictions in Puritanism, the divergent emphases on the spirit and the law, individual experience and social order, self-examination and the commitment to history. . . . The colonists wrought the synthesis by a gargantuan act of will and imagination. We can trace their effort through all forms of the literature: sermons that integrate the stages of regeneration with communal good works; elegies that render the saint's glorification a preview of New England's destiny; journals that blend mysticism and apocalypse; hagiographies whose subjects are microcosms of the colony; federal exhortations couched in the vocabulary of the covenant of grace" (Bercovitch, *The American Puritan Imagination*, 7, 9).

12. Ann Bradstreet, *The Works of Ann Bradstreet*, edited by Jennine Hensley (Cambridge: Belknap Press of Harvard University Press, 1967).

13. Despite Lord's use of the male pronoun, there were some women singers, too.

14. Some have asked whether the pedagogy I propose will silence boys/men who are also students in classrooms that I suggest can be

revitalized through feminist theory. I would argue as a profound irony
that what passes for male knowledge in schools is not a boy's/man's
experience any more than it is a girl's/woman's. This book proposes a
model for bringing the body back into the classroom: the body to be
interpreted *can be male, too.* One significant outcome of my own efforts
to begin this work, starting with reading in the fledgling men's studies
literature and offering similar writing opportunities to male and female
students, has been the discovery that, despite men's apparent access to
the "public rhetoric," access to things and to themselves has been denied
men—indeed, they have denied these to themselves—often just as
effectively as they have denied them to women. I believe much could be
written about men's silence, and feminist explorations of their own
silencing can be rich models to help unlock a world of interpretation and
connection for men in classrooms, too.

Conclusion

1. *The Ridgeleaf,* #184, May, 1991, Bangor, Pennsylvania, 18013.
This is an occasional newsletter from *Kirkridge,* a retreat center in the
Pennsylvania mountains.

2. *The Ridgeleaf,* #184, May, 1991.

3. Cf. especially Grumet, "Curriculum As Theatre" and "In Search
of Theatre."

4. Linda Flower and John Hayes, "A Cognitive Process Theory of
Writing" in College Composition and Communication, 32:4 (December
1981) 365–387.

5. Cf. especially Genevieve Lloyd, *The Man of Reason: "Male" and
"Female" in Western Philosophy.* (Minneapolis, Minnesota: U. of Minnesota
Press, 1984).

BIBLIOGRAPHY

Abel, Elizabeth, ed. *Writing and Sexual Difference*. Chicago: University of Chicago Press, 1980.

Alighieri, Dante. *The Divine Comedy*. Translated by Henry F. Cary. New York: P. F. Collier, 1909.

Arnold, Matthew. *The Complete Prose Works of Matthew Arnold*. Vols. 1–3. Edited by R. H. Super. Ann Arbor: University of Michigan, 1962.

———. *The Poetical Works of Matthew Arnold*. Edited by Miriam Allott and R. H. Super. London: Oxford University Press, 1986.

Auerbach, Nina. *Woman and the Demon: The Life of Victorian Myth*. Cambridge: Harvard University Press, 1982.

Bachelard, Gaston. *The Poetics of Space*. Translated by Maria Jolas. Boston: Beacon Press, 1964.

Bakhtin, M. M. *Speech Genres and Other Essays*. Translated by Vern W. McGee. Edited by Michael Holquist. Austin: University of Texas Press, 1986.

Bal, Mieke. *Narratology: Introduction to the Theory of Narrative*. Toronto: University of Toronto Press, 1985.

Barthes, Roland. *A Barthes Reader*. Edited by Susan Sontag. New York: Hill & Wang, 1982.

———. *A Lover's Discourse: Fragments*. Translated by Richard Howard. New York: Hill & Wang, 1978.

———. *Writing Degree Zero and Elements of Semiology*. Translated by Annette Lavers and Colin Smith. Boston: Beacon Press, 1968.

Belenky, Mary Field, Blythe McVicker Clinchy, Nancy Rule Goldberger, and Jill Mattuck Tarule. *Women's Ways of Knowing: The Development of Self, Voice, and Mind.* New York: Basic Books, 1986.

Bell, Diane. *Daughters of the Dreaming.* North Sydney, Australia: McPhee Gribble, 1988.

Benstock, Shari, ed. *The Private Self: Theory and Practice of Women's Autobiographical Writings.* Chapel Hill: University of North Carolina Press, 1988.

Bercovitch, Sacvan, ed. *The American Puritan Imagination: Essays in Revaluation.* New York: Cambridge University Press, 1974.

Bergson, Henri. *The Creative Mind.* Translated by Mabelle L. Andison. New York: Philosophical Library, 1946.

———. *Matter and Memory.* Translated by Nancy Margaret Paul and W. Scott Palmer. London: Allen & Unwin, 1911.

Bale, William. *The Complete Poetry and Prose of William Blake.* Edited by David Erdman. Berkeley: University of California Press, 1982.

Bloom, Benjamin, ed. *Taxonomy of Educational Objectives.* New York: Longman, Green, 1956.

Bronte, Charlotte. *Jane Eyre.* New York: Bantam, 1981.

Brooks, Gwendolyn. *Selected Poems.* New York: Harper, 1963.

Buber, Martin. *I and Thou.* New York: Scribner & Sons, 1958.

Butcher, S. H. and A. Lang, translators. *The Odyssey of Homer.* New York: P. F. Collier & Son, 1909.

Byron, George Gordon Noel Byron, Baron. *The Poetical Works of Byron.* Edited by Robert F. Gleckner. Boston: Houghton Mifflin, 1975.

Campbell, Joseph. *Myths to Live By.* New York: Bantam, 1973.

Campbell, Joseph, and Bill Moyers. *The Power of Myth.* Edited by Betty Sue Flowers. New York: Doubleday, 1988.

Carroll, Lewis. *Through the Looking Glass, and What Alice Found There*. Berkeley: University of California Press, 1983.

Carson, Anne. *EROS the Bittersweet: An Essay*. Princeton: Princeton University Press, 1986.

Chatwin, Bruce. *The Songlines*. New York: Penguin, 1987.

Chernin, Kim. *Reinventing Eve: Modern Woman in Search of Herself*. New York: Harper & Row, 1988.

Chicago, Judy. *The Dinner Party: A Symbol of Our Heritage*. New York: Anchor Press, 1979.

Chodorow, Nancy. *The Reproduction of Mothering: Psychoanalysis and the Sociology of Gender*. Berkeley: University of California Press, 1978.

Christ, Carol P. *Laughter of Aphrodite: Reflections on a Journey to the Garden*. San Francisco: Harper & Row, 1987.

Cixous, Hélène. "The Laugh of the Medusa," in Marks, Elaine and Isabelle deCourtivron, eds. *New French Feminisms*. New York: Schocken Books, for the University of Massachusetts Press, 1980.

Coleridge, Samuel Taylor. *Selected Poetry and Prose of Coleridge*. Edited by Donald A. Stauffer. New York: Random House, 1951.

Conley, Verena Andermatt. *Helene Cixous: Writing the Feminine*. Lincoln: University of Nebraska Press, 1984.

Conrad, Joseph. *The Secret Agent*. Garden City, N.Y.: Doubleday, 1953.

Craighead, Meinrad. *The Mother's Songs: Images of God the Mother*. New York: Paulist Press, 1986.

Culley, Margo, ed. *A Day at a Time: The Diary Literature of American Women from 1764 to the Present*. New York: Feminist Press, 1985.

De Pisan, Christine. *The Book of the City of Ladies*. New York: Persea Press, 1982.

Desmond, John F., ed. *A Still Moment: Essays on the Art of Eudora Welty.* New York: Scarecrow Press, 1978.

Dick, Susan, transcriber and ed. *To the Lighthouse: The Original Holograph Draft.* Toronto: University of Toronto Press, 1982.

Dickens, Charles. *Bleak House.* edited by George Ford and Sylvère Monod. New York: Norton, 1977.

———. *Martin Chuzzlewit.* New York: Scribner, 1905.

Dillard, Annie. "Sight into Insight." *Harper's.* February 1974, 39–46.

Dinnerstein, Dorothy. *The Mermaid and the Minotaur: Sexual Arrangements and Human Malaise.* New York: Harper Colophon, 1977.

DuBois, Page. *Sowing the Body: Psychoanalysis and Ancient Representations of Women.* Chicago: University of Chicago Press, 1988.

Duerr, Hans Peter. *Dreamtime: Concerning the Boundary between Wilderness and Civilization.* Translated by Felicitas Goodman. Oxford: Basil Blackwell, 1987.

Eagleton, Mary, ed. *Feminist Literary Theory: A Reader.* Oxford: Basil Blackwell, 1986.

Eisenstein, Hester, and Alice Jardine, eds. *The Future of Difference.* New Brunswick: Rutgers University Press, 1985.

Eliade, Mircea. *Cosmos and History: The Myth of the Eternal Return.* New York: Harper, 1954.

———. *Myth and Reality.* New York: Harper, 1963.

Eliot, T. S. *The Complete Poems and Plays 1909–1950.* New York: Harcourt, 1971.

———. *Selected Essays.* London: Faber & Faber, 1932.

Emig, Janet. *The Web of Meaning: Essays on Writing, Teaching, Learning and Thinking.* Edited by Dixie Goswami and Maureen Bulter. Montclair, N.J.: Boynton/Cook, 1983.

Fetterley, Judith. *The Resisting Reader: A Feminist Approach to American Fiction.* Bloomington: Indiana University Press, 1978.

Field, Joanna [Marion Milner]. *An Experiment in Leisure.* Los Angeles: Tarcher, 1937.

———. *A Life of One's Own.* Los Angeles: Tarcher, 1936.

———. *On Not Being Able to Paint.* Los Angeles: Tarcher, 1957.

Flynn, Elizabeth A., and Patrocinio P. Schweickart, eds. *Gender and Reading: Essays on Readers, Texts, and Contexts.* Baltimore: Johns Hopkins University Press, 1986.

Forster, E. M. *Howard's End.* New York: Vintage, 1921.

Franck, Frederick. *The Zen of Seeing.* New York: Vintage, 1973.

Fynsk, Christopher. *Heidegger: Thought and Historicity.* Ithaca: Cornell University Press, 1986.

Gallagher, Catherine, and Thomas Laqueur, eds. *The Making of the Modern Body: Sexuality and Society in the Nineteenth Century.* Berkeley: University of California Press, 1987.

Gallop, Jane. *Reading Lacan.* New York: Cornell University Press, 1985.

Gardner, Howard. *Frames of Mind: The Theory of Multiple Intelligences.* New York: Basic Books, 1983.

Garry, Ann, and Marilyn Pearsall, eds. *Women, Knowledge, and Reality: Explorations in Feminist Philosophy.* Boston: Unwin Hyman, 1989.

Gates, Henry Louis, Jr. *The Signifying Monkey: A Theory of Afro-American Literary Criticism.* New York: Oxford University Press, 1988.

Gilbert, Sandra Caruso Mortola, and Susan Dreyfuss David Gubar. "Ceremonies of the Alphabet: Female Grandmatologies and the Female Authorgraph," in *The Female Autograph,* ed. by Domna Stanton. Chicago: University of Chicago Press, 1984.

Gilbert, Sandra M., and Susan Gubar. *The Madwoman in the Attic: The Woman Writer and the Nineteenth-Century Literary Imagination.* New Haven: Yale University Press, 1979.

Gilligan, Carol. *In a Different Voice.* Cambridge: Harvard University Press, 1982.

Giovanni, Nikki. *Cotton Candy on a Rainy Day.* New York: Quill, 1978.

Griffin, Susan. *Woman and Nature: The Roaring inside Her.* New York: Harper, 1978.

Grumet, Madeleine R. *Bitter Milk: Women and Teaching.* Amherst: University of Massachusetts Press, 1988.

———. "Curriculum as Theater: Merely Players." *Curriculum Inquiry* 8, no. 1 (1978): 37–64.

———. "In Search of Theater: Ritual, Confrontation and the Suspense of Form." *Journal of Education* 162 (1980): 93–110.

———. "The Politics of Personal Knowledge." *Curriculum Inquiry* 17, no. 3 (1987).

Hall, Roberta M. "The Classroom Climate: A Chilly One for Women." Project on the Status and Education of Women, Association of American Colleges, 1818 R. Street, NW, Washington, DC 20009.

Hardy, Thomas. *Tess of the d'Urbervilles.* Edited by Scott Elledge. New York: W. W. Norton, 1965.

Harrison, Regina. *Signs, Songs, and Memory in the Andes: Translating Quechua Language and Culture.* Austin: University of Texas, 1989.

Hawthorne, Nathaniel. *The Complete Novels and Selected Tales of Nathaniel Hawthorne.* Edited by Norman Holmes Pearson. New York: Modern Library, 1937.

Heidegger, Martin. *The Basic Problems of Phenomenology*. Translated by Albert Hofstadter. Bloomington: Indiana University Press, 1982.

———. *Being and Time*. Translated by John Macquarrie and Edward Robinson. New York: Harper, 1962.

———. *Discourse on Thinking*. Translated by John M. Anderson and E. Hans Freund. New York: Harper, 1959.

———. *On the Way to Language*. Translated by Peter Hertz and John Stambaugh. New York: Harper, 1971.

———. *Poetry, Language, Thought*. Translated by Albert Hofstadter. New York: Harper, 1971.

———. *What Is a Thing?* Translated by W. B. Barton, Jr., and Vera Deutsch. Chicago: Henry Regnery, 1967.

Heilbrun, Carolyn. *Writing a Woman's Life*. New York: Ballantine, 1988.

Heilbrun, Carolyn, and Nancy K. Miller, eds. *Reading Woman: Essays in Feminist Criticism*. New York: Columbia University Press, 1986.

Hill, Alette Olin. *Mother Tongue, Father Time: A Decade of Linguistic Revolt*. Bloomington: Indiana University Press, 1986.

Homans, Margaret. *Bearing the Word: Language and Female Experience in Nineteenth-Century Women's Writing*. Chicago: University of Chicago Press, 1986.

Homer. *The Odyssey*. Translated by W. H. D. Rouse. New York: New American Library, 1973.

Irigaray, Luce. *This Sex Which Is Not One*. Translated by Catherine Porter. New York: Cornell University Press, 1985.

James, Henry. *The Portrait of a Lady*. Edited by Robert D. Bamberg. New York: Norton, 1975.

Jardine, Alice A. *Gynesis: Configurations of Woman and Modernity*. New York: Cornell University Press, 1985.

Jeffrey, Julie Roy. *Frontier Women: The Trans-Mississippi West 1840–1880*. New York: Hill & Wang, 1979.

Keats, John. *The Complete Poems*. Edited by John Barnard. New York: Penguin, 1977.

Keneally, Thomas. "Dreamscapes." *New York Times Magazine*, 13 November 1988, 52–58.

Kenner, Hugh. *The Pound Era*. Berkeley: University of California Press, 1971.

Kern, Stephen. *The Culture of Time and Space 1881–1918*. Cambridge: Harvard University Press, 1983.

Kincaid, Jamaica. "On Seeing England for the First Time." *Harper's Magazine*, August 1991, 13–17.

Knight, Chris. "Lévi-Strauss and the Dragon: *Mythologiques* Reconsidered in the Light of an Australian Aboriginal Myth." *Man* 18, no. 1 (1983): 21–50.

Kohlberg, Lawrence. *The Philosophy of Moral Development: Moral Stages and the Idea of Justice*. San Francisco: Harper & Row, 1981.

Kristeva, Julia. *Desire in Language: A Semiotic Approach to Literature and Art*. Edited by Leon S. Roudiez. New York: Columbia University Press, 1980.

———. *The Kristeva Reader*. Edited by Toril Moi. New York: Cornell University Press, 1986.

———. *Revolution in Poetic Language*. Translated by Margaret Waller. New York: Cornell University Press, 1984.

Lacan, Jacques. *Écrits: A Selection*. Translated by Alan Sheridan. New York: Norton, 1977.

———. *Feminine Sexuality*. Edited by Juliet Mitchell and Jacqueline Rose. Translated by Jacqueline Rose. New York: Norton, 1982.

LaChapelle, Dolores. *Sacred Land, Sacred Sex—Rapture of the Deep: Concerning Deep Ecology—and Celebrating Life.* Silverton, Colorado: Finn Hill Arts, 1988.

Langbaum, Robert. *The Mysteries of Identity.* New York: Oxford University Press, 1977.

Langer, Susanne K. *Philosophy in a New Key.* Cambridge: Harvard University Press, 1982.

Lauter, Estella. *Women As Mythmakers: Poetry and Visual Art by Twentieth-Century Women.* Bloomington: Indiana University Press, 1984.

Lawrence, D. H. *Lady Chatterley's Lover.* New York: Bantam, 1968.

Layton, Robert. "The Cultural Context of Hunter-Gatherer Rock Art." *Man* 20, no. 3 (1985): 434–53.

Lerner, Gerda. *The Creation of Patriarchy.* New York: Oxford University Press, 1986.

Lessing, Doris. *The Golden Notebook.* New York: Bantam, 1973.

Levertov, Denise. *Candles in Babylon.* New York: New Directions, 1982.

Lord, Albert B. *The Singer of Tales.* Cambridge: Harvard University Press, 1964.

Lowry, Howard Foster. *The Letters of Mathew Arnold to Hugh Clough.* Oxford: Clarendon Press, 1986.

Luijpen, William A. *Existential Phenomenology.* Pittsburgh: Duquesne University Press, 1960.

Makward, Christine. "To Be or Not to Be . . . a Feminist Speaker." In *The Future of Difference,* edited by Hester Eisenstein and Alice Jardine. New Jersey: Rutgers University Press, 1980.

Marks, Elaine, and Isabelle de Courtivron, eds. *New French Feminisms: An Anthology.* New York: University of Massachusetts Press, 1980.

May, Rollo. *The Courage to Create*. New York: Bantam, 1976.

———. *Love and Will*. New York: Delta, 1969.

McDonnell, Thomas P., ed. *Through the Year with Thomas Merton: Daily Meditations from His Writings*. New York: Image Books, 1985.

Merlan, Francesca. "Australian Aboriginal Conception Beliefs Revisited." *Man* 21, no. 3 (1986): 474–93.

Meyers, Fred. Review of *The Australian Aborigines: A Portrait of Their Society*, by Kenneth Maddock. *Ocenia* 57, no. 1 (1986): 55–58.

Miller, Jean Baker. *Toward a New Psychology of Women*. Boston: Beacon Press, 1976.

Miller, Nancy K., ed. *The Poetics of Gender*. New York: Columbia University Press, 1986.

Moffat, Mary Jane, and Charlotte Painter. *Revelations: Diaries of Women*. New York: Vintage, 1974.

Morton, John. "The Effectiveness of Totemism: 'Increase Ritual' and Resource Control in Central Australia." *Man* 22, no. 3 (1987): 453–74.

Muller, John P., and William J. Richardson. *Lacan and Language: A Reader's Guide to* Écrits. New York: International University Press, 1982.

Murray, Janet. *Strong-Minded Women and Other Lost Voices from Nineteenth-Century England*. New York: Pantheon, 1982.

Neisser, Ulric, ed. *Memory Observed: Remembering in Natural Contexts*. New York: Freeman, 1982.

Neumann, Erich. *The Origins and History of Consciousness. Part 1: The Psychological Stages and the Evolution of Consciousness*. New York: Harper, 1954.

Nicholson, Linda, editor. *Feminism/Postmodernism*. New York: Routledge, 1990.

O'Brien, Mary. *The Politics of Reproduction*. Boston: Routledge & Kegan Paul, 1983.

Olsen, Tillie. *Silences*. New York: Dell, 1965.

Ong, Walter J. *Fighting for Life: Contest, Sexuality, and Consciousness*. New York: Cornell University Press, 1981.

———. *Orality and Literacy: The Technologizing of the Word*. New York: Methuen, 1982.

———. *The Presence of the Word: Some Prolegomena for Cultural and Religious History*. Minneapolis: University of Minnesota Press, 1967.

Ornstein, Robert E. *The Psychology of Consciousness*. Middlesex, England: Penguin, 1975.

Pearson, Carol. *The Hero Within: Six Archetypes We Live By*. San Francisco: Harper, 1986.

Peradotto, John, and J. P. Sullivan, eds. *Women in the Ancient World: The Arethusa Papers*. Albany: State University of New York Press, 1984.

Perry, William G. *Forms of Intellectual and Ethical Development in the College Years*. New York: Holt, Rinehart & Winston, 1970.

Piercy, Marge. *Circles on the Water: Selected Poems*. New York: Knopf, 1982.

Plath, Sylvia. *Ariel*. New York: Harper, 1961.

Polkinghorne, Donald E. *Narrative Knowing and the Human Sciences*. Albany, New York: State University of New York Press, 1988.

Prenshaw, Peggy Whitman, ed. *Conversations with Eudora Welty*. New York: Washington Square Press, 1984.

Rich, Adrienne. *Blood, Bread, and Poetry: Selected Prose 1979–1985*. New York: Norton, 1986.

———. *The Fact of a Doorframe: Poems Selected and New 1950–1984*. New York: Norton, 1984.

———. *On Lies, Secrets, and Silence: Selected Prose 1966–1978*. New York: Norton, 1979.

———. *Poems Selected and New, 1950–1974*. New York: Norton, 1975.

———. *A Wild Patience Has Taken Me This Far: Poems 1978–1981*. New York: Norton, 1981.

———. *Of Woman Born: Motherhood As Experience and Institution*. New York: Norton, 1976.

Rogers, Katharine M., and William McCarthy. *The Meridian Anthology of Early Women Writers: British Literary Women from Aphra Behn to Maria Edgeworth 1660–1800*. New York: New American Library, 1987.

Rohman, Gordon. "Pre-Writing: Models for Concept Formation in Writing." Textual basis of a talk given at Janice Lauer's seminar on rhetoric and rhetorical theory at Purdue University, 1981.

Rossi, Alice S., ed. *The Feminist Papers: From Adams to de Beauvoir*. New York: Bantam, 1974.

Roszak, Betty, and Theodore Roszak, eds. *Masculine/Feminine: Readings in Sexual Mythology and the Liberation of Women*. New York: Harper, 1969.

Sacks, Oliver. *The Man Who Mistook His Wife for a Hat and Other Clinical Tales*. New York: Harper, 1970.

Said, Edward. *The World, the Text, and the Critic*. Cambridge: Harvard University Press, 1983.

Sarton, May. *I Knew a Phoenix: Sketches for an Autobiography*. New York: Norton, 1959.

———. *Journal of a Solitude*. New York: Norton, 1973.

———. *Mrs. Stevens Hears the Mermaids Singing*. New York: Norton, 1965.

———. *Plant Dreaming Deep*. New York: Norton, 1968.

Sartre, Jean-Paul. *Nausea*. Norfolk, Virginia: New Directions, 1959.

Schachtel, Ernest. "On Memory and Childhood Amnesia," in *Memory Observed: Remembering in Natural Contexts*, edited by U. Neisser. New York: Freeman, 1982.

Schechner, Richard. "Towards a Poetics of Performance." In *Alcheringa: A First International Symposium*, edited by Benamou and Rothenberg. Boston: Alcheringa, with Boston University Press, 1976.

Schlissel, Lillian. *Women's Diaries of the Westward Journey*. New York: Schocken, 1982.

Schlissel, Lillian, Vicki L. Ruiz, and Janice Monk, eds. *Western Women: Their Land, Their Lives*. Albuquerque: University of New Mexico, 1988.

Scholes, Robert, and Robert Kellogg. *The Nature of Narrative*. London: Oxford University Press, 1966.

Schwartz, Sanford. *The Matrix of Modernism: Pound, Eliot, and Early Twentieth-Century Thought*. Princeton: Princeton University Press, 1985.

Shahn, Ben. *The Shape of Content*. New York: Vintage, 1957.

Shin, Nan [Nancy Amphoux]. *Diary of a Zen Nun: Every Day Living*. New York: E. P. Dutton, 1986.

Showalter, Elaine. *The Female Malady: Women, Madness, and English Culture, 1830–1980*. New York: Penguin, 1985.

Smith, Sidone. *A Poetics of Women's Autobiography: Marginality and the Fictions of Self-Representation.* Bloomington: Indiana University Press, 1987.

Spelman, Elizabeth. *Inessential Woman: Problems of Exclusion in Feminist Thought.* Boston: Beacon, 1988.

Stanton, Domna C., ed. *The Female Autograph.* Chicago: University of Chicago Press, 1984.

Starhawk. *Dreaming the Dark: Magic, Sex and Politics.* Boston: Beacon, 1982.

Sternburg, Janet, ed. *The Writer on Her Work.* New York: Norton, 1980.

Stewart, Elinore Pruitt. *Letters of a Woman Homesteader.* Boston: Houghton Mifflin, 1988.

Suleiman, Susan Rubin, ed. *The Female Body in Western Culture: Contemporary Perspectives.* Cambridge: Harvard University Press, 1986.

Sutherland, Donald. *The Bacchae of Euripides: A New Translation with a Critical Essay.* Lincoln: University of Nebraska, 1968.

Taylor, Gordon Rattray. *The Natural History of the Mind.* New York: Penguin, 1981.

Thich Nhat Hanh. *The Miracle of Mindfulness: A Manual on Meditation.* Translated by Mobi Ho. Boston: Beacon Press, 1987.

Tuchman, Gaye, and Nina E. Fortin. *Edging Women Out: Victorian Novelists, Publishers, and Social Change.* New Haven: Yale University Press, 1989.

Turnbull, Colin M. *The Forest People: A Study of the Pygmies of the Congo.* New York: Simon & Schuster, 1961.

Versenyi, Laszlo. *Heidegger, Being, and Truth.* New Haven: Yale University Press, 1965.

Walker, Alice. *In Search of Our Mothers' Gardens*. San Diego: Harvest, 1983.

———. *Living by the Word: Selected Writings 1973–1987*. New York: Harcourt, 1988.

Wandor, Michelene, ed. *On Gender and Writing*. London: Pandora, 1983.

Washington, Mary Helen, ed. *Invented Lives: Narratives of Black Women 1860–1960*. New York: Anchor, 1987.

Welty, Eudora. *The Collected Stories of Eudora Welty*. New York: Harcourt, 1980.

———. *The Eye of the Story: Selected Essays and Reviews*. New York: Vintage, 1979.

———. *One Writer's Beginnings*. New York: Warner, 1983.

Wollstonecraft, Mary. *A Vindication of the Rights of Woman*. Edited by Carol H. Poston. New York: Norton, 1988.

Woolf, Virginia. *Between the Acts*. New York: Harcourt, Brace & World, 1941.

———. *Collected Essays: Vols. 1–4*. New York: Harcourt, Brace & World, 1967.

———. *Jacob's Room and The Waves: Two Complete Novels*. New York: Harcourt, 1931.

———. *The Letters of Virginia Woolf: Vol. 4; 1929–1931*. Edited by Nigel Nicolson and Joanne Trautmann. New York: Harcourt Brace Jovanovich, 1978.

———. *To the Lighthouse*. New York: Harcourt, 1927.

———. *Moments of Being: Unpublished Autobiographical Writings*. Edited by Jeanne Schulkind. New York: Harcourt, 1976.

———. "Professions for Women." In *Women and Writing,* edited by Michele Barrett. New York: Harcourt, 1979.

———. *A Room of One's Own.* New York: Harcourt, Brace & World, 1957.

———. *A Writer's Diary.* New York: Harcourt Brace Jovanovich, 1953.

Wordsworth, William. *The Prose Works of William Wordsworth.* Vol. 1. Edited by J. B. Owens and Jane Worthington Smyse. Oxford: Clarendon Press, 1974.

Wynter, Sylvia. "Ethno or Socio Poetics." In *Alcheringa: A First International Symposium,* edited by Benamou and J. Rothenberg. Boston, Mass.: Alcheringa with Boston University Press, 1976.

Zinsser, William, ed. *Inventing the Truth: The Art and Craft of Memoir.* Boston: Houghton Mifflin, 1987.

INDEX

intimate, 102, 112, 116, 119, 121, 131, 138, 151, 227n
intimate immensity, 86, 99, 104, 199. *See also* Gaston Bachelard; phenomenology of intimacy; Virginia Woolf, the problematic of intimacy

J

James, Henry, 120
work: *The Portrait of a Lady*, 73–74
Jamieson, Sandra, 212–13n
Jardine, Alice, *Gynesis*, 82–83, 223n
Jefferson, Thomas, 187
Jeffrey, Julie Roy, *Frontier Women*, 229n
Jonah, 139
jouissance, 71, 83, 165, 236n. *See also* Julia Kristeva
Joyce, James, 176
Jung, Carl, 96–97

K

Keats, John, 8–9, 16–17, 32
works: "Ode on a Grecian Urn," 9; "Ode to a Nightingale," 9
Kern, Stephen, *The Culture of Time and Space*, 120–21
Kincaid, Jamaica, "*On Seeing England for the First Time*," 173–74, 189
Kipling, Rudyard, 42–43
Knight, Chris, "Levi-Strauss and the Dragon," 37, 68–69, 213n, 225–26nn
koans, 184–85, 247n
Kohlberg, Lawrence, 237n
Kristeva, Julia, xvii, 26–27, 40, 71–72, 163, 165, 218n
works: *Desire in Language*, 219–20n, 223n, 235–36n, 244–45nn, 246–47n; "Women's Time," 201–02

L

Lacan, Jacques, 46–47, 50, 139, 183, 222–23n, 224n
law of the Father, 139, 224n
mirror stage, 175–81, 194
LaChapelle, Delores, *Sacred Land, Sacred Sex, Rapture of the Deep*, 96–99, 231nn, 233n, 235n
Lamia, 13
Langbaum, Robert, *The Mysteries of Identity*, 16, 219
Lawrence, D. H., *Lady Chatterley's Lover*, 75
Levertov, Denise, "Poet and Person," 31
Lewis, Wyndham, xxi
work: *Blast*, 213
the vortex, xxi, 213
See also vorticism
Lincoln, Abraham, 187
literacy, xvii, 13–14, 36, 42, 56–57, 65, 121–22, 182–83, 218n. *See also* orality; Walter Ong
and cities, 13
and eroticism, 121–22
literate, xviii, 14, 17, 37, 39, 48, 121, 182, 190–91, 193. *See also* pre-literate, post-literate
Locke, John, 16
Logos, 218n. *See also* symbolic
Lord, Albert, *The Singer of Tales*, 13–14; 17, 19–21, 36, 190–91
Lorenz, Konrad, 97
Luijpen, William, 212n, 218n, 232n. *See also* facticity

M

Makic, Sulejman, 20
Marcel, Gabriel, *Homo Viator*, 117, 234n
Marxism, 83
mask, xii
mastoi, 83
material imagination, 78. *See also* Bachelard